CASEBOOK SERIES

JANE AUSTEN: *Emma* David Lodge
JANE AUSTEN: *'Northanger Abbey' & 'Persuasion'* B. C. Southam
JANE AUSTEN: *'Sense and Sensibility', 'Pride and Prejudice' & 'Mansfield Park'* B. C. Southam
BECKETT: *Waiting for Godot* Ruby Cohn
WILLIAM BLAKE: *Songs of Innocence and Experience* Margaret Bottrall
CHARLOTTE BRONTË: *'Jane Eyre' & 'Villette'* Miriam Allott
EMILY BRONTË: *Wuthering Heights* Miriam Allott
BROWNING: *'Men and Women' & Other Poems* J. R. Watson
CHAUCER: *Canterbury Tales* J. J. Anderson
COLERIDGE: *'The Ancient Mariner' & Other Poems* Alun R. Jones & W. Tydeman
CONRAD: *'Heart of Darkness', 'Nostromo' & 'Under Western Eyes'* C. B. Cox
CONRAD: *The Secret Agent* Ian Watt
DICKENS: *Bleak House* A. E. Dyson
DICKENS: *'Hard Times', 'Great Expectations' & 'Our Mutual Friend'* Norman Page
DICKENS: *'Dombey and Son' & 'Little Dorrit'* Alan Shelston
DONNE: *Songs and Sonets* Julian Lovelock
GEORGE ELIOT: *Middlemarch* Patrick Swinden
GEORGE ELIOT: *'The Mill on the Floss' & 'Silas Marner'* R. P. Draper
T. S. ELIOT: *Four Quartets* Bernard Bergonzi
T. S. ELIOT: *'Prufrock', 'Gerontion' & 'Ash Wednesday'* B. C. Southam
T. S. ELIOT: *The Waste Land* C. B. Cox & Arnold P. Hinchliffe
T. S. ELIOT: *Plays* Arnold P. Hinchliffe
HENRY FIELDING: *Tom Jones* Neil Compton
E.M. FORSTER: *A Passage to India* Malcolm Bradbury
WILLIAM GOLDING: *Novels 1954–64* Norman Page
HARDY: *The Tragic Novels* R. P. Draper
HARDY: *Poems* James Gibson & Trevor Johnson
HARDY: *Three Pastoral Novels* R. P. Draper
GERARD MANLEY HOPKINS: *Poems* Margaret Bottrall
HENRY JAMES: *'Washington Square' & 'The Portrait of a Lady'* Alan Shelton
JONSON: *Volpone* Jonas A. Barish
JONSON: *'Every Man in his Humour' & 'The Alchemist'* R. V. Holdsworth
JAMES JOYCE: *'Dubliners' & 'A Portrait of the Artist as a Young Man'* Morris Beja
KEATS: *Odes* G.S. Fraser
KEATS: *Narrative Poems* John Spencer Hill
D.H. LAWRENCE: *Sons and Lovers* Gamini Salgado
D.H. LAWRENCE: *'The Rainbow' & 'Women in Love'* Colin Clarke
LOWRY: *Under the Volcano* Gordon Bowker
MARLOWE: *Doctor Faustus* John Jump
MARLOWE: *'Tamburlaine the Great', 'Edward II' & 'The Jew of Malta'* J. R. Brown
MARLOWE: *Poems* Arthur Pollard
MAUPASSANT: *In the Hall of Mirrors* T. Harris
MILTON: *Paradise Lost* A. E. Dyson & Julian Lovelock
O'CASEY: *'Juno and the Paycock', 'The Plough and the Stars' & 'The Shadow of a Gunman'* Ronald Ayling
EUGENE O'NEILL: *Three Plays* Normand Berlin
JOHN OSBORNE: *Look Back in Anger* John Russell Taylor
PINTER: *'The Birthday Party' & Other Plays* Michael Scott
POPE: *The Rape of the Lock* John Dixon Hunt
SHAKESPEARE: *A Midsummer Night's Dream* Antony Price
SHAKESPEARE: *Antony and Cleopatra* John Russell Brown
SHAKESPEARE: *Coriolanus* B. A. Brockman

SHAKESPEARE: *Early Tragedies* Neil Taylor & Bryan Loughrey
SHAKESPEARE: *Hamlet* John Jump
SHAKESPEARE: *Henry IV Parts I and II* G.K. Hunter
SHAKESPEARE: *Henry V* Michael Quinn
SHAKESPEARE: *Julius Caesar* Peter Ure
SHAKESPEARE: *King Lear* Frank Kermode
SHAKESPEARE: *Macbeth* John Wain
SHAKESPEARE: *Measure for Measure* C. K. Stead
SHAKESPEARE: *The Merchant of Venice* John Wilders
SHAKESPEARE: *'Much Ado About Nothing' & 'As You Like It'* John Russell Brown
SHAKESPEARE: *Othello* John Wain
SHAKESPEARE: *Richard II* Nicholas Brooke
SHAKESPEARE: *The Sonnets* Peter Jones
SHAKESPEARE: *The Tempest* D. J. Palmer
SHAKESPEARE: *Troilus and Cressida* Priscilla Martin
SHAKESPEARE: *Twelfth Night* D. J. Palmer
SHAKESPEARE: *The Winter's Tale* Kenneth Muir
SPENSER: *The Faerie Queene* Peter Bayley
SHERIDAN: *Comedies* Peter Davison
STOPPARD: *'Rosencrantz and Guildenstern are Dead', 'Jumpers' & 'Travesties'* T. Bareham
SWIFT: *Gulliver's Travels* Richard Gravil
SYNGE: *Four Plays* Ronald Ayling
TENNYSON: *In Memoriam* John Dixon Hunt
THACKERAY: *Vanity Fair* Arthur Pollard
TROLLOPE: *The Barsetshire Novels* T. Bareham
WEBSTER: *'The White Devil' & 'The Duchess of Malfi'* R. V. Holdsworth
WILDE: *Comedies* William Tydeman
VIRGINIA WOOLF: *To the Lighthouse* Morris Beja
WORDSWORTH: *Lyrical Ballads* Alun R. Jones & William Tydeman
WORDSWORTH: *The 1807 Poems* Alun R. Jones
WORDSWORTH: *The Prelude* W. J. Harvey & Richard Gravil
YEATS: *Poems 1919–35* Elizabeth Cullingford
YEATS: *Last Poems* Jon Stallworthy

Issues in Contemporary Critical Theory Peter Barry
Thirties Poets: 'The Auden Group' Ronald Carter
Tragedy: Developments in Criticism R.P. Draper
Epic Ronald Draper
Poetry Criticism and Practice: Developments since the Symbolists A.E. Dyson
Three Contemporary Poets: Gunn, Hughes, Thomas A.E. Dyson
Elizabethan Poetry: Lyrical & Narrative Gerald Hammond
The Metaphysical Poets Gerald Hammond
Medieval English Drama Peter Happé
The English Novel: Developments in Criticism since Henry James Stephen Hazell
Poetry of the First World War Dominic Hibberd
The Romantic Imagination John Spencer Hill
Drama Criticism: Developments since Ibsen Arnold P. Hinchliffe
Three Jacobean Revenge Tragedies R.V. Holdsworth
The Pastoral Mode Bryan Loughrey
The Language of Literature Norman Page
Comedy: Developments in Criticism D.J. Palmer
Studying Shakespeare John Russell Brown
The Gothic Novel Victor Sage
Pre-Romantic Poetry J.R. Watson

Emily Brontë

Wuthering Heights

A CASEBOOK

EDITED BY

MIRIAM ALLOTT

Revised Edition

B L O O M S B U R Y

NEW DELHI • LONDON • OXFORD • NEW YORK • SYDNEY

BLOOMSBURY INDIA
Bloomsbury Publishing India Pvt. Ltd
Second Floor, LSC Building No. 4, DDA Complex, Pocket C–6&7,
Vasant Kunj, New Delhi 110070

BLOOMSBURY, BLOOMSBURY ACADEMIC INDIA and the Diana logo are trademarks of Bloomsbury Publishing Plc

First published in India 2024

This edition published with permission from Bloomsbury Publishing Plc,
50 Bedford Square, London, WC1B3DP, UK

A catalogue record for this book is available from the British Library.
A catalog record for this book is available from the Library of Congress.

ISBN: 978-93-61319-03-7
For sale in the Indian subcontinent only

Printed and bound in India by Replika Press Pvt. Ltd.

To find out more about our authors and books
visit www.bloomsbury.com and sign up for our newsletters

CONTENTS

ACKNOWLEDGEMENTS

The editor and publishers wish to thank the following for permission to use copyright material: Lascelles Abercrombie, *Brontë Society Transactions* (1924) (Martin Secker & Warburg Ltd); Virginia Woolf, '*Jane Eyre* and *Wuthering Heights*', from *The Common Reader* (copyright 1925 by Harcourt, Brace & World Inc., copyright 1953 by Leonard Woolf); C. P. Sanger, *The Structure of Wuthering Heights* (Hogarth Press Ltd); E. M. Forster, *Aspects of the Novel* (Edward Arnold (Publishers) Ltd); H. W. Garrod, introduction to the 1930 World's Classics edition of *Wuthering Heights* (Oxford University Press); Q. D. Leavis, *Fiction and the Reading Public* (Chatto & Windus Ltd); David Cecil, 'Emily Brontë and *Wuthering Heights*', from *Early Victorian Novelists* (Constable & Co. Ltd); Irene Cooper Willis, *The Authorship of Wuthering Heights* (Hogarth Press Ltd); Mark Schorer, *The World We Imagine* (Mark Schorer, Chatto & Windus Ltd and Farrar, Straus & Giroux Inc., copyright 1949, © 1968 by Mark Schorer); Derek Traversi, '*Wuthering Heights* after a Hundred Years', from *Dublin Review* (1949) (Derek Traversi); Dorothy Van Ghent, 'Dark "otherness" in *Wuthering Heights*', from *The English Novel: form and function* (Holt, Rinehart & Winston Inc., New York, copyright 1953 by Dorothy Van Ghent); Miriam Allott 'The Rejection of Heathcliff?', from *Essays in Criticism* (1958) (Miriam Allott); Mary Visick, 'The Genesis of *Wuthering Heights*', from *The Genesis of Wuthering Heights* (University of Hong Kong); Jacques Blondel, 'Literary Influences on *Wuthering Heights*', from *Emily Brontë* (Presses Universitaires de France); Philip Drew, 'Charlotte Brontë as a Critic of *Wuthering Heights*', from *Nineteenth-Century Fiction*, XVIII (1964) (© the Regents of the University of California 1964); Terry Eagleton, extracts from *Myths of Power: A Marxist Study of the Brontës* (1975) by permission of Macmillan, London and Basingstoke; Margaret Homans, extracts from *Women Writers and Poetic Identity: Dorothy Wordsworth, Emily Brontë and Emily Dickinson* (1980). Copyright © 1980 Princeton University Press, by permission of Princeton University Press; G. D. Klingopulos, 'Wuthering Heights as Dramatic Poem', *Scrutiny*, 14 (1946–7) by permission of Cambridge University Press; J. Hillis Miller, extracts from *Fiction and Repetition: Seven English Novels* (1982). Copyright © 1982 by J. Hillis Miller, by permission of Harvard University Press.

Every effort has been made to trace all the copyright holders but if any have been inadvertently overlooked the publishers will be pleased to make the necessary arrangement at the first opportunity.

System of Titling: Here and in the Selection, exterior quotemarks are used for editorially devised captions. In other cases, the caption employs the original title of the writer's book, chapter or section of a book, article or essay (in some instances abbreviated from that), and it is displayed without exterior quotemarks.

GENERAL EDITOR'S PREFACE

The Casebook series, launched in 1968, has become a well-regarded library of critical studies. The central concern of the series remains the 'single-author' volume, but suggestions from the academic community have led to an extension of the original plan, to include occasional volumes on such general themes as literary 'schools' and genres.

Each volume in the central category deals either with one well-known and influential work by an individual author, or with closely related works by one writer. The main section consists of critical readings, mostly modern, collected from books and journals. A selection of reviews and comments by the author's contemporaries is also included, and sometimes comment from the author himself. The Editor's Introduction charts the reputation of the work or works from the first appearance to the present time.

Volumes in the 'general themes' category are variable in structure but follow the basic purpose of the series in presenting an integrated selection of readings, with an Introduction which explores the theme and discusses the literary and critical issues involved.

A single volume can represent no more than a small selection of critical opinions. Some critics are excluded for reasons of space, and it is hoped that readers will pursue the suggestions for further reading in the Select Bibliography. Other contributions are severed from their original context, to which some readers may wish to turn. Indeed, if they take a hint from the critics represented here, they certainly will.

A. E. Dyson

INTRODUCTION

'*Wuthering Heights* is now generally regarded to be one of the greatest English novels', declared a modern reader in his centennial attempt to map the growth of Emily Brontë's literary reputation since her death in 1848, 'but it has gained this recognition only after a battle with the critics and the general public which has lasted a large part of the hundred years since its publication.'[1] The critical attention now devoted to Emily Brontë's single novel certainly contrasts dramatically in quality and kind with the reception it received from its earliest reviewers. Nowadays all aspects of its meaning and structure are explored by critics who take its importance for granted. Their commentaries still appear frequently in literary periodicals and occupy considerable space in books about the Brontës. From where we are today this proliferation can be seen in part as one consequence of the vast growth since the 1940s of modern professional criticism, especially as it developed in the academies. Any overview of Emily Brontë criticism besides illustrating the remarkable course of her critical reputation will also provide a register of the intellectual movements shaping critical theory and practice from her time to ours. These lead from the late nineteenth century, which inaugurated the tradition of serious systematic critical and biographical study, to the period from the 1940s to 1960s, when detailed close readings of the novel reflected the influence of what came to be called the New Criticism, and culminate in the years since the 1970s, which have brought energetically into play controversial, sometimes incompatible, psycho-social and linguistic preoccupations associated with latter-day Freudian, Marxist, feminist, structuralist, and post-structuralist, modes of critical inquiry. This diversity in itself testifies to the powerful fascination which Emily Brontë's still mysterious and impenetrable work has managed to exercise, even for hostile critics, from its first appearance. For one modern critic this continuing power of appeal combined with openness to multiplicity of response is what defines the 'classic'.[2] What modern criticism also shows, recently in particular, is the gulf which separates – for good or ill – the language and concerns of many professional readings from the natural responses of the 'ordinary' reader.

The latter description has a wide application, for it includes those who naturally enjoy reading and talking about books socially, or perhaps a little more formally in non-academic literary groups around the country, or those again who may also be regular followers of literary reviews in newspapers and book programmes on radio and television. The discussions in such instances are quickened for the most part by the compelling 'reality' of the novel's characters and their setting, the power and skill of the author, including her command of plot and narrative, her insight into both violent and harmonising potentialities of human passion, and the mystery of where her sympathies really lie, since she speaks only through narrators and abjures authorial comment. The mystery, the power, and the passion account for the immediacy with which so many of these 'ordinary' readers have responded to the book's romantic appeal. What is 'romantic' for them is the passionate love story and exciting narrative, the larger-than-life emotions, and the gloomy grandeur and mysterious 'Gothick' atmosphere which is identified with the setting of the Heights and the 'Byronic' hero, Heathcliff, and which contrasts so dramatically with the calm life of Thrushcross Grange in the valley below. The novel is read at school; it has been repeatedly filmed, dramatised, and televised; it is known to almost everyone in the country, whether they are 'literary' or not. This wide response is not owed to scholarly weighing of the novel's moral, political or metaphysical significance, to minute structural, symbolic or textual analysis, or to attempts to measure the extent of its relationship with English and European Romanticism – which is a different thing indeed from the popular conception of what is 'romantic'. But it may be added, perhaps, that this wide popular response has also begun to draw fresh nourishment from informed ideas about the book's social and historical context and the consequent pressures, conscious or unconscious, exerted upon a young woman living in such a place and at such a time, the weight of them helping to urge unique expressive gifts into the making of a remarkable literary document.

Scrupulous investigations by critics and scholars may not have solved the riddle of *Wuthering Heights*: Clement Shorter called its author 'the sphinx of our modern literature'.[3] But they have achieved something. Setting aside the difficult language of some recent literary theorists, and the stridences which can attend the sometimes disturbingly narrow application of favourite theories, specialist criticism of all kinds has demonstrated that the mind and imagination which produced this book were tough, profound and original, and far from encouraging self-indulgent fantasy, were engaged in the projection of a daring statement about certain kinds of human conflict. That statement as it came into being drew on a sense of external as well as inner debate about these matters, and has contributed in its turn to continuing dialogue about their nature and consequences.

One might say that Emily Jane Brontë came into the world in order to write her one remarkable book and then to die. She was born on 30 July 1818 at Thornton, near Bradford in Yorkshire, as the fifth of the six children of the Reverend Patrick Brontë and his wife, Maria. The two eldest children, Maria and Elizabeth, died in childhood; the third child was Charlotte, the fourth Branwell, and the sixth Anne. In April 1820, a few months before Emily's second birthday, Patrick Brontë moved his family to the small town of Haworth, which lies between Bradford and Keighley, and here, except for three short intervals, Emily stayed for the rest of her life. She died at the age of thirty from the family disease, tuberculosis, on 19 December 1848, having survived the publication of her novel by one year.

She knew, then, little about the outside world and was even more unfamiliar with literary society than her sister Charlotte. Her reluctance to venture outside her family circle is partly explained by the extreme awkwardness and constraint felt by all three Brontë sisters when they met strangers. But it seems that she experienced a special need for the freedom of the wild moorland country surrounding her home. She pined when she was obliged to leave it: first in 1835, when at sixteen she went to Roe Head School and was released after only three months because her unhappiness had begun to affect her health; then in 1837 when she tried once more to endure a period of exile, this time as a teacher in Miss Patchett's school at Law Hill; and finally in 1842, when from February to November she studied with Charlotte at the Pensionnat Heger in Brussels. Although she was not a solemn recluse, and appears to have been at her brightest and gayest when wandering on the moors with her sisters, she clearly preferred her remote and sometimes – when there was no one else at home but old Patrick Brontë – almost hermit-like existence.

In spite of this seclusion, Emily was not cut off from literature. She and her family knew the older authors, Shakespeare especially, and, nearer their own time, Cowper; they also grew up on a diet of Scott, Wordsworth and Byron, and read the articles, reviews and stories – many of the latter strongly 'Gothick' in flavour – published in *Blackwood's Magazine*.[4] 'Romantic' influences are strongly felt in the stories which the Brontë children made up for themselves, and, above all, in the fantasy worlds which they created and kept alive from their childhood to their early maturity: in Angria, created by Charlotte and Branwell, and in Gondal, created by Emily and Anne. When Emily eventually turned to the task of writing a novel for publication, she must certainly have given some thought to the kind of story and to the manner of telling it that would be most likely to interest and hold a contemporary audience. The popular success of the 'dark' tales in *Blackwood's* and the family admiration for Scott, which was in agreement with a taste widespread in the 1840s,[5] almost certainly had their part to play in affecting her narrative style. She was also in sympathy with the familiar tradition that the heroine of a novel must be beautiful and attractive: Charlotte was rounded upon by both Emily and Anne for her decision to make the heroine of her second novel a Plain Jane.[6]

That her re-working of various influences which played upon her imagination would produce an effect of such complete unconventionality in her novel, Emily Brontë seems not to have foretold or even to have recognised when it was pointed out to her. 'Having formed these beings [Heathcliff, Earnshaw, Catherine]', writes Charlotte in her preface of 1850, 'she did not know what she had done.' When she read aloud to her sisters from her manuscript, she thought them guilty of affectation as they 'shuddered at her portrayal of natures so relentless and implacable, of spirits so lost and fallen' (p. 62 below). Wasted by illness and near to death, she still smiled, 'half amused and half in scorn', as Charlotte read out to her from the notice in the *North American Review* the description of herself (she and her sisters were, of course, then known only pseudonymously as Currer, Ellis and Acton Bell) as 'a man of uncommon talents', but dogged, brutal and morose.[7]

She was about twelve or thirteen when she and Anne brought the Gondal world into being, and perhaps about twenty-two when they began to write down its prose chronicles. As everyone knows, these are lost, and scholars have been able to piece together some notion of

Gondal and its people only from poems in which Emily dramatises the highly charged emotional experiences of certain of its inhabitants and situations.[8] It is also well known that Emily was secretive about the full extent of her poetic activity. Just how many of the poems accidentally discovered by Charlotte in the autumn of 1845, when Emily was twenty-seven, were 'Gondal' poems and how many were 'personal' (the distinction is not necessarily easy to make) is unrecorded. But both kinds are represented, along with poems by Charlotte and Anne, in the little pseudonymous volume, *Poems by Currer, Ellis and Acton Bell*, published by Aylott & Jones in May 1846, after heroic efforts by Charlotte first to overcome Emily's fierce distaste for having her 'rhymes' read at all, let alone printed, and then to master the difficulties of getting a manuscript accepted and finally seen through the press. The pseudonyms, Charlotte explains, were a deliberately 'ambiguous choice'; the sisters' scruples did not allow them to assume 'christian names positively masculine', but they hoped to be taken for men and so avoid the prejudice which, according to their 'vague impression', usually greeted women writers.[9]

The book sold only two copies, but long before they knew its failure the sisters had begun writing their novels. 'The mere effort to succeed', Charlotte tells us, 'had given a wonderful zest to existence; it must be pursued.' It is generally agreed that Emily probably began to write *Wuthering Heights* towards the end of 1845, though it is possible that she may have conceived the story earlier. It was completed by the summer of 1846, when in company with Charlotte's *The Professor* and Anne's *Agnes Grey* it set out on its year's journey in search of a publisher. (Aylott & Jones, who had taken the *Poems*, were approached, but replied that they did not publish novels.) In summer 1847, Thomas Cautley Newby agreed to publish *Wuthering Heights* and *Agnes Grey*, but not *The Professor*, which failed to find a publisher in Charlotte's lifetime. He accepted the two books in July and sent proof-sheets by mid-August; but he delayed the printing until suddenly stung into action by the dramatic success of Charlotte ('Currer Bell') with her second novel, *Jane Eyre*, published by Smith, Elder & Company in October 1847, only six weeks after its prompt acceptance. Two months later, in December 1847, Newby published the two novels in a three-volume edition, with *Wuthering Heights*, by 'Ellis Bell', occupying two volumes, and *Agnes Grey*, by 'Acton Bell', making up the third.

Newby's part in the early history of *Wuthering Heights* is hardly glorious. According to his contract with Emily and Anne, there were to be 350 copies of the edition; the sisters were to pay £50 towards the expenses and to share the risks of publication; and on the sale of 250 copies their £50 would be refunded and they would be paid £100. With her own more generous contract from Smith, Elder in front of her, Charlotte recognised the hardness with which Newby had driven a bargain, but neither then nor later could she persuade Emily or Anne to transfer to her own publishers. Indeed Anne offered Newby her second novel, *The Tenant of Wildfell Hall*, which had something of a *succès de scandale* the following summer and brought him more profit than he deserved.

Charlotte's distrust of Newby was justified. For one thing, although the edition sold well, the sisters' original payment of £50 was never returned. For another, Newby shamelessly exploited the mystery of the identity of his unknown authors, which became a favourite subject of literary gossip in 1847–8. Not content with phrasing his advertisements so that nobody should miss the connection between his own authors and George Smith's best-selling success, he went on to hint that 'Ellis Bell' was in fact also the author of *Jane Eyre* (a notion reflected in some current reviews), and then, on publishing Anne's *The Tenant of Wildfell Hall*, printed extracts from reviews of the other 'Bell' novels, arranging them so that one might infer that 'Acton' was the sole author of all the tales. The climax of this behaviour came in his correspondence with Harper Brothers of New York when – hoping that this would influence them to take it – he claimed that 'Acton's' new novel was by the author of *Jane Eyre* and that all the Bell novels were the product of a single writer.[10] It was when the sisters heard this that Charlotte and Anne made their celebrated journey from Haworth to London on 7 July 1848 in order to clear up matters with George Smith by presenting at least two of the 'brothers Bell' for the first time in person: that there was a third had to be taken on trust, for Emily would not be dislodged.[11] Newby's part in the history of the 'Bells' and their reputation came to an end in 1850, when George Smith obtained from him his rights in Emily's and Anne's novels and published Charlotte's single-volume memorial edition of *Wuthering Heights* and *Agnes Grey*. This contains the biographical sketch in which Charlotte hoped to settle for ever any lingering doubts about the separate identities of Currer, Ellis and Acton Bell.

It is hard to say how long Emily Brontë's novel would have had to wait for general recognition without that eager popular interest in the Brontës which was prompted by the immediate success of *Jane Eyre* in 1847, stimulated further by its author's tribute to her dead sisters in 1850, and later given further life by the absorbing biographical material in Mrs Gaskell's *The Life of Charlotte Brontë*, published in 1857. And yet, when we have all the evidence before us, it seems right to say that the individual qualities of this remarkable work never went completely unrecognised or unsung, as indeed George Lewes pointed out as early as 1850 (see below, p. 64). The first reviewers of 1847 and 1848 convey, in their perplexity at its apparent moral unorthodoxy and in the urgency of their distress at its violence, the strong impression made upon them by this unusual addition to the output of new novels. They were certainly upset by its deserting the accepted convention which required the author to provide clear moral signposts for the reader's guidance. Emily Brontë's indirect narrative method, which precludes explicit authorial comment, has of course been familiar since the days of James and Conrad, who helped to make readers at home with the 'multiple perspectives' which their procedures afforded. Nowadays 'who says what to whom, and why?' is a key hermeneutical concern. The variety of possible answers may be seen as the text's self-reflexive comment on its own fictionality, but this does not prevent those still in pursuit of the authorial voice sometimes formulating self-reflexive interpretations on their own account, for example that the mixed feelings and interventions of the principal narrator, Nelly Dean, mean that she must be the true villain of the piece; that the clue to the novel's meaning lies in the sardonic rendering of Branderham's long-winded sermon, one part of the famous dream which frightens Lockwood who is himself the narrator of Nelly's narrative; or that the book must be read as a document of sexual repression because of the 'Freudian' use of locks and keys as a feature of the plot involving both the Catherines.[12]

Considering what has happened since, it is perhaps hardly surprising that when the indirect method was new in the 1840s it was especially troubling for readers. The violent and destructive passions in the story seemed, in the conventions of the day, to call out for open condemnation, and yet were dramatised with an intensity that suggested the author's sympathetic identity with them. The combination has had the effect ever since of overshadowing for many readers what could be termed the more 'normal' elements in the novel, which probably tells us something about the sort of stimulus to which this author's creativity was most likely to respond. Yet the second half of her novel seems to come into being to set forward the contrasting qualities of brightness, gaiety and warmth which – ostensibly – make successful headway against the increasingly fitful darkness of the second generation story. The relationship between this 'dark' and 'light' remains one of the novel's famously unresolved puzzles (see below, pp. 32–3).

In spite of the early worries we find in 1847–8 more than one commentator expressing in the same breath his disapproval of the book's subject-matter and his acknowledgement of its originality and genius. Clearly *Wuthering Heights* was something more than 'only a novel' for the *Britannia*, *Douglas Jerrold's Weekly Newspaper* and the *Atlas*, from all of which Newby was able to cull commendatory passages for use when puffing *The Tenant of Wildfell Hall*. Each of these periodicals contains bewildered allusions to the book's gloom, its violence, its so-called 'coarseness' of language, but at the same time it was felt to be 'strangely original'. 'It reminds us of *Jane Eyre*. The author is a Salvator Rosa (see below, p. 41n) with his pen' (*Britannia*); 'the writer . . . wants but the practised skill to make a great artist; perhaps a great dramatic artist' (*Douglas Jerrold's Weekly Newspaper*); it is a 'colossal' performance (*Atlas*). The *Britannia*, in spite of blindness to the author's considerable powers of craftsmanship, which are now usually taken for granted, understood that the book's weaknesses and strengths were both related to its origin in 'a mind of limited experience but of original energy and of a singular and distinctive cast'.

Clippings of these reviews, together with clippings of the brief *Examiner* notice and the encouraging undated review reprinted by Charles Simpson in his *Emily Brontë* (1929)[13] – all of which are represented here – are included among the Brontë papers collected at Haworth Parsonage Museum. They were certainly known to Charlotte, who none the less insists in her memorial preface of 1850 that the 'immature but very real powers in *Wuthering Heights* were scarcely recognised'. She is right, though, in feeling that the novel's 'import and nature were misunderstood', and that its author's identity was 'misrepresented'. She would be remembering with especial poignancy, perhaps, those American conjectures concerning 'Ellis Bell's' embittered nature and the 'coarseness' of the work which this nature produced.

In fact, although it is chiefly English reviewers whom literary historians have in mind when referring to the initial disapproval of *Wuthering Heights* on moral grounds, it is from America that many of the sternest moral criticisms arrive. Several American reviewers warn their readers off the book, and it is not until the 1870s, when a lengthy biographical and critical study of Emily Brontë appeared in the New York *Galaxy*, that any substantial *amende honorable* is made in an American literary periodical. One early reviewer regarded the book as 'the last desperate attempt to corrupt the virtue of the sturdy descendants of the Puritans' (see below, p. 51).

In England, however, feelings about *Wuthering Heights* took a fresh direction during the 1850s. Charlotte's edition of 1850 prompted renewed interest; so too did her death in 1855, which inspired Matthew Arnold's poem, 'Haworth Churchyard', and Mrs Gaskell's biography of her in 1857, which was widely reviewed, often by notable Victorians who took this opportunity to survey all the Brontë novels and were eager to incorporate references to Emily's individual achievement as a poet and novelist. But even before the 1850 edition, though in the same year, *Wuthering Heights* had received the first of what were to be a growing number of tributes from practising authors. Sidney Dobell's article in the *Palladium* of September 1850 must be placed beside Swinburne's essay of 1883 and Mary Ward's work on the Brontë's in 1899–1900 as landmarks in the critical standing of *Wuthering Heights* during the nineteenth century.

Dobell reflects the prevalent confusion over the identity of the 'Bells'. In spite of 'Currer Bell's' disclaimer in the third edition of *Jane Eyre* he persists in believing that all the Brontë novels were written by a single author.[14] The innovation here is that for the first time it is not *Jane Eyre* but *Wuthering Heights*, although 'earlier in date and ruder in execution', to which the critic gives his whole-hearted response, stressing in particular the 'freshness' of the conception, its atmospheric vividness and the poetic concentration of its style. Dobell's own style in this essay is hardly pithy, but his analysis is governed by the practitioner's informed admiration for a fellow-writer's skill.

Dobell's reservations about Heathcliff sustain the habit of debate that places this character at the centre of much of what has come to be thought and felt about the novel. Dobell sees him to be 'as wonderfully strong and original' in conception as Catherine Earnshaw, but 'spoilt in detail'. 'The authoress has too often disgusted where she should have terrified, and allowed us a familiarity with her fiend which has ended in unequivocal contempt.' Reviewers had frequently located the source of the book's troubling effects in him, but Dobell is the first to hint at the mixture of the naturalistic and non-naturalistic in his characterisation, anticipating Mary Ward on this aspect of the novel in her 1900 Introduction for the Howarth edition of the Brontë novels.

Heathcliff is certainly at the centre of Charlotte Brontë's anxiety about her sister's work in her suggestive Preface of 1850, itself the subject of later scrutiny (see p. 29 below). It is plain to her, as to Dobell and other earlier commentators, that Heathcliff is a 'villain' and intended to be one.[15] The idea that he could be anything else began to take hold in the 1920s, stemming first from the kind of enthusiasm represented by Lascelles Abercrombie's piece on *Wuthering Heights* (see below, p. 106), and encouraged by David Cecil's influential essay of 1934. Cecil saw *Wuthering Heights* as a 'metaphysical' novel in which principles of 'storm' and 'calm' are temporarily in conflict but are ultimately shown to be components in a total harmony (see below, p. 120). The radical shift of opinion came with the social preoccupations of Marxist critiques, which centred the book's conflicts in the class differences separating the Lintons from the Earnshaws and placing Heathcliff in an anomalous position in relation to both, a position seen as leading to his desire for revenge on both their houses. The best known early example is Arnold Kettle's sympathetic defence in his *An Introduction to the English Novel* of 1951, where Heathcliff, sinned against before sinning, is a rebel dealing out rough justice to ruling-class oppressors who is himself corrupted in the process: 'the very forces which drove him to rebelling for a higher freedom have themselves entrapped him in their own values and determined the nature of this revenge' (p. 140). Resistance to such 'social' readings of the novel usually meant that judgement was upheld against Heathcliff, as in the 1960s by Philip Drew (see below, p. 197) and John Hagan in 'The Control of Sympathy in *Wuthering Heights*' (see below, p. 237), who are uncompromising about his 'villainy' but impressed by the skill and feeling with which the author arouses sympathy for him. Terry Eagleton's chapter in *The Myths of Power* (p. 209 below), which begins where Kettle leaves off, inaugurates a period of more stringent social and political analysis. His Heathcliff, as 'contradiction incarnate', harnesses the 'agrarian capitalist forces of Thrushcross Grange' to beat it at its own game but does this 'with an unLinton like' extremism because his real commitment is to Catherine, and thus to a more ancient world 'of absolute personal value which capitalist social relations cancel'. The relative primitivism with which subsequent psycho-social, and especially feminist, critiques have charged this suggestive analysis lends piquancy to the author's corrective self-review in his introduction to the 1988 edition of his book (see below, p. 213), but also helps to light up for us the movements of critical dialogue which collections of the present kind try to reflect and of which the continuing argument about Heathcliff is a sharply representative particular instance.

Charlotte in 1850 was making her own contribution to the debate by differing from the first reviewers in finding that the troubling matter was not so much that Heathcliff should have been conceived at all (though she glances uneasily at this), but precisely that he should have been so powerfully portrayed. The combination of villainy and poetic power was to lead some of Emily Brontë's later nineteenth-century readers to make comparisons between *Wuthering Heights* and poetic drama: thirty years later, in 1883, Swinburne was to speak of the book's 'fresh dark air of tragic passion' and to refer the reader to Shakespeare and Webster. Something of the same imaginative response is felt in certain modern essays written during the 1940s, some sixty years or so after Swinburne's, which find that the novel exacts for its full appreciation the same kind of attention as verse drama. The theme surfaces less frequently as a central concern today but was more than once explored in connection with the novel's style and formal structure in some notable essays of the 1940s, including G. D. Klingopulos's piece in *Scrutiny* (see below, p. 129), and Melvin Watson on 'tempest in the soul' as the main theme of *Wuthering Heights* (see p. 34, n. 12), which went so far as to claim that the novel was 'consciously organised into a five-act tragedy'.

The general feeling of wonder once Charlotte had revealed the true identity of the unknown authors is reflected in almost every review of the 1850 edition and marks the beginning of an unfailing appetite for biographical studies of the Brontës which still finds a lively market today. The first reviewers, though, were usually too engrossed by the new information to do more than record it, and perhaps to register even more surprise than before at the sisters' exceptional subject-matter. George Henry Lewes, who was later to review Charlotte's own novels and to conduct a correspondence with her, is a notable exception. 'Curious it is to read *Wutherhing Heights* and *The Tenant of Wildfell Hall*,' he remarks, 'and remember that the writers were two retiring, solitary, consumptive girls'; one senses that the knowledge increases his admiration, quickening especially his romantic delight in Heathcliff, who 'is drawn with a sort of dusky splendour which fascinates'.[16] Emily's treatment of Catherine's loving him 'with a passionate abandonment which sets culture, education, the world at defiance' shows 'real mastery . . . and more genius . . . than you will find in a thousand novels . . .'. He salutes Charlotte's insight in her preface into the nature of the creative imagination, and he defends the validity of its statements, which do not have to do with ordinary 'moral' considerations. At the same time he does find a lesson in the book: moral anarchy follows the display of untamed natural passions. Moreover, in depicting this moral anarchy, the artist errs – through extravagance, through exaggeration, through the excessive indulgence of horrors.

Such 'indulgence' was still capable of alienating critics, as with the writer in the *Eclectic Review* of 1851 who found the book 'repellent', or at least eliciting excuses from others, for example Harriet Martineau, who tried to explain the reason for the 'repulsiveness' in Anne's and Emily's novels in her obituary notice for Charlotte in 1855. On the other hand, in 1854 and 1855 we find D. G. Rossetti and Matthew Arnold responding as ardently as Lewes to Emily's poetic power.

The publication of Mrs Gaskell's *The Life of Charlotte Brontë* in 1857 helped to establish two major preoccupations in Brontë studies. One of them is that excited interest already referred to which fastens on all biographical facts concerning the entire Brontë family. The other is the critical weighing of the relative literary merits of Charlotte and Emily which, as the century proceeded, worked more and more in Emily's favour and, as the century closed, reached a considerable degree of critical sophistication with Mrs Humphry Ward's shrewd series of assessments. One modern attempt to redress the balance in Charlotte's favour occurs in the apology for neglect of her social and political perceptions included by Eagleton in the afterthoughts about his study of the Brontës. But it was the biographical emphasis that was to keep the upper hand until critical practice in the 1940s and 1950s shifted towards the

New Critics' concentrated analysis of theme, structure and texture, a methodology to which *Wuthering Heights* in particular seemed especially ready to lend itself.

It has to be said that the fascination which the Brontë story came to hold for Victorian readers and their successors has in many respects done all the Brontës a critical disservice. The engrossing circumstances of their lives – impoverished, shadowed with fatal disease and restricted in almost everything except passionate imagination and intensity of feeling – and the vividness with which these circumstances throw into relief the workings of creative genius, have again and again since 1857 drawn attention away from the writings to concentrate it on the writers. It is in the years between 1857 and 1899 that the Brontë legends begin to grow, Emily perhaps in the end suffering most from fanciful speculations about her life and character. Mrs Gaskell had not met Emily, had not read her succinct, matter-of-fact, rather childlike diary-papers in which – poignantly to us now – she tries to guess what the future has in store.[17] Mrs Gaskell makes no allusion to the mischievous girl who lost her reserve when rambling on the moors with her sisters or playing the piano for them in the parlour at home, and who was remembered affectionately by Charlotte's old school-friend Ellen Nussey.[18] She knew Emily chiefly from listening to her still grief-haunted sister Charlotte, and from reading Charlotte's letters written between September and December 1848, when Emily stubbornly refused to accept any medical help and obliged her family to stand by helplessly as she grew weaker.[19] Mrs Gaskell calls her a 'Titan' and refers to her briefly with more wonder than warmth.

The first attempt to rectify matters was made by Mary Robinson who published the earliest full-length biography in 1883, drawing on fresh materials from Charlotte's friend Ellen Nussey and displaying particular interest in the religious and autobiographical sources of Emily's novel, including the innovative suggestion of a link with the Gondal poems, an idea explored more fully in this century by Mary Visick (see below, p. 181). Charles Simpson's agreeably straightforward *Emily Brontë* (1929) is one of the earliest twentieth-century biographies. On the wilder shores of fancy are Romer Wilson's colourful reconstruction, *All Alone: The Life and Private History of Emily Jane Brontë* (1928) and Virginia Moore's *The Life and Eager Death of Emily Brontë* (1936). Modern expansion upon Mrs Gaskell's *Life* virtually begins with Margaret Lane's 'reconstruction' in *The Brontë Story* (1953), which incorporates into the original text distinctively set out passages of up-to-date material. Since then at least one new substantial biographical study has appeared in each decade, notably by John Hewish (1969), Winifred Gérin (1971), Tom Winnifrith (1973), and Edward Chitham (1987), all in effect concerned with separating fact and fiction in existing Brontë studies (see Select Bibliography, p. 236 below). Hewish, Gérin and Chitham devote themselves exclusively to Emily and to the assessment of connections between the few known facts about her life and the nature of her novel and poems; Edward Chitham's eminently sensible recent finding is that nothing in what we know of her life is at all incompatible with her work.

The 'mystery' about her personality in Mrs Gaskell's *Life* prompted reviewers of the book to look again at her achievement, particularly in relation to that of Charlotte and Anne (who is still overshadowed by her sisters). Of those cited here it is an American alone who – ten years after the novel's publication – still finds it possible to dismiss *Wuthering Heights* as grotesque (see below, p. 76). For the others, who continued to overlook the warmer elements in the book, Emily is certainly 'dark', 'grim' and 'gloomy', and altogether takes more swallowing than Charlotte, but John Skelton in *Fraser's Magazine* sensed that her work belonged to a different, more poetic region of the imagination, and was the first to point to the parallel between Catherine's delirium and Ophelia's madness in *Hamlet* (see below, p. 70n). William Roscoe in the *National Review* commented on the 'personal impress' in all the Brontë writings – thus foreshadowing the emphasis laid on their Romantic *amour de soi* by Mrs Humphry Ward in 1900 and again by Jacques Blondel in 1958 – and was in the end carried away by the 'whole wild harmony' of Emily's book. In *Blackwood's Magazine*, E. S. Dallas – anticipating in some respects Swinburne in 1883 and G. D. Klingopulos in 1947 – spoke of her novel's approaching the predominating idea of fatality in Greek tragedy. In the same period, Émile Montégut, again anticipating Swinburne (as he pointed out with pride when reprinting his essay in 1887) saluted her 'dark' poetic imagination, and G. H. Lewes reaffirmed the special strength of his feelings for this *bête fauve*, in a private letter to Mrs Gaskell. Perhaps it was on Lewes's advice that *Wuthering Heights* was packed in the baggage which travelled with him and Marian Evans (recently transformed into George Eliot) to Germany in 1858.[20]

Thirty years later, in 1887, the conventional 'lady novelist' Mrs Oliphant, referring to 'the extraordinary and feverish romance, *Wuthering Heights*, which in very painfulness and horror made an impression upon the mind of the public, greater perhaps than its merits justify', attributed part of its fame to the interest stimulated in the Brontës by Mrs Gaskell's *Life*, and spoke rather loosely of the 'respectful oblivion' into which so many of the once-celebrated earlier Victorian novelists had by this time fallen: in 'circulating libraries in watering places' one might have the best chance of still discovering old copies of *Jane Eyre* or *Mary Barton*.[21] In fact, during these thirty years Emily Brontë's reputation had been consolidated by Thomas Wemyss Reid's references to her in his monograph *Charlotte Brontë* (1877) and by Mary Robinson's 1883 biography, which engaged with Reid over his view that Heathcliff was drawn directly from Emily's brother Branwell, whose moral and physical disintegration had darkened the Brontë home between the years of 1845 and 1848 (see below, pp. 86–7).

Mary Robinson's book stimulated further debate by prompting Swinburne's seminal essay, which first appeared in the *Athenaeum* as a review of this pioneering biography. Swinburne's piece set a seal on the conception of *Wuthering Heights* as an outstanding work of the poetic imagination, which could be best understood if approached in the same way as *King Lear* or *The Duchess of Malfi*. For Swinburne, even Mary Robinson makes too much of Branwell's effect on Emily, whose naturally sombre vision, as he understands it, did not have to rely for its stimulus on this kind of experience. Haunted as he is by the pure tragic feeling which the novel seems to him to express, he nevertheless devotes considerable space to defending its 'story-within-a-story' narrative method, which he felt to be a clumsy, though perfectly familiar and justifiable, literary device. In spite of this, the method remained for many readers until the 1930s a sign of the author's technical awkwardness and uncertainty; it mars what is otherwise a masterpiece for Violet Paget in 1895 and, again, for H. W. Garrod in 1930.

In the sixty years or so between 1883 and the Second World War the most significant appraisals of Emily Brontë's achievement were almost certainly Mrs Humphry Ward's introduction to the volume containing *Wuthering Heights* in the Haworth edition of works by the Brontë sisters, published in 1899–1900, and David Cecil's 'Emily Brontë and *Wuthering Heights*' in his *Early Victorian Novelists*

(1934). This was itself a landmark in the revaluation of the nineteenth-century novel, which had by then fallen far out of favour and was still a long way from its huge revival, though its tremendous popularity may be on the turn, judging by recent sounds of deconstruction which suggest the beginning of a withdrawing roar.

Mary Ward's essay, now rather less well known than it should be, displays the breadth and range of reference that would probably have pleased her uncle Matthew Arnold. Her interest in a writer's processes of recreating actual experience, and her familiarity with English, French, German and Russian literature, enabled her to come as close as anyone had yet done to seeing what was non-parochial in Charlotte and Emily's artistic achievement, especially its relation to the English and European romanticism with whose movements they were themselves familiar. This does not prevent her from distinguishing sharply between Emily's native vigour as a writer and Charlotte's responsiveness to the French 'dithyrambs' of Victor Hugo and George Sand. It is probably true that she overestimated the importance of sensational German 'Gothick' influences on Emily, who had learnt some German in Brussels in 1842 and, it is generally agreed, was familiar with tales from the German published in *Blackwood's Magazine* in the 1830s and 1840s. For a corrective we can go to the modern French scholar, Jacques Blondel, who weighs the relative importance of the various literary influences probably affecting Emily Brontë's writings in his full-length study, *Emily Brontë: expérience spirituelle et création poetique* (1958). Mary Ward in her final assessments of the relative weaknesses and strengths of the three Brontë sisters speaks comparatively little, though not slightingly, of Anne; recognises in Charlotte and Emily, in spite of the dithyrambs and amateurish 'lack of literary reticence' of the one and the occasional crudities of the other, a similar foundation of 'stern and simple realism' and a 'singular faculty of observation at once shrewd and passionate'; and finds in the end that the differences between them 'are almost wholly in Emily's favour'. She admires in particular what she sees as the fundamental saneness, wholeness, and imaginative health underlying the violent sweep of events in *Wuthering Heights*, a reading which separates her at once both from her predecessors among reviewers and from many of her recent successors, for whom the oppositions in the work – whether 'social', 'metaphysical' or exclusively those of conflicting human passions – resist resolution.

Mary Ward's introduction to *Jane Eyre* drew attention to the fact that interest in the Brontës on the part of the general reading public was firmly established by 1899. The founding of the Brontë Society in the 1890s, the setting up of a Brontë Museum in Haworth Parsonage, and the regular publication from 1895 onwards of the *Brontë Society Transactions* had the effect of fostering this kind of enthusiasm. Such enthusiasm is certainly reflected in the rhapsodical style of several biographical and critical studies of the Brontës in the 1920s, a period which also produced notable short studies by Herbert Read, Lascelles Abercrombie and C. P. Sanger, and the first attempts by Mabel Hope Dodds (followed in the 1930s by Fanny Ratchford) to explore in detail the connection between Emily Brontë's novel and her Gondal poems.[22]

Twenty-two years ago, when the first edition of this Casebook appeared, it seemed possible to say at this point that after Mary Ward's Haworth edition the 'modern' history of *Wuthering Heights* really began with David Cecil's essay of 1934, since it seemed to have affected directly or indirectly much that had been written about the book in the interval. But that was then and, as always, the landscape of the 'modern' shifts with time. As it happens, Cecil does not differ essentially from Mrs Ward in judging Emily as a greater writer than Charlotte, in whom he too sees weaknesses which in any writers less passionate would be fatally crippling. It was sometimes claimed that his pronouncements put an end to Charlotte's pre-eminence for the modern reader, but a movement of taste is involved which is far more general than this judgement allows for. The recognition of Emily's power had begun to glimmer in some sensibilities in the late 1850s and by the end of the century had won considerable allegiance. Charlotte's more explicit narrative style and seemingly simpler moral certainties were bound to lose some of their appeal in a period which reacted against the overt moral strenuousness of the Victorians and also produced such complex 'impressions of life' as the novels of Hardy, James and Conrad. The older fashion survived perhaps in the 1890s in Leslie Stephen, though his repudiation of Emily Brontë – compensated for by his daughter Virginia Woolf some twenty years later – may be thought to be in keeping with a certain coolness of temperament which leads him to distrust this kind of romantic sensibility. The same thing might be said of Frederic Harrison, who like Stephen regards *Wuthering Heights* as a kind of nightmare.[23]

Nevertheless Cecil's essay, described over thirty years later as 'woolly' in Mrs Leavis's also influential 'A Fresh Approach to *Wuthering Heights*' of 1969 (which appeared while the Casebook was first in preparation), did provide two important points of departure for subsequent discussion. It drew together and confirmed what many readers had come to feel about the strength of the novel's formal structure, the firmness of its grip on the actual, and the vivid particularity of its incidental detail. Such qualities had been underlined earlier by C. P. Sanger in his remarkable monograph, *The Structure of Wuthering Heights* (1926), which was originally prepared as a paper to be read before the Heretics Society at Cambridge, and later by Irene Cooper Willis, whose study of Emily Brontë's forceful, disciplined handling of language in *The Authorship of Wuthering Heights* (1936) was undertaken in order to disprove the now long-exploded theory that Branwell was the true author of his sister's book.[24] Emily's full individuality as a prose writer had been first revealed to many modern readers in 1930, when H. W. Garrod reproduced for the Worlds Classics the original text of 1847. In the 1850 edition Charlotte had 'improved' Emily in the interests of correctness, smoothing away some of her pungent dialect and correcting her punctuation. Since Charlotte's recension of the original, hers had been the familiar text.

Cecil's second contribution of historical importance was to offer for the first time a reassuringly coherent reading of the book's total meaning, which seemed to many readers to take care of several of its most puzzling features, especially its 'moral unorthodoxy' and its mixture of the naturalistic and non-naturalistic in its treatment of events and characters. The reading encouraged assumptions about the 'organicism' of important art which no longer compels anything like the same degree of critical assent. At the time, therefore, it was not the coherency or 'closure' of Cecil's reading that prompted discussion about its validity, but his view of the principles of 'storm' and 'calm' which he took to be the work's governing principles. Readers tended either to lean towards his belief in the book's harmonious resolution of contraries, or to agree that it aspired to such a resolution in spite of irreducible elements of conflict. The latter view took account of the author's possible emotional ambivalence towards her central figure and was prone to resist 'metaphysical' interpretations. Derek Traversi in his centennial essay was indeed readier than Cecil to contemplate real anomalies in Emily Brontë's creative achievement, and the notion of the daemonic, emphasised by Cecil and by Dorothy Van Ghent in her well-known discussion of the 'window-image' in the novel, was repudiated by, among others, Philip Drew, who brought the critical wheel full circle by taking a fresh look of approval at Charlotte's 1850 Preface. The notion was also rejected in my own, now shortened, essay, which would certainly be alert to other matters if properly recast. It would still agree with Drew and Traversi that the novel's passionate discrimination between the 'agreeable' and the 'necessary' is at odds with belief that its major principles are 'not conflicting' and that Heathcliff is destructive only because in 'the cramped condition of . . . earthly incarnation' he is diverted 'from the course his nature dictates'. But it would need to take into account fresh ideas of the kind looked at below (see e.g. pp. 30–1), in particular attempts to assess the importance of the novel's social context, the dilemma of 'Ellis Bell' as an author seeking to escape the limitations of gender, and above all perhaps the reasons why her book should have inspired so many extraordinarily diverse readings and interpretations throughout its history. Such considerations have encouraged critics to look with suspicion on the need – obviously in reaction to a prevailing emphasis on the novel's 'strange otherness' and as such prominent in the original version of my own essay – to stress the fresh, even sunny 'normality' of, say, the novel's treatment of the younger Catherine's childhood, its feeling for the ordinary human emotions of affection and grief (for example, in Edgar and Francis), and the progress of one part of the second generation story towards consolidation and commitment to qualities of personal kindness and care. Recognition of such 'human' qualities found enthusiastic culminating expression in Mrs Leavis's 'fresh approach' of 1969. Her essay for this reason has come to be regarded by representatives of other ideologies as a typically debilitating instance of liberal humanist criticism, and thus a good deal more 'woolly' even than Cecil's essay had seemed to her. But critical attention generally has been drawn away from what is informative and genuinely 'fresh' in her approach to the novel by her attitude to its discordances, which she sees as vestiges of earlier versions surviving in the 'true' text, most notably in the incompletely realised portrait of Heathcliff (see Select Bibliography, p. 236 below).

Belief in an author's individual responsibility for the organisation and discipline of his or her work has taken some knocking in latterday discussions about the nature of texts, but in the 1950s those who believed in Emily Brontë's conscious attempt to shape the materials presented to her creative imagination could find what is still strong support in Mary Visick's helpful examination of the reworking in *Wuthering Heights* of figures and situations from the Gondal fantasy, and in scholarly accounts such as Jacques Blondel's of the use which Emily Brontë made of her early reading. Regrettably, the extract from the latter's lengthy study appearing in this collection can only provide a hint of his main conception of her achievement as a highly individual blend of realism and romanticism in which her *amour de soi* prompts the creation of a powerful myth – one which apparently permits her to impose order on a vast and divided universe – at the same time as it precludes the accomplishment of anything like a true 'Shakespearian' detachment. This may risk over-emphasising the quality which has led so many of her readers to speak of her with more fervour than accuracy as a visionary or 'mystic' (a term usefully placed in perspective by Margaret Lane in *The Brontë Story*, and by Tom Winnifrith in his characteristically comprehensive account of the Brontës' religious attitudes). At the same time, Blondel's emphasis on the strong, independent movements of her feeling and thought does help us to perceive what it was in her that enabled her Brussels teacher, M. Heger, to speak so confidently of her masculine cast of mind – she should have been, he thought, 'a man – a great navigator' – and how it was that her sister Charlotte could say, while 'Ellis Bell' was yet alive, 'he broaches ideas which strike my sense as much more daring and original than practical; his reason may be in advance of mine, but it certainly often travels a different road. Ellis will not be seen in his full strength till he is seen as an essayist . . .'.[25]

The allusion to Emily's 'masculine' cast of mind, a reference to gender unlikely now to pass without further comment, provides a useful cue for reference to the new material included in this revised edition. Even before the developments of the past twenty years, which include some powerful revaluations from feminist critics, the difficulty of adequately representing Brontë criticism was acute. It may be gauged by glancing at the six columns of close print devoted to the Brontës in *The New Cambridge Bibliography of English Literature*, 111 (1969). The first three columns list important studies appearing before 1940, the rest represent the vast proliferation of work up to the 1960s, the striking feature being the enormous weight of attention centred on Emily at the expense of Charlotte. Some idea of the number of column inches now needing to be added is conveyed by the selected bibliographies included in such recent studies as Lyn Pykett's *Emily Brontë* (1989), which includes a thirteen-page final chapter on 'Reading Women's Writing: Emily Brontë and the Critics', and supplements this useful survey with a bibliography which lists over thirty separate studies published since 1970, of which at least twenty are feminist critiques. The 'Guide to Further Reading' in U. C. Knoepflmacher's *Emily Brontë. Wuthering Heights*, which appeared in the same year, though a much briefer survey, is again helpful in indicating the range of recent criticism (for both books see Select Bibliography, p. 236 below). Knoepflmacher points to 'ideological' readings, for instance by Terry Eagleton (1975) and James Kavanagh (1985), whose psycho-social Freudian study builds on Eagleton and is singled out here for the critical insights which manage to survive its 'relentless' insistence on utilising and glossing specialist terms. (An early 'social' reading of Emily Brontë, published by David Wilson in 1947 and recently rescued from neglect in the new critical climate, but omitted by Knoepflmacher, is likewise included in the Select Bibliography below). Knoepflmacher's record of significant feminist readings includes those by Sandra Gilbert and Susan Gubar (1979), Nina Auerbach (1982), and Margaret Homans (1980).[26] Lyn Pykett's list, necessarily more comprehensive and indispensable for this area of interest, also includes the informative and, so to speak, 'pre-feminist' critique of the Brontë sisters as 'early-Victorian female novelists', published in 1966 by Inga-Stina Ewbank (again see Select Bibliography, below). The third of Knoepflmacher's important groupings refers to those who have encouraged us to challenge assumptions about the act of reading and interpretation, notably Frank Kermode (1973), Hillis Miller (1982), and James R. Kincaid (1987), who are referred to again below. It should be added that the 'Short Bibliography' attached to Rod Mengham's *Wuthering Heights* for Penguin Critical Studies (1989) rectifies another omission by reminding us of the papers prepared by David Musselwhite (1976) and P. M. Stoneham (1976) as contributions to symposia from the University of Essex on the Sociology of Literature.

It will be clear from all this how necessary and welcome must be the projected New Casebook on *Wuthering Heights*, which it is hoped will appear shortly. It is certainly welcome to the present editor, who can take comfort from knowing that the task of finding space for a proper representation of what has happened since 1970 will be met elsewhere. In revising the present Casebook it has been found possible to make room for extracts from commentaries representing the three main lines of approach indicated above. This has been managed not by excluding altogether any of the existing passages but by taking pains to reduce their length wherever possible, a measure which aims to preserve the book's dual interest in tracing the history of its subject's critical reputation along with the critical fashions which helped to shape, and were in turn shaped by, the various responses called out by Emily Brontë's novel over the years.

Among the new materials, then, are the extracts from Terry Eagleton's discussion of Heathcliff in *Myths of Power. A Marxist Study of the Brontës* (1975), with the addition of brief passages from his introduction to the 1988 edition, both of which have received comment above with special reference to their illustration of, and openness to, the rapid growth of fresh ideas since the 1970s. Eagleton is particularly, and perhaps a little too rawly, self-critical about his former neglect of Emily Brontë as a woman writer, with all that this entails for the incompleteness of his socially orientated reading. I have represented this region of feminist concern by passages from Margaret Homans's discussion in her *Women Writers and Poetic Identity: Dorothy Wordsworth, Emily Brontë, and Emily Dickinson* (1980), which is admirable for its breadth in dealing with these three writers, and for its discussion of Emily Brontë's handling of nature in her poems as this relates to images and concepts of nature in Wordsworth and Coleridge. Homans's study of the poems incorporates a commentary, extracted here, on the greater success of the novel over the poetry as a means of freeing the author from the constricting association of poetic creativity with the idea of 'male' inspiration.

That these and all other readings, whatever their range, can only be 'partial' is the natural corollary of radical investigations into the meaning and nature of texts which have engrossed professional critics interested in exploring the literary application of structuralist theories. These theories have encouraged us to look out for the arbitrariness of the patterns we may be tempted to impose on what we read and see. There are several first-rate attempts to look at *Wuthering Heights* in this light, including Frank Kermode's essay, already referred to, which argues that such an overplus of 'signs' is a determinant of the abiding appeal which identifies 'the classic' (see below, p. 237). James R. Kincaid's 'Coherent Readers, Incoherent Texts' (1977), uses four contrary readings to illustrate his own argument for the book's insistence on divergence. Both critics are properly exercised by the huge diversity in interpretations of the novel, some of them incompatible with each other as well as failing on their own terms to resolve puzzling contradictions within the text. The final decision to select passages from Hillis Miller's chapter on *Wuthering Heights* in *Fiction and Repetition: Seven English Novels* (1982) was in part decided by his taking some direction from, and obliquely addressing, analyses such as these, and also by his own listing of major differences of approach, which seemed useful for present purposes. His material also seemed appropriate because of his reference to movements of critical opinion helping to shape his own responses, from preoccupation with the New Criticism to his redeployment of its attentiveness to detail in the interests of concern with present day textual inquiry. To get some grip on his central argument one should of course read his explanatory introduction on 'Two Kinds of Repetition', but his comments on *Wuthering Heights* may indicate the special oddity and mysteriousness associated with the inherency of repetition in fictions and its potentially disturbing effects on the reader, especially in this novel where repetitions are performed with endlessly renewed variations which forbid final resolution while perpetually haunting us with expectations of its imminence.

I must add that I have also included for the first time a brief extract from G. D. Klingopulos's 1947 essay on the novel 'as a dramatic poem', which seems to fill a gap, thematically as well as chronologically, since the idea of 'dramatic' presentation underlies much of what one now thinks of as characteristic of both nineteenth-century poetry and also the modern 'non-authorial' narrative procedures engaging present-day critical attention. The inclusion of this piece may hint at a personal interest in the idea of 'dialogue' as a continuous without-which-not in the formulations of literature and our critical engagements with it.

NOTES

1. Melvin Watson, '*Wuthering Heights* and the Critics', *Trollopian*, III (1948), p. 243.

2. Frank Kermode, *The Classic: Literary Images of Permanency and Change* (1983). See below, p. 237.

3. Clement Shorter, *Charlotte Brontë and Her Circle* (1896), p. 144.

4. For discussions of the Brontës' reading see Mrs Humphry Ward and Jacques Blondel (pp. 96–9, 157 below).

5. Cp. the eulogy in 'The Historical Romance', *Blackwood's Magazine*, LVIII (September 1845), pp. 341–56.

6. Harriet Martineau's obituary notice for Charlotte Brontë in the *Daily News*, April 1855, repr. *Life and Letters*, IV, 182; Mrs Gaskell's *Life*, ch. 15.

7. From Charlotte's letter to W. S. Williams, 22 Nov. 1848, *Life and Letters*, II, 287. For the review referred to see below, p. 51.

8. F. E. Ratchford's 'The Brontës' Web of Dreams', *Yale Review*, XVIII (1931); *The Brontës' Web of Childhood* (New York, 1941); and *Gondal's Queen: a novel in verse* (Austin, 1955). Another reconstruction appears in Laura L. Hinkley's *The Brontës: Charlotte and Emily* (New York, 1945). See also n.22 below.

9. Charlotte Brontë's biographical notice in the 1850 edition of *Wuthering Heights* and *Agnes Grey*.

10. Cp. the attribution of *Wuthering Heights* to 'Acton Bell' in E. Whipple's notice in *North American Review* (p. 51 below).

11. Charlotte inadvertently disclosed Emily's identity to George Smith; see her letter to him from Haworth, 31 July 1848, '... the words "we are three sisters" escaped me before I was aware ... I regret [the avowal] bitterly now, for I find it against every feeling and intention of Ellis Bell' (*Life and Letters*, II, 241).

12. Many of these essays appeared during the 1950s–1960s in *Nineteenth-Century Fiction* (*NCF*), which provided a platform for debate and is thus a valuable source of information on prevailing critical ideas about Emily Brontë's novel as well as about nineteenth-century fiction generally. Arguments about Nelly Dean's role appear in James Hafley, 'The Villain in *Wuthering Heights*', *NCF*, CIII (June 1958); J. K. Mathison, 'Nelly Dean and the Power of *Wuthering Heights*', *NCF*, XV (Sept. 1960); and John Fraser, who argues against 'sentimental depreciations' of Nelly Dean in 'The Name of Action', *NCF*, XX (Dec. 1965); see Select Bibliography, p. 236 below). Edgar F. Shannon refers to Branderham in 'Lockwood's dreams and the exegesis of *Wuthering Heights*', *NCF*, XIV (Sept. 1959), and Thomas Moser looks at possible reflections of sexual repression in 'What is the Matter with Emily Jane?', *NCF*, XVII (June 1962). Other essays on focal topics include Philip Drew on Charlotte Brontë's 1850 Preface (see below, p. 197; A. R. Brick on Lewes's review of *Wuthering Heights* (see n.16 below); Melvin Watson on the dramatic structure of *Wuthering Heights*, *NCF*, IV (1950) (see also p. 21 and n.1 above); R. C. McKibben on 'The Image of the Book in *Wuthering Heights*', *NCF*, XV (Sept. 1960); E. Solomon on 'The Incest Theme in *Wuthering Heights*, *NCF*, XIV (June 1959); and Carl Woodring on

'The Narrators of *Wuthering Heights*', *NCF*, XII (March 1957). Dorothy Van Ghent's discussion of the window image first appeared in *NCF*, VII (Dec. 1952; see below p. 152).

13. A cutting of this review was found in Emily's writing desk, but no details of its source have survived.

14. The matter was cleared up after 8 Dec. 1850 when Charlotte sent him a copy of her 1850 memorial edition of *Wuthering Heights* and *Agnes Grey* (*Life and Letters*, III, 186–7).

15. See Charlotte's remarks about Heathcliff written when Emily was still alive, and cp. the emphasis given by Émile Montégut, the Brontës' French reviewer in 1857, on Emily Brontë's defying us to despise him however bad he seems to be.

16. Alan Brick notes Lewes's critical insight while overlooking his romantic feeling in 'Lewes's Review of *Wuthering Heights*', *Nineteenth-Century Fiction*, XIV (March 1960), pp. 355–9.

17. These papers, dated respectively 24 Nov. 1834, 26 June 1837, 30 July 1841 and 30 July 1845, did not come to light until the 1890s. They are now in the Brontë Parsonage Museum.

18. See Ellen Nussey's 'Reminiscences of Charlotte Brontë', *Scribner's Magazine*, May 1871 (repr. *Brontë Society Transactions* 1899, and *Life and Letters*, II, 273–5).

19. *Life and Letters*, II, 386–95.

20. G. S. Haight writes of their stay in Munich during spring 1858: 'In the evenings they tried to keep up their habit of reading aloud, taking *Mary Barton* and *Wuthering Heights* in the first weeks with a little Wordsworth and Tennyson' (*George Eliot: a biography*, 1968, p. 258).

21. M. O. Oliphant, 'The Literature of the Last Fifty Years', *Blackwood's Magazine*, CXLI (Jan. 1887), p. 758).

22. M. H. Dodds, 'Gondaliand', *Modern Language Review*, XVIII (1923); 'A Second Visit to Gondaliand', *Modern Language Review*, XXI–XXII (1926–7). See also her 'Heathcliff's Country', *Modern Language Review*, XXXIX (1944). For F. E. Ratchford see n.8 above.

23. 'Emily Brontë's gruesome phantasmagoria ... we always feel in reading it, that *Wuthering Heights* is merely a grisly dream, not a novel at all' (Frederic Harrison, *Forum*, March 1895; repr. *Studies in early Victorian Literature*, 1895).

24. This theory was first put forward by Branwell's friend F. A. Leyland, in his partisan study, *The Brontë Family, with special reference to Patrick Branwell Brontë*, 2 vols (1886). The harshly sardonic flavour characterising the atmosphere in Lockwood's dream about Branderham has been singled out by some readers as a possible instance of Branwell's lingering influence.

25. Letter to W. J. Williams, 5 Feb. 1848, *Life and Letters*, II, 189.

26. Nina Auerbach, *Woman and the Demon: The Life of a Victorian Myth* (1982). For Margaret Homans see below, pp. 216, 240; for Sandra Gilbert and Susan Gubar see Select Bibliography, p. 237 below.

PART ONE

Contemporary Reviews 1847–8

1. ENGLISH REVIEWS

Spectator, 18 December 1847

An attempt to give novelty and interest to fiction, by resorting to those singular 'characters' that used to exist everywhere, but especially in retired and remote places. The success is not equal to the abilities of the writer; chiefly because the incidents are too coarse and disagreeable to be attractive, the very best being improbable, with a moral taint about them, and the villainy not leading to results sufficient to justify the elaborate pains taken in depicting it. The execution, however, is good: grant the writer all that is requisite as regards matter, and the delineation is forcible and truthful.

Athenaeum, 25 December 1847

Here are two tales [*Wuthering Heights* and *Agnes Grey*] so nearly related to *Jane Eyre* in cast of thought, incident and language as to excite some curiosity. All three might be the work of one hand, – but the first issued remains the best. In spite of much power and cleverness; in spite of its truth to life in the remote nooks and corners of England *Wuthering Heights* is a disagreeable story. . . . The brutal master of the lonely house on 'Wuthering Heights' – a prison which might be pictured from life – has doubtless had his prototype in those uncongenial and remote districts where human beings, like the trees, grow gnarled and dwarfed and distorted by the inclement climate; but he might have been indicated with far fewer touches, in place of so entirely filling the canvas that there is hardly a scene untainted by his presence. It was a like dreariness – a like unfortunate selection of objects – which cut short the popularity of Charlotte Smith's novels – rich though they be in true pathos and faithful descriptions of Nature. . . .[1] If the Bells, singly or collectively, are contemplating future or frequent utterances in Fiction, let us hope that they will spare us further interiors so gloomy as the one here elaborated with such dismalness. . . .

NOTE

1. Charlotte Smith (1749–1806) was the author of *Elegiac Sonnets and Other Essays* (1784; 9th edn 1800) and of many equally popular novels, notably *Emmeline, or the Orphan of the Castle* (1788), *Celestina* (1792), *The Old Manor House* (1793).

Examiner, 8 January 1848

This is a strange book. It is not without evidences of considerable power: but, as a whole, it is wild, confused, disjointed and improbable; and the people who make up the drama, which is tragic enough in its consequences, are savages ruder than those who lived before the days of Homer. . . . Heathcliff may be considered as the hero of the book, if hero there be. He is an incarnation of evil qualities; implacable hate, ingratitude, cruelty, falsehood, selfishness, and revenge . . . there is one portion of his nature, one only, wherein he appears to approximate to humanity. Like the Corsair, and other such melodramatic heroes, he is

> Linked to one virtue and a thousand crimes . . .[1]

and it is with difficulty that we can prevail upon ourselves to believe in the appearance of such a phenomenon, so near our own dwellings as the summit of a Lancashire or Yorkshire moor. . . .

If this book be . . . the first work of the author, we hope that he will produce a second, – giving himself more time in its composition than in the present case, developing his incidents more carefully, eschewing exaggeration and obscurity, and looking steadily at human life, under all its moods, for those pictures of the passions that he may desire to sketch for our public benefit. It may be well also to be sparing of certain oaths and phrases, which do not materially contribute to any character, and are by no means to be reckoned among the evidence of a writer's genius. . . .[2]

NOTES

1. Misquotes the closing line of Byron's *The Corsair* (1814), III, 1864, 'Linked with one virtue, and a thousand crimes'. For Emily Brontë and Byron, see below pp. 160 and n, 174, 209.
2. The 'coarseness' of Emily's language is a common theme in many early reviews. See especially the American reviewers G. W. Peck and E. W. Whipple and Charlotte's 1850 Preface (pp. 49, 51 and 60 below).

Britannia, 15 January 1848

The uncultured freedom of native character presents more rugged aspects than we meet with in educated society. Its manners are not only more rough, but its passions are more violent. . . . It is more subject to brutal instinct than to divine reason.

It is humanity in this wild state that the author of *Wuthering Heights* essays to depict. His work is strangely original. It bears a resemblance to some of those irregular German tales in which the writers, giving the reins to their fancy, represent personages as swayed and impelled to evil by supernatural influences.[1] But they gave spiritual identity to evil impulses, while Mr Bell more naturally shows them as the natural offspring of the unregulated heart. He displays considerable power in his creations. They have all the angularity of mis-shapen growth, and form in this respect a striking contrast to those regular forms we are accustomed to meet with in English fiction. . . . They are so new, so grotesque, so entirely without art, that they strike us as proceeding from a mind of limited experience but original energy and of a singular and distinctive cast.

In saying this we indicate both the merits and faults of the tale. It is in parts very unskilfully constructed; many passages in it display neither the grace of art nor the truth of nature, but only the vigour of one positive idea – that of passionate ferocity. . . . The author is a Salvator Rosa with his pen.[2] He delineates forms of a savage grandeur when he wishes to represent sylvan beauty. His Griseldas are furies and his swains Polyphemi.[3] For this reason his narrative leaves an unpleasant effect on the mind. There are no green spots in it on which the mind can linger with satisfaction. The story rushes onwards with impetuous force, but it is the force of a dark and sullen torrent, flowing between high and rugged rocks. ... It is difficult to pronounce any decisive judgement on a work in which there is so much rude ability displayed yet in which there is so much matter for blame. The scenes of brutality are unnecessarily long and unnecessarily frequent; and as an imaginative writer the author has to learn the first principles of his art. But there is singular power in his portraiture of strong passion. He exhibits it as convulsing the whole frame of nature, distracting the intellect to madness, and snapping the heartstrings. The anguish of Heathcliff on the death of Catherine approaches to sublimity. ...

We do not know whether the author writes with any purpose; but we can speak of one effect of his production. The story shows the brutalising influence of unchecked passion.[4] His characters are a commentary on the truth that there is no tyranny in the world like that which thoughts of evil exercise in the daring and reckless breast. ...

The tale ... is but a fragment, yet of colossal proportion and bearing evidence of some great design. With all its power and originality, it is so rude, so unfinished and so careless, that we are perplexed to pronounce an opinion on it or to hazard a conjecture on the future of the author. As yet it belongs to the future to decide whether he will remain a rough hewer of marble or become a great and noble sculptor.

NOTES

1. One of the earliest attempts in print to relate Emily Brontë's novel to German romantic tales. For the first reference in the commentaries in this collection to a direct influence from E. T. A. Hoffmann's supernatural tale *Das Majorat* ('The Entail'), published 1817, see Émile Montégut's essay of 1857 on the Brontë sisters (p. 74 and n, below).

2. The reviewer in the *Atlas* of 22 January 1848 makes the same comparison (p. 43 below). The Italian painter Salvator Rosa (1615–73) was admired in England for the energy and picturesque grandeur of his landscapes.

3. 'Griseldas ... Polyphemi': the story of Griselda, the model of patience and fidelity, is related by, among others, Boccaccio (*Decameron*, x, x), Petrarch ('De Obedientia et Fidë Uxoria Mythologia') and Chaucer ('The Clerkes Tale'): for the Cyclops Polyphemus, the one-eyed giant who imprisoned Odysseus and his men, see *Odyssey*, IX.

4. A reading which agrees with that of G. H. Lewes in 1850 (p. 77 below).

Douglas Jerrold's Weekly Newspaper, 15 January 1848

Wuthering Heights is a strange sort of book, baffling all regular criticism; yet it is impossible to begin and not to finish it, and quite as impossible to lay it aside afterwards and say nothing about it. In the midst of the reader's perplexity the ideas predominant in his mind concerning this book are likely to be – brutal cruelty and semi-savage love.

What may be the moral which the author wishes the reader to deduce from the work it is difficult to say, and we refrain from assigning any, because, to speak honestly, we have discovered none but mere glimpses of hidden morals or secondary meanings. There seems to us great power in this book, but it is a purposeless power, which we feel a great desire to see turned to better account. We are quite confident that the writer of *Wuthering Heights* wants but the practised skill to make a great artist; perhaps a great dramatic artist. His qualities are, at present, excessive; a far more promising fault, let it be remembered, than if they were deficient. He may tone down, whereas the weak and inefficient writer, however carefully he may write by rule and line, will never work up his productions to the point of beauty and art. In *Wuthering Heights* the reader is shocked, disgusted, almost sickened by details of cruelty, inhumanity and the most diabolical hate and vengeance, and anon come passages of powerful testimony to the supreme power of love – even over demons in the human form. The women in the book are of a strange, fiendish-angelic nature, tantalising and terrible, and the men are indescribable out of the book itself. . . . We strongly recommend all our readers who love novelty to get this story, for we can promise them that they have never read anything like it before.

Atlas, 22 January 1848

Wuthering Heights is a strange, inartistic story. There are evidences in every chapter of a sort of rugged power – an unconscious strength – which the possessor seems never to think of turning to the best advantage. The general effect is inexpressibly painful. . . . *Jane Eyre* is a book which affects the reader to tears; it touches the most hidden sources of emotion. *Wuthering Heights* casts a gloom over the mind not easily to be dispelled. . . . There are passages in it which remind us of the *Nowlans* of the late John Banim,[1] but of all pre-existent works the one which it most recalls to our memory is the *History of Matthew Wald.*[2] It has not however, the unity and concentration of that fiction; but is a *sprawling* story, carrying us, with no mitigation of anguish, through two generations of sufferers – though one presiding evil genius sheds a grim shadow over the whole, and imparts a singleness of malignity to the somewhat disjointed tale. A more natural unnatural story we do not remember to have read. Inconceivable as are the combinations of human degradation which are here to be found moving within the circle of a few miles, the *vraisemblance* is admirably preserved. . . .

Wuthering Heights is not a book the character of which it is very easy to set forth in extract; but the . . . scene in which Catherine and Heathcliff – the lovers of early days, each wedded to another – are the actors, will afford a glimpse of Ellis Bell's power. [Quotes from chapter 15 the account of Heathcliff's last meeting with Catherine.] . . . This is at least forcible writing; but, to estimate it aright, the reader must have all the scenic accompaniments before him. He must . . . fancy himself . . . in an old north-country manor-house, situated on 'the dreary, dreary moorland',[3] far from the haunts of civilised men. There is, at all events, keeping[4] in the book – the groups of figures and the scenery are in harmony with each other. There is a touch of Salvator-Rosa[5] in all . . . *Jane Eyre* and *Wuthering Heights* are not things to be forgotten. The work of Currer Bell is a great performance; that of Ellis Bell is only a promise, but it is a colossal one.

NOTES

1. John Banim (1798–1842), 'the Scott of Ireland', novelist, dramatist and poet, published *The Nowlans* in 1826 as a contribution to *Tales by the O'Hara Family*, second series (first series 1825); 'The O'Hara Family' was a pseudonym adopted by John Banim and his brother Michael (1796–1874).
2. *The History of Matthew Wald: a novel* (1824) by J. G. Lockhart.
3. Tennyson's 'Locksley Hall' (1842) line 40: 'O the dreary, dreary moorland! O the barren, barren shore . . .'
4. The word 'keeping' was frequently in use in the later eighteenth and earlier nineteenth centuries for the maintenance of harmony and composition (*O.E.D.*). It is used again with reference to *Wuthering Heights* by Sidney Dobell (p. 58 and n below).
5. See above, p. 41 and n.

New Monthly Magazine, January 1848

Wuthering Heights, by Ellis Bell, is a terrific story, associated with an equally fearful and repulsive spot. It should have been called *Withering* Heights, for any thing from which the mind and body would more instinctively shrink, than the mansion and its tenants, cannot be imagined. . . . Our novel reading experience does not enable us to refer to anything to be compared with the personages we are introduced to at this desolate spot – a perfect misanthropist's heaven.

Tait's Edinburgh Magazine, February 1848

This novel contains undoubtedly powerful writing, and yet it seems to be thrown away. We want to know the object of a fiction. Once people were contented with a crude collection of mysteries. Now they desire to know why the mysteries are revealed. Do they teach mankind to avoid one course and take another? Do they dissect any portion of existing society, exhibiting together its weak and its strong points? If these questions were asked regarding *Wuthering Heights*, there could not be an affirmative answer given. . . .

Mr Ellis Bell, before constructing his novel, should have known that forced marriages, under threats and in confinement are illegal, and parties instrumental thereto can be punished. And second, that wills made by young ladies' minors are invalid.

The volumes are powerfully written records of wickedness and they have a moral – they show what Satan could do with the law of Entail.[1]

NOTE

1. Possibly an allusion to E. T. A. Hoffmann's *Das Majorat* (1817); see above, p. 41 and n. On Emily Brontë's legal knowledge, see C. P. Sanger, p. 109 below.

An unidentified review of 1847–8 (reproduced, from the cutting preserved at Haworth Parsonage Museum, by Charles Simpson in his *Emily Brontë*, 1929).

This is a work of great ability, and contains many chapters, to the production of which talent of no common order has contributed. At the same time, the materials which the author has placed at his own disposal have been but few. In the resources of his own mind, and in his own manifestly vivid perceptions of the peculiarities of character – in short, in his knowledge of human nature – has he found them all. An antiquated farm-house, a neighbouring residence of a somewhat more pretending description, together with their respective inmates, amounting to some half a dozen souls in each, constitute the material and the personal components of one of the most interesting stories we have read for many a long day. The comfortable cheerfulness of the one abode, and the cheerless discomfort of the other – the latter being less the result of a cold and bleak situation, old and damp rooms, and . . . of a sort of 'haunted house' appearance, than of the strange and mysterious character of its inhabitants – the loves and marriages, separations and hatreds, hopes and disappointments, of two or three generations of the gentle occupants of the one establishment, and the ruder tenants of the other, are brought before us at a moment with a tenderness, at another with a fearfulness, which appeals to our sympathies with the truest tones of the voice of nature; and it is quite impossible to read the book – and this is no slight testimony to the merits of a work of the kind – without feeling that, if placed in the same position as any one of the characters in any page of it, the chances would be twenty to one in favour of our conduct in that position being precisely such as the author has assigned to the personages he has introduced into his domestic drama. . . .

ELIZABETH RIGBY [LADY EASTLAKE]: *Quarterly Review*, December 1848[1]

. . . there can be no interest attached to the writer of *Wuthering Heights* – a novel succeeding *Jane Eyre* and purporting to be written by Ellis Bell – unless it were for the sake of a more individual reprobation. For though there is a decided family likeness between the two, yet the aspect of the Jane and Rochester animals in their native state, as Catherine and Heathfield [*sic*], is too odiously and abominably pagan to be palatable even to the most vitiated class of English reader. With all the unscrupulousness of the French school of novels it combines that repulsive vulgarity in the choice of its vice which supplies its own antidote. . . .[2]

NOTES

1. These remarks form part of the celebrated hostile review by Elizabeth Rigby (later Lady Eastlake) of *Jane Eyre*, which she describes as coarse, 'anti-Christian' and certainly not the work of a woman writer.

2. Cp. the attitude to French writers in 'The Historical Romance', in *Blackwood's Magazine*, LVIII (Sept. 1845), 'the modern romance writers of France – Victor Hugo, Janin, Madame Dudevant [George Sand], and Sue – by whom vice and licentiousness are exhibited with vast power' (p. 356).

2. AMERICAN REVIEWS

Paterson's Magazine, March 1848

We rise from the perusal of *Wuthering Heights* as if we had come fresh from a pest-house. Read *Jane Eyre* is our advice, but burn *Wuthering Heights*. . . .

Graham's Lady's Magazine, July 1848

How a human being could have attempted such a book as the present without committing suicide before he had finished a dozen chapters, is a mystery. It is a compound of vulgar depravity and unnatural horrors. . . .

Literary World, April 1848

The extraordinary popularity of *Jane Eyre* will give this book a reputation which it would not, perhaps, have otherwise acquired for itself. Few of those who read that work will find in this a worthy successor, for, although possessing far more strength and power in its darker portions, yet it lacks the relief necessary to make it as pleasing as *Jane Eyre*. It is 'a dark tale darkly told'; a book that seizes upon us with an iron grasp, and makes us read its story of passions and wrongs whether we will or no. Fascinated by strange magic we read what we dislike . . . and are made subject to the immense power, of the book, – a rough, shaggy, uncouth power. . . . In the whole story not a single trait of character is elicited which can command our admiration . . . yet, spite of this, spite of the disgusting coarseness of much of the dialogue, and the improbabilities and incongruities of the plot, we are spell-bound, we cannot choose but read. ... the following extract will, we think, give a fair estimate of [the book's] various peculiarities, its strange power, its coarse feeling, its unnatural characters, and its dark fascination. [Quotes from chapter 15 the account of Heathcliff's last meeting with Catherine.]

G. W. PECK: *American Review: A Whig Journal of Politics*, June 1848

... If we did not know that this book has been read by thousands of young ladies in the country, we should esteem it our first duty to caution them against it simply on account of the coarseness of the style. ...[1] We may express the deepest thoughts, the most ardent passions, the strongest emotions, without in the least offending propriety. We are not called upon to affect surliness or bluntness of speech; and where a whole book is in this style, whatever may be its merits, this is a simple obvious defect, the first to impress itself upon the reader, and by no means the least serious. ... The book is original; it is powerful; full of suggestiveness. But still it is coarse. ... Setting aside the profanity, which if a writer introduces into a book, he offends against both politeness and good morals, there is such a general roughness and savageness in the soliloquies and dialogues here given as never should be found in a work of art. The whole tone of the style of the book smacks of lowness. It would indicate that the writer was not accustomed to the society of gentlemen, and was not afraid, indeed, rather gloried, in showing it. ... A person may be unmannered from want of delicacy of perception, or cultivation, or ill-mannered intentionally. The author of *Wuthering Heights* is both. His rudeness is chiefly real but partly assumed ... he is rude, because he prefers to be so. ... It is evident that [he] has suffered not disappointment in love, but some great mortification of pride. Possibly his position in society has given him manners that have prevented him from associating with those among whom he feels he has intellect enough to be classed, and he is thus in reality the misanthropist he claims to be. Very likely he may be a young person who has spent his life, until within a few years, in some isolated town in the North of England. It is only by some such supposition that his peculiarities of style and thought can be accounted for. ... The influence which this book cannot but have upon manners, must be bad. For the coarseness extends farther than the mere style; it extends all through. ...

Yet with all this faultiness *Wuthering Heights* is, undoubtedly, a work of many singular merits. In the first place it is not a novel which deals with the shows of society, the surfaces and conventionalities of life. ... It lifts the veil and shows boldly the dark side of our depraved nature. ... the rapid hold it has taken of the public shows how much truth there is hidden under its coarse extravagance. ...

Next to the merit of this novel as a work of thought and subtle insight, is its great power as a work of the imagination. In this respect it must take rank very high, if not among the highest. It is not flowingly written; the author can hardly be an easy writer. Yet he has the power, with all his faults of style, of sometimes flashing a picture upon the eye, and the feeling with it, in a few sentences. The snow-storm which occurs in the second and third chapters of the first volume, is an example. ... The dialogue is also singularly effective and dramatic. The principal characters ... stand before us as definite as so many individuals. ... That [the book] is original all who have read it need not be told. ... And this is the reason of its popularity. It comes upon a sated public a new sensation. Nothing like it has ever been written before; it is to be hoped that in respect of its faults, for the sake of good manners, nothing will be hereafter. Let it stand by itself, a coarse, original, powerful book. ... It will live a short and brilliant life, and then die and be forgotten. For when the originality becomes familiarised, there will not be truth enough left to sustain it. The public will not acknowledge its men and women to have the true immortal vitality. Poor Cathy's ghost will not walk the earth forever; and the insane Heathcliff will soon rest quietly in his coveted repose. ...

NOTE

1. This review, which is exceptionally lengthy and does at least salute the author's imaginative power, also contains the most detailed of the various attacks made on the language of the novel: see above, p. 41n

E. Whipple: North American Review, October 1848[1]

. . . Not many months ago, the New England States were visited by a distressing mental epidemic, passing under the name of the 'Jane Eyre fever'. . . . The book which caused the distemper would probably have been inoffensive, had not some sly manufacturer of mischief hinted that it was a book which no respectable man should bring into his family circle. Of course, every family soon had a copy of it, and one edition after another found eager purchasers. The hero, Mr Rochester . . . became a great favourite in the boarding-schools and in the worshipful society of governesses. That portion of Young America known as ladies' men began to swagger and swear in the presence of the gentler sex, and to allude darkly to events in their lives which excused impudence and profanity.

While fathers and mothers were much distressed at this strange conduct of their innocents, and with a pardonable despair were looking for the dissolution of all the bonds of society, the publishers of *Jane Eyre* announced *Wuthering Heights* by the same author.[2] When it came, it was purchased and read with universal eagerness; but, alas! it created disappointment almost as universal. . . . Society returned to its old condition, parents were blessed in hearing their children talk common sense, and rakes and battered profligates of high and low degree fell instantly to their proper level. Thus ended the last desperate attempt to corrupt the virtue of the sturdy descendants of the Puritans. . . . The truth is, that the whole firm of Bell & Co. seems to have a sense of the depravity of human nature peculiarly their own. It is the yahoo, not the demon, that they select for representation; their Pandemonium is of mud rather than fire.

This is especially the case with Acton Bell [*sic*], the author of *Wuthering Heights*, *The Tenant of Wildfell Hall*, and, if we mistake not, of certain offensive but powerful portions of *Jane Eyre*. Acton . . . seems to take a morose satisfaction in developing a full and complete science of human brutality. In *Wuthering Heights* he has succeeded in reaching the summit of this laudable ambition. He [has] . . . made a compendium of the most striking qualities of tiger, wolf, cur, and wild-cat, in the hope of framing out of such elements a suitable brute-demon to serve as the hero of his novel. . . . Compared with Heathcote [*sic*], Squeers is considerate and Quilp humane. He is a deformed monster, whom the Mephistopheles of Goethe would have nothing to say to, whom the Satan of Milton would consider as an object of simple disgust, and to whom Dante would hesitate in awarding the honour of a place among those whom he has consigned to the burning pitch. This epitome of brutality . . . Mr Acton Bell attempts in two whole volumes to delineate, and certainly he is to be congratulated on his success. As he is a man of uncommon talents, it is needless to say that it is to his subject and his dogged manner of handling it that we are to refer the burst of dislike with which the novel was received. . . . He details all the ingenuities of animal malignity, and exhausts the whole rhetoric of stupid blasphemy, in order that there may be no mistake as to the kind of person he intends to hold up to the popular gaze. . . . This coarseness, though the prominent, is not the only characteristic of the writer . . . he aims further to exhibit the action of the sentiment of love on the nature of the being whom his morbid imagination has created. This is by far the ablest and most subtle portion of his labours, and indicates that strong hold upon the elements of character, and that decision of touch in the delineation of the most evanescent qualities of emotion, which distinguish the mind of the whole family. For all practical purposes, however, the power evinced in *Wuthering Heights* is power thrown away. Nightmares and dreams, through which devils dance and wolves howl, make bad novels.

NOTES

1. This is the review referred to by Charlotte in her letter to W. S. Williams of 22 November 1848 (Emily died 19 December 1848), 'The *North American Review* is worth reading. There is no mincing the matter there. What a bad set the Bells must be! What appalling books they wrote! Today, as Emily appeared a little easier, I thought the *Review* would amuse her, so I read it aloud to her and Anne. As I sat between them at our quiet but now somewhat melancholy fireside, I studied the two ferocious authors. Ellis, the "man of uncommon talents, but dogged, brutal and morose", sat leaning back in his easy-chair drawing his impeded breath as he best could, and looking, alas! piteously pale and wasted; it is not his wont to laugh, but he smiled half-amused and half in scorn as he listened. Acton was sewing, no emotion ever stirs him to loquacity, so he only smiled too. . . . I wonder what the reviewer would have thought of his own sagacity could he have beheld the pair as I did' (*Life and Letters*, II, p. 287).

2. See Introduction, p. 16 above.

3. 'CURRER BELL' ON 'ELLIS BELL' (1847–8)

Ellis has a strong, original mind, full of strange though sombre power. When he writes poetry that power speaks in language at once condensed, elaborated, and refined, but in prose it breaks forth in scenes which shock more than they attract. Ellis will improve, however, because he knows his defects.

SOURCE: from a letter to W. S. Williams, 21 December 1847

Heathcliff . . . exemplifies the effects which a life of continued injustice and hard usage may produce on a naturally perverse, vindictive, and inexorable disposition. Carefully trained and kindly treated, the black gipsy-cub might possibly have been reared into a human being, but tyranny and ignorance made of him a mere demon. The worst of it is, some of his spirit seems breathed through the whole narrative in which he figures: it haunts every moor and glen, and beckons in every fir-tree of the Heights.

SOURCE: from a letter to W. S. Williams, 14 August 1848.

PART TWO

Wuthering Heights in the 1850s

Sidney Dobell 'The Stamp of High Genius' (1850)

. . . placing in an assumed order of production (though not of publication) the novels called *Wuthering Heights*, *Wildfell Hall*, *Jane Eyre* and *Shirley*, as the works of one author under sundry disguises, we should have deemed, a few days since, that an analysis of the first (and, by our theory, the earliest) of these was the amplest justice she [i.e. 'Currer Bell'] could at present receive. Opening, however, the third edition of *Jane Eyre*, published before the appearance of *Shirley*, we find a preface in which all other works are disclaimed. A nom de guerrist has many privileges, and we are willing to put down to a double entendre all that is serious in this disclaimer. That any hand but that which shaped *Jane Eyre* and *Shirley* cut out the rougher earlier statues, we should require more than the evidence of our senses to believe[1] . . . the author of *Jane Eyre* need fear nothing in acknowledging these yet more immature creations of one of the most vigorous of modern idiosyncrasies. . . . We look upon *Wuthering Heights* as the flight of an impatient fancy fluttering in the . . . exultation of young wings . . . a youthful story, written for oneself in solitude, and thrown aside till other successes recall the eyes to it in hope. In this thought let the critic take up the book; lay it down in what thought he will, there are some things in it he can lay down no more.

That Catherine Earnshaw – at once so wonderfully fresh, so fearfully natural . . . what can surpass the strange compatibility of her simultaneous loves; the involuntary art with which her two natures are so made to co-exist, that in the very arms of her lover we dare not doubt her purity; the inevitable belief with which we watch the oscillations of the old and new elements in her mind, and the exquisite truth of the last victory of nature over education, when the past returns to her as a flood, sweeping every modern landmark from within her, and the soul of the child, expanding, fills the woman? . . . Heathcliff *might* have been as unique a creation. The conception in his case was as wonderfully strong and original, but he is spoilt in detail. The authoress has too often disgusted, where she should have terrified, and has allowed us a familiarity with her fiend which has ended in unequivocal contempt. If *Wuthering Heights* had been written as lately as *Jane Eyre*, the figure of Heathcliff, symmetrised and elevated, might have been one of the most natural and most striking portraits in the gallery of fiction.

Not a subordinate place or person in this novel but bears more or less the stamp of high genius. Ellen Dean is the ideal of the pleasant playmate and servant of 'the family'. The substratum in which her mind moves is finely preserved. Joseph, as a specimen of the sixty years' servitor of 'the house', is worthy a museum case. We feel that if Catherine Earnshaw bore her husband a child, it must be that Cathy Linton, and no other. The very Jane Eyre, of quiet satire, peeps out in such a paragraph as this: – 'He told me to put on my cloak, and run to Gimmerton for the doctor and the parson. I went through wind and rain, and brought one, the doctor, back with me: the other said, he would come in the morning' [ch. 5]. What terrible truth, what nicety of touch, what 'uncanny' capacity for mental aberration in the first symptoms of Catherine's delirium. 'I'm not wandering; you're mistaken, or else I should believe you really were that withered hag, and I should think I was under Penistone Crags: and I'm conscious it's night, and there are two candles on the table making the black press shine like jet.' What an unobtrusive, unexpected sense of keeping[2] in the hanging of Isabella's dog.

The book abounds in such things. But one looks back at the whole story as to a world of brilliant figures in an atmosphere of mist; shapes that come out upon the eye, and burn their colours into the brain, and depart into the enveloping fog. It is the unformed writing of a giant's hand: the 'large utterance'[3] of a baby god . . . there are passages in this book of *Wuthering Heights* of which any novelist, past or present, might be proud. Open the first volume at the fourteenth page, and read to the sixty-first.[4] There are few things in modern prose to surpass these pages for native power. . . . The thinking out of some of these pages – of pp. 52, 53, and 60[5] – is the masterpiece of a poet, rather than the hybrid creation of the novelist . . . the images in these pages will live – when every word that conveyed them is forgotten – as a recollection of things heard and seen. This is the highest triumph of description. . . . We are at a loss to find anywhere in modern prose . . . such wealth and such economy, such apparent ease, such instinctive art. . . . When Currer Bell writes her next novel, let her remember, as far as possible, the frame of mind in which she sat down to her first. She cannot now commit the faults of that early effort; it will be well for her if she be still capable of the virtues. . . . She will not let her next dark-haired hero babble away the respect of her reader and the awe of his antecedents; nor will she find another housekeeper who remembers two volumes literatim. Let her rejoice if she can again give us such an elaboration of a rare and fearful form of mental disease . . . with such nicety in its transitions, such intimate symptomatic truth in its details, as to be at once a psychological and medical study. It has been said of Shakespeare, that he drew cases which the physician might study; Currer Bell has done no less. She will not, again, employ her wonderful pencil on a picture so destitute of moral beauty and human worth. Let her exult, if she can still invest such a picture with such interest. . . . Let Currer Bell prize the young intuition of character which dictated Cathy's speech to Ellen: page 223.[6] There is a deep, unconscious philosophy in it. There are minds whose crimes and sorrows are not so much the result of intrinsic evil as of a false position in the scheme of things, which clashes their energies with the arrangements of surrounding life. It is difficult to cure such a soul from within. The point of view, not the eye or the landscape, is in fault. Move that, and as at the changing of a stop, the mental machine assumes its proper relative place, and the powers of discord become, in the same measure, the instruments of harmony. It was a fine instinct which saw this. Let Currer Bell be passing glad if it is as vigorous now as then. . . .

SOURCE: from 'Currer Bell', in *Palladium*, September 1850, reprinted in *Life and Letters of Sydney Dobell*, ed. E. Jolly (1878).

NOTES

1. See Introduction, p. 16 above.
2. Cp below, 'easy strength and instinct of keeping' and 'never sin so much against consistent keeping'. See above, p. 41 and n.
3. Keats's 'Hyperion', I (1820) lines 50–1, 'O how frail/To that large utterance of the early Gods!'
4. The sequence of events from the opening of ch. 2 to the moment in ch. 3 when Lockwood settles down for the rest of the night on the bench in the kitchen at *Wuthering Heights*. Dobell's page-references throughout this review are of course to the first edition.
5. Lockwood's nightmare in ch. 3, from his grasping the 'little ice-cold hand' to his waking up in terror (pp. 52–3); Heathcliff's calling for Catherine through the open window in the same chapter (p. 60).
6. Catherine's speech in ch. 10 from 'The event of this evening has reconciled me to God . . .' to 'I'm an angel'.

Charlotte Brontë 'A Spirit more Sombre than Sunny, more Powerful than Sportive' (1850)

I have just read over *Wuthering Heights*, and, for the first time, have obtained a clear glimpse of what are termed (and, perhaps, really are) its faults; have gained a definite notion of how it appears to other people – to strangers who knew nothing of the author; who are unacquainted with the locality where the scenes of the story are laid; to whom the inhabitants, the customs, the natural characteristics of the outlying hills and hamlets in the West Riding of Yorkshire are things alien and unfamiliar.

To all such *Wuthering Heights* must appear a rude and strange production. The wild moors of the north of England can for them have no interest; the language, the manners, the very dwellings and household customs of the scattered inhabitants of those districts, must be to such readers in a great measure unintelligible, and – where intelligible – repulsive. Men and women who, perhaps naturally very calm, and with feelings moderate in degree, and little marked in kind, have been trained from their cradle to observe the utmost evenness of manner and guardedness of language, will hardly know what to make of the rough, strong utterance, the harshly manifested passions, the unbridled aversions, and headlong partialities of unlettered moorland hinds and rugged moorland squires, who have grown up untaught and unchecked, except by mentors as harsh as themselves. A large class of readers, likewise, will suffer greatly from the introduction into the pages of this work of words printed with all their letters, which it has become the custom to represent by the initial and final letter only – a blank line filling the interval. I may as well say at once that, for this circumstance, it is out of my power to apologise; deeming it, myself, a rational plan to write words at full length. The practice of hinting by single letters those expletives with which profane and violent persons are wont to garnish their discourse, strikes me as a proceeding which, however well meant, is weak and futile, I cannot tell what good it does – what feeling it spares – what horror it conceals.

With regard to the rusticity of *Wuthering Heights*, I admit the charge, for I feel the quality. It is rustic all through. It is moorish, and wild, and knotty as a root of heath. Nor was it natural that it should be otherwise; the author being herself a native and nursling of the moors. Doubtless, had her lot been cast in a town, her writings, if she had written at all, would have possessed another character. Even had chance or taste led her to choose a similar subject, she would have treated it otherwise. Had Ellis Bell been a lady or a gentleman accustomed to what is called 'the world', her view of a remote and unreclaimed region, as well as of the dwellers therein, would have differed greatly from that actually taken by the homebred country girl. Doubtless it would have been wider – more comprehensive: whether it would have been more original or more truthful is not so certain. As far as the scenery and locality are concerned, it could scarcely have been so sympathetic: Ellis Bell did not describe as one whose eye and taste alone found pleasure in the prospect; her native hills were far more to her than a spectacle; they were what she lived in, and by, as much as the wild birds, their tenants, or as the heather, their produce. Her descriptions, then, of natural scenery, are what they should be, and all they should be.

Where delineation of human character is concerned, the case is different. I am bound to avow that she had scarcely more practical knowledge of the peasantry amongst whom she lived, than a nun has of the country people who sometimes pass her convent gates. My sister's disposition was not naturally gregarious; circumstances favoured and fostered her tendency to seclusion; except to go to church or take a walk on the hills, she rarely crossed the threshold of home. Though her feeling for the people round was benevolent, intercourse with them she never sought; nor, with very few exceptions, ever experienced. And yet she knew them: knew their ways, their language, their family histories; she could hear of them with interest, and talk of them with details, minute, graphic, and accurate; but *with* them, she rarely exchanged a word. Hence it ensued that what her mind had gathered of the real concerning them, was too exclusively confined to those tragic and terrible traits of which, in listening to the secret annals of every rude vicinage, the memory is sometimes compelled to receive the impress. Her imagination, which was a spirit more sombre than sunny, more powerful than sportive, found in such traits material whence it wrought creations like Heathcliff, like Earnshaw, like Catherine. Having formed these beings she did not know what she had done. If the auditor of her work when read in manuscript, shuddered under the grinding influence of natures so relentless and implacable, of spirits so lost and fallen; if it was complained that the mere hearing of certain vivid and fearful scenes banished sleep by night, and disturbed mental peace by day, Ellis Bell would wonder what was meant, and suspect the complainant of affectation. Had she but lived, her mind would of itself have grown like a strong tree, loftier, straighter, wider-spreading, and its matured fruits would have attained a mellower ripeness and sunnier bloom; but on that mind time and experience alone could work: to the influence of other intellects, it was not amenable.

Having avowed that over much of *Wuthering Heights* there broods 'a horror of great darkness';[1] that, in its storm-heated and electrical atmosphere, we seem at times to breathe lightning, let me point to those spots where clouded daylight and the eclipsed sun still attest their existence. For the specimen of true benevolence and homely fidelity, look at the character of Nelly Dean; for an example of constancy and tenderness, remark that of Edgar Linton. (Some people will think these qualities do not shine so well incarnate in a man as they would do in a woman, but Ellis Bell could never be brought to comprehend this notion: nothing moved her more than any insinuation that the faithfulness and clemency, the long-suffering and loving kindness which are esteemed virtues in the daughters of Eve, become foibles in the sons of Adam. She held that mercy and forgiveness are the divinest attributes of the Great Being who made both man and woman, and that what clothes the Godhead in glory, can disgrace no form of feeble humanity.) There is a dry saturnine humour in the delineation of old Joseph, and some glimpses of grace and gaiety animate the younger Catherine. Nor is even the first heroine of the name destitute of a certain strange beauty in her fierceness, or of honesty in the midst of perverted passion and passionate perversity.

Heathcliff, indeed, stands unredeemed; never once swerving in his arrow-straight course to perdition, from the time when 'the little black-haired swarthy thing, as dark as if it came from the Devil', was first unrolled out of the bundle and set on its feet in the farmhouse kitchen, to the hour when Nelly Dean found the grim, stalwart corpse laid on its back in the panel-enclosed bed, with wide-gazing eyes that seemed 'to sneer at her attempt to close them, and parted lips and sharp white teeth that sneered too'.

Heathcliff betrays one solitary human feeling, and that is *not* his love for Catherine; which is a sentiment fierce and inhuman; a passion such as might boil and glow in the bad essence of some evil genius; a fire that might form the tormented centre – the ever-suffering soul of a magnate of the infernal world: and by its quenchless and ceaseless ravage effect the execution of the decree which dooms him to carry Hell with him wherever he wanders. No; the single link that connects Heathcliff with humanity is his rudely-confessed regard for Hareton Earnshaw – the young man who he has ruined; and then his half-implied esteem for Nelly Dean. These solitary traits omitted, we should say he was child neither of Lascar nor gipsy, but a man's shape animated by demon life – a Ghoul – an Afreet.

Whether it is right or advisable to create beings like Heathcliff, I do not know: I scarcely think it is. But this I know: the writer who possesses the creative gift owns something of which he is not always master – something that, at times, strangely wills and works for itself. He may lay down rules and devise principles, and to rules and principles it will perhaps for years lie in subjection; and then, haply without any warning of revolt, there comes a time when it will no longer consent to 'harrow the valleys, or be bound with a band in the furrow'[2] – when it 'laughs at the multitude of the city, and regards not the crying of the driver'[3] – when, refusing absolutely to make ropes out of sea-sand any longer, it sets to work in statue-hewing, and you have a Pluto or a Jove, a Tisiphone or a Psyche, a Mermaid or a Madonna, as Fate or Inspiration direct. Be the work grim or glorious, dread or divine, you have little choice left but quiescent adoption. As for you – the nominal artist – your share in it has been to work passively under dictates you neither delivered nor could question – that would not be uttered at your prayer, nor suppressed nor changed at your caprice. If the result be attractive, the World will praise you, who little deserve praise; if it be repulsive, the same World will blame you, who almost as little deserve blame.

Wuthering Heights was hewn in a wild workshop, with simple tools, out of homely materials. The statuary[4] found a granite block on a solitary moor; gazing thereon, he saw how from the crag might be elicited a head, savage, swart, sinister; a form moulded with at least one element of grandeur – power. He wrought with a rude chisel, and from no model but the vision of his meditations. With time and labour, the crag took human shape; and there it stands colossal, dark, and frowning, half statue, half rock: in the former sense, terrible and goblin-like; in the latter, almost beautiful, for its colouring is of mellow grey, and moorland moss clothes it; and heath, with its blooming bells and balmy fragrance, grows faithfully close to the giant's foot.

SOURCE: from the Preface to the 1850 edition.

NOTES

1. Genesis 15 : 12, 'And when the sun was going down, a deep sleep fell upon Abram; and, lo, an horror of great darkness fell upon him. . . . '
2. Job 39 : 10, 'Canst thou bind the unicorn with his band in the furrow? or will he harrow the valleys after these? . . .'
3. Job 39 : 7, 'He scorneth the multitude of the city, neither regardeth he the crying of the driver. . . . '
4. 'The statuary': the sculptor.

G. H. Lewes 'Sombre, Rude, Brutal, yet True' (1850)

There are various points of interest in this republication [*Wuthering Heights* and *Agnes Grey*], some arising from the intrinsic excellence of the works themselves, others from the lustre reflected on them by *Jane Eyre*. The biographical notice of her two sisters is plainly and touchingly written by Currer Bell. With their early struggles in authorship thousands will sympathise [quotes Charlotte's account of their first publications from her 1850 preface]. . . . Critics, we are told, failed to do them justice. But to judge from the extracts given of articles in the *Britannia* and *Atlas*, the critics were excessively indulgent, and we take it the great public was the most recalcitrant, and would *not* be amused with these strange wild pictures of incult humanity, painted as if by lurid torchlight, though painted with unmistakeable power – the very power only heightening their repulsiveness. . . .

And yet, although there is a want of air and light in the picture we cannot deny its truth; sombre, rude, brutal, yet true. The fierce ungoverned instincts of powerful organisations,[1] bred up amidst violence, revolt, and moral apathy, are here seen in operation; such brutes we should all be, or the most of us, were our lives as insubordinate to law; were our affections and sympathies as little cultivated, our imaginations as undirected. And herein lies the moral of the book, though most people will fail to draw the moral from very irritation at it.

Curious enough it is to read *Wuthering Heights* and *The Tenant of Wildfell Hall*, and remember that the writers were two retiring, solitary, consumptive girls! Books, coarse even for men, coarse in language and coarse in conception, the coarseness apparently of violent and uncultivated men – turn out to be the productions of two girls living almost alone, filling their loneliness with quiet studies, and writing these books from a sense of duty, hating the pictures they drew, yet drawing them with austere conscientiousness! There is matter here for the moralist or critic to speculate on.

That it was no caprice of a poor imagination wandering in search of an 'exciting' subject we are most thoroughly convinced. The three sisters have been haunted by the same experience. Currer Bell throws more humanity into her picture; but Rochester belongs to the Earnshaw and Heathcliff family. . . . The power, indeed, is wonderful. Heathcliff, devil though he be, is drawn with a sort of dusky splendour which fascinates, and we feel the truth of his burning and impassioned love for Catherine, and of her inextinguishable love for him. It was a happy thought to make her love the kind, weak, elegant Edgar, and yet without lessening her passion for Heathcliff. Edgar appeals to her love of refinement, and goodness, and culture; Heathcliff clutches her soul in his passionate embrace . . . although she is ashamed of her early playmate she loves him with a passionate abandonment which sets culture, education, the world, at defiance. It is in the treatment of this subject that Ellis Bell shows real mastery, and it shows more genius, in the highest sense of the word, than you will find in a thousand novels. . . .

Creative power is so rare and so valuable that we should accept even its caprices with gratitude. Currer Bell, in a passage on this question, doubts whether the artist can control his power; she seems to think with Plato (see his argument in the *Ion*), that the artist does not possess, but is possessed [see above, p. 63]. . . . We suppose every writer will easily recall his sensations of being 'carried away' by the thoughts which in moments of exaltation possessed his soul – will recall the headlong feeling of letting the reins slip – being himself as much astonished at the result as any reader can be. There is at such time a *momentum* which propels the mind into regions inaccessible to calculation, unsuspected in our calmer moods. . . .[2]

SOURCE: from the *Leader*, 28 December 1850.

NOTES

1. See also p. 77 below for Lewes's continued fascination for Emily Brontë as '*un bête fauve*'.
2. Used here to mean 'living beings'.
3. Cp Dobell's emphasis on Emily's 'involuntary' and intuitive art pp. 58–9 above.

Eclectic Review 'One of the Most Repellent Books We Ever Read' (1851)

Jane Eyre was instantaneously popular; but not so the productions of Ellis and Acton Bell. We are not surprised at this. . . . The successful work was attractive as well as talented, while *Wuthering Heights* – we know little of *Agnes Grey* – is one of the most repellent books we ever read. . . . That the work has considerable merit we admit. The scenery is laid in the North, the bleak, moorish, wild, character of which is admirably preserved. Ellis Bell was evidently attached to her native hills. She was at home amongst them; and there is, therefore, a vividness and graphic power in her sketches which present them actually before us. So far we prefer no complaint, but the case is different with the dramatis personæ. Such a company we never saw grouped before; and we hope never to meet with its like again. Heathcliff is a perfect monster. . . . Hindley Earnshaw is a besotted fool . . . his son Hareton is at once ignorant and brutish, until, as by the wand of an enchanter, he takes polish in the last scene of the tale. . . . The two Catherines, mother and daughter, are equally exaggerations, more than questionable in some part of their procedure, and absurdly unnatural in the leading incidents of their life. Isabella Linton is one of the silliest and most credulous girls that fancy ever painted . . . the enduring affection and tenderness of her brother Edgar are so exhibited as to produce the impression of a feeble rather than of a virtuous character . . . the minor personages . . . with slight exceptions . . . are in keeping with their superiors.

As the characters of the tale are unattractive, so the chief incidents are sadly wanting in probability. They are devoid of truthfulness, are not in harmony with the actual world, and have, therefore, but little more power to move our sympathies than the romances of the middle ages, or the ghost stories which made our granddames tremble.

SOURCE: from *Eclectic Review*, 5th series, I, February 1851.

D. G. Rossetti 'The Action is Laid in Hell' (1855)

I've been greatly interested in *Wuthering Heights*, the first novel I've read for an age and the best (as regards power and sound style) for two ages. . . . But it is a fiend of a book – an incredible monster. . . . The action is laid in hell, – only it seems places and people have English names there. . . .

SOURCE: from a letter to William Allingham, 19 September 1854.

Matthew Arnold 'Haworth Churchyard' (1855)

. . . and she
(How shall I sing her?) whose soul
Knew no fellow for might,
Passion, vehemence, grief,
Daring, since Byron died,
That world-famed son of fire – she, who sank
Baffled, unknown, self-consumed;
Whose too bold dying song
Shook, like a clarion-blast, my soul . . .'.[1]

SOURCE: from *Fraser's Magazine*, April 1855; reprinted 1877.

NOTE

1. 'Whose too bold . . . soul': Arnold noted in 1877, 'See the last verses by Emily Brontë in Poems by *Currer, Ellis and Acton Bell* [1846]'. He was probably thinking of Emily's 'No coward soul is mine . . .', which was first published not in the 1846 volume but in Charlotte's 1850 memorial edition of *Wuthering Heights* and *Agnes Grey* with the note, 'The following are the last lines my sister ever wrote'. In C. W. Hatfield's *The Complete Poems of Emily Jane Brontë* (1941) the poem is dated 2 January 1846 and followed by two pieces dated, 14 September 1846 and 13 May 1848. The song was 'too bold' presumably because of its assertions in stanzas 3–4,

> Vain are the thousand creeds
> That move men's hearts, unutterably vain,
> Worthless as withered weeds
> Or idlest froth amid the boundless main
>
> To waken doubt in one
> Holding so fast by thy infinity
> So surely anchored on
> The steadfast rock of Immortality . . .

Harriet Martineau 'A Terrible Experience of Life' (1855)

In her obituary notice[1] of her two sisters 'Currer' reveals something of their process of authorship, and their experience of failure and success. How terrible some of their experience of life was, in the midst of the domestic freedom and indulgence afforded them by their studious father, may be seen by the fearful representatives of masculine nature of character found in the novels and tales of Emily and Anne. They considered it their duty . . . to present life as they knew it, and they gave us *Wuthering Heights* and *The Tenant of Wildfell Hall*. Such an experience as this indicates is really perplexing to English people in general, and all that we have to do with it is to bear it in mind when disposed to pass criticism on the coarseness which to a certain degree pervades the works of all the sisters, and the repulsiveness which makes the tales by Emily and Anne really horrible to people who have not iron nerves.

SOURCE: from obituary notice of Charlotte Brontë, *Daily News*, April 1855.

NOTE

1. Charlotte's biographical sketch of Emily and Ann in the 1850 memorial edition of *Wuthering Heights* and *Agnes Grey*.

John Skelton 'Fierce Poetry'[1] (1857)

Emily Brontë . . . is . . . the most powerful of the Brontë family. They are a remarkable race. . . . But Emily is a Titan. Charlotte loved her with her whole heart; to her the implacable sister is 'mine bonnie love'; but Emily . . . is stern, taciturn, untameable. . . . Her affections . . . are spent on her moorland home, and the wild animals she cherishes. . . . On her death-bed she accepts no assistance – does not admit that she suffers even. Her death, Charlotte said afterwards, 'was very terrible. She was torn, conscious, panting, reluctant, yet resolute, out of a happy life.'

Wuthering Heights is not unworthy of its grim parentage. Emily's novel is not, perhaps, more powerful than her sister's; but we meet in it, I think, with more subtle diversities of character than we do in any of them. . . . There is a refrain of fierce poetry in the men and women she draws . . . Heathcliff, the boy, is ferocious, vindictive, wolfish; but we understand the chain of fire that binds Cathy to him. . . . As he stands moodily in the presence of his fastidious, courtly, and well-bred rival, we feel that though his soul is the fouler, he is the greater, the more loveable of the two. He may be an imp of darkness . . . but he has come direct from the affluent heart of nature, and the hardy charm of her bleak hill-sides and savage moorlands rests upon the boy. On the boy only, however; for the man develops and degenerates; it is then a tiger-cat's passion, a ghoul's vindictiveness, a devil's remorse.

The elder Cathy, too, is very subtly conceived. . . . Her childish delight in arranging on her death-bed the lapwing, the mallard, and the moor-fowl's feathers – the wild birds she had followed with Heathcliff in their childish rambles across the moorland, – is sad and true as the 'coronet flowers' of Ophelia. . . . there is a genuine reminiscence of the Shakespearian madness.[2] This richness and affluence of poetic life in which Emily invests the creations of her brain, these delicacies and subtleties of insight, are all the more striking, from the grave, sombre, and resolutely homely form in which her tale is narrated. She may describe abnormal characters; but, whatever they are, she describes them with startling genuineness.

SOURCE: from the review of Mrs Gaskell's *Life of Charlotte Brontë*, in *Fraser's Magazine*, June 1857.

NOTES

1. Sir John Skelton (1831–97), author and essayist, was an extensive reviewer, chiefly in *Blackwood's Magazine*.
2. The parallel between *Hamlet* IV V 180–6 and Catherine's musings about the feathers from her pillow (ch. 12) has also been noticed by recent readers, for example, Arnold P. Drew in 'Emily Brontë and *Hamlet*', in *Notes & Queries*, NS I (1954), pp. 81–2, and Lew Girdler in '*Wuthering Heights* and Shakespeare', in *Huntington Library Quarterly*, XIX, no. 4 (Aug. 1956), pp. 389–90.

W. C. Roscoe 'Dark, Intense, Powerful' (1857)

The close shadow of the Brontës' churchyard-home, the bitter winds, and the wild dark aspect of their moors, have left the mark of their influence upon the writings as well as upon the characters of the sisters. ... A personal impress is strongly marked on them. It is curious that, though the writers all had strong imaginations, not one of them had the power to get rid for a moment of her own individuality. It permeates with its subtle presence every page they write. ... They had been brought into close contact with the darker shades of character, and they instinctively studied them and reproduced them; too often they used light to give a greater depth to shadow, rather than shadow to set off light. It is in Emily's works, as in her own nature, that the darkness lies deepest. None of them are at home in sunny weather; but Emily has drawn mid-winter and thunderous skies. The clouds are ragged and dreadful, illumined for short glimpses by tempest fire:

Storm and hail and thunder,
And the winds that rave,

are the material correspondents of those dread perturbations of the human spirit in which she found herself at home. Her temperament was a strange, even a distorted one. There must have been a fund of ferocity in her own nature strangely mingled with tenderness. 'Stronger than a man, simpler than a child, her whole nature stood alone.' So says her sister. She could not tolerate the contact of other wills. Isolation became a necessary of her life; she could not endure her reserve to be infringed, and the demonstrations at least of her affection were reserved for the dumb creation. . . . Concentrated on few objects, love may become more strong; but the more it is concentrated, the closer it approaches to self-love. How mere a self-love it may become, how mere a passionate wilful surrender to native instincts, has nowhere received a more vivid and terrible artistic delineation than in Emily Brontë's tale of *Wuthering Heights*. In force of genius, in the power of conceiving and uttering intensity of passion, Emily surpassed her sister Charlotte. On the other hand, her range seems to have been still more confined. The atmosphere of the book obscures the elements of character and incident; it is like gazing on a storm which melts together and shrouds in rain and gloom all the distinctive features of the landscape. It is idle to deny that the book is revolting. That a wickedness, whose only claim to attention is its intensity, that the most frightful excesses of degrading vices, snarling hypocrisy, an almost idiotic imbecility of mind and body, combined with a cruel and utterly selfish nature, – that these things should not excite abhorrence is impossible; and they occupy so large a space in the book, they seem displayed so much for their own sake, that it is impossible the whole work should not obtain a share of the sentiment. We may admire, but not without horror, the stern, unflinching hand with which the author drives her keen plough through the worst recesses of the human heart, nothing surprised at what she finds there, nothing concerned at what she uproots. . . . In the original temperament of Emily, there must have been some strange sympathy with the fierce natures she revels in delineating. We cannot help shrinking from a mind which could conceive and describe, even as occurring in a dream, the rubbing backwards and forwards of a child's hand along the jagged glass in a broken window-pane till the blood flowed down upon the bed.

'Having formed these beings,' says Charlotte, 'she did not know what she had done. . . . '

In *Wuthering Heights* there is an unmistakeable tendency to subordinate differences of character to vividness of narration. . . . All the characters . . . are within a very narrow range, and have a tendency to run into one another. Yet the whole story embodies a wonderful effort of imagination. . . . All is fused together as by fire; and the reader has neither power nor inclination to weigh probabilities or discuss defects. . . . the laceration of his feelings deadens him to the bearings of details. There is humour in Joseph, rude and harsh though it be; a quality not discernible in any of the other writings of the sisters (we do not except the curate scene[2]); and once, though once only, Heathcliff shows in such a light that it is possible for pity to mingle with our detestation. It is when, after Catherine's death, he stands on his hearthstone, his passion spent, and his spirit overwhelmed by the sense of his desolation. [Quotes from ch. 17 Isabella's narrative, beginning 'Heathcliff did not glance my way . . .' and ending, 'The clouded windows of hell flashed a moment towards me; the fiend which usually looked out, however, was so dimmed and drowned that I did not fear to hazard another sound of derision.']

'The clouded windows of hell flashed a moment towards me!' What a wealth of tragic utterance there is in the phrase! Entirely out of place, indeed, in the mouth by which it is uttered, as is the whole of this description; but in true keeping with the strain which underlies the whole wild harmony. Never, perhaps, has unbridled ferocity and unassuageable vindictiveness found so adequate a delineator as in this young girl. If her book have any moral, it serves, as we before observed, to show how fierce, how inhuman a passion, personal attachment to another may become, and how reckless of the welfare of its object; and this, too, not the love which sinks from the human level into the sensual appetite of the brutes, but the pure love of souls. For such is the passion of Heathcliff and Catherine. The life-like presentation of how such a love may be compatible with selfishness utterly unredeemed is, if not the conscious teaching of the author, yet the prominent lesson of her rude titanic story, 'rich with barbaric gems and crusted gold.'. . .

SOURCE: from the review of Mrs Gaskell's *Life of Charlotte Brontë*, in *National Review*, July 1857; reprinted in W. C. Roscoe, *Poems and Essays*, vol. II (1860).

NOTES

1. William Caldwell Roscoe (1823–59), poet and essayist, was the grandson of the historian William Roscoe (1753–1831) and the friend of Walter Bagehot and R. H. Hutton (whom he met at University College London).
2. Charlotte Brontë's *Shirley* (1849), ch. I.

E. S. Dallas Approaching the 'Pitiless Fatality . . . of Greek Tragedy'[1] (1857)

. . . Mrs Gaskell, who . . . probably was never troubled in her life with a doubt as to her own excellent qualities, has no idea of Emily Brontë's reserve proceeding from any other source than indifference and selfishness. . . . How tenderly Emily Brontë could feel, how large and steadfast was her heart, [her] poems and her novel of *Wuthering Heights* amply testify. In this latter work . . . we find the developed expression of her despairing nature – a hopelessness which paralyses every power, and is intimately mingled with the most deadly fatalism. Although all the characters are more or less finely conceived, there is only one man of will and action in the book, and that is Heathcliff. . . . He is surrounded by people who might easily master him, or who, at all events, might get out of his reach, but there they remain motionless where he places them, and he has only to say 'Dilly, dilly, dackling,' and they come to be killed without an effort of resistance . . . he too . . . is actuated by a blind fate, is as helpless and hopeless as the other mortals who lie passive in his grasp. The whole gloomy tale is in its idea the nearest approach that has been made in our time to the pitiless fatality which is the dominant idea of Greek tragedy. . . .

SOURCE: from the review of Mrs Gaskell's *Life of Charlotte Brontë*, in *Blackwood's Magazine*, July 1857.

NOTE

1. Eneas Sweetland Dallas (1828–79) was a lively journalist and aesthetic theorist; his published works include *Poetics* (1852), an abridgement of Richardson's *Clarissa* (1858) and *The Gay Science* (1866).

Émile Montégut 'A Dark Poetic Imagination'[1] (1857)

. . . Emily Brontë's novel, *Wuthering Heights*, is quite different [from Anne's *Agnes Grey*]. Terror predominates from start to finish and we assist at a succession of scenes of which some possess an intensity of horror recalling Hoffmann's *Das Majorat*.[2] Emily's dark imagination sets before us characters and scenes that are all the more fearful because the terror which they inspire is above all a moral one. They do not threaten us with apparitions or marvellous happenings, but with ferocious passions and criminal impulses. At first glance . . . the characters . . . seem like worthy country folk, if somewhat rough and uncouth; but before long their eyes – as wild as a madman's, as cruel as a tiger's, or as full of mockery as those of a sorceress casting a spell of whose certain effectiveness she is convinced – fix themselves upon us, and hold us fascinated and disturbed. The poetic effect gains peculiar power from the fact that the author never shows herself behind her characters. Her energetic firmness of style indicates a spirit which is familiar with such terrible emotions and makes sport with fear. . . . I have referred to Charlotte's talent for detecting the spirit's hidden perversities; but in the end the perversities which she describes are avowable, for they are of the kind which we all carry within us. Emily goes much further; she describes the secrets of guilty passions and . . . the play of guilty instincts. The subject of her novel is strange, and she treats it without hypocrisy, prudishness or false reserve. Her characters are guilty: she knows this to be so, says as much, and yet defies us not to admire them. . . . Catherine is wilful, energetic and filled with savage and poetic impulses – a flower of the moorland armed with thorns. . . . Emily observes marvellously well the law of mysterious attraction. We understand very readily how Catherine can prefer Heathcliff – this brutal, savage being . . . who given the occasion will not hesitate to commit murder or shrink from revenge – to the good, devoted and charming Edgar Linton. [He] does not possess a spirit strong enough for Catherine, and in consequence she feels a certain pity for him; what she had loved in him was nothing more than wealth and beauty. . . . With Heathcliff she is, as it were, completely at one; they make from their two identities a hybrid monster, with two sexes and two souls. ... Catherine sees in him her own energies ... uncurbed by the restraint which her sex imposes; she sees her own hidden perversities blossoming forth in him like poisoned poetic flowers. The scene in which she confesses the secret of her love for Heathcliff is fine and terrible. 'He is so much myself,' she says, 'that he is more myself than I am; he is the thunderbolt of which I am nothing more than the lightning flash.'[3] The occasion of another outstanding scene is the moment when, as Edgar Linton calls on his servants to throw Heathcliff out of his house, Catherine quietly puts the keys in her pocket and looks at her husband with calm contempt [ch. 11]. Catherine does not want to be saved, the thought never once crosses her mind; her terrible passion is irresistible and rages on through the most appalling sufferings. ...

SOURCE: translated from 'Charlotte Brontë, IV: Les Œuvres' (August 1857), reprinted in *Ecrivains modernes de l'Angleterre*, Première série (1885).

NOTES

1. Émile Montégut (1825–95), critic and essayist, was associated from 1847 with the *Revue des Deux Mondes* in which many of his best articles on English, American and French writers appeared. His books include *Libres Opinions: morales et historiques* (1858), *Essais sur la littérature anglaise* (1883) and *Ecrivains modernes de l'Angleterre* (1885–92).

2. Ernst Theodor Amadeus Hoffmann (1776–1822), German romantic writer and music critic, celebrated for his supernatural tales. His best-known stories include *Das Majorat* ('The Entail'), published in the two-volume collection *Nachstücke* (1817), translated into English by F. Gillies as 'Rolandsitten or the Deed of Entail' (1826) and referred to at length by Scott, with substantial quotations from the English version, in his review of Hitzig's *Life of Hoffmann* and Hoffmann's *Die Serapionsbrüder* and *Nachstücke* (*Quarterly Review*, 1827). A modern translation by J. M. Cohen appears in the latter's collection, *Tales from Hoffmann* (translated by various hands, 1951). Many other readers have seen some resemblances to *Das Majorat* in *Wuthering Heights*, but there is no evidence that Emily Brontë had read Hoffmann either in the original or in translation. The similarities in incidental details and the differences in imaginative quality between the two stories are discussed by Jacques Blondel (pp. 160–1 below). Other allusions to Hoffmann at p. 42n. above and p. 99 below.

3. A free paraphrase rather than literal translation of Catherine's speech to Nelly Dean in ch. 9. Montégut's subsequent description of the scene in ch. 11 is not altogether accurate.

North American Review 'A Nightmare' (1857)

. . . The power of the creation is as great as it is grotesque, and there is, after all, a fearful fascination in turning over the pages of *Wuthering Heights*. It calls for no harsh judgment as a moral utterance; for its monstrosity removes it from the range of moralities altogether, and can no more be reduced to any practical application than the fancies which perplex a brain in a paroxysm of nightmare.

SOURCE: from the review of Mrs Gaskell's *Life of Charlotte Brontë*, in *North American Review*, October 1857.

Peter Bayne 'Rich in Promise, Monstrous in Execution'[1] (1857)

Emily Brontë was . . . one of the most extraordinary women that ever lived . . . her genius more powerful, her promise more rich, than those of her gifted sister Charlotte. . . . It were a strange and surely distempered criticism which hesitated to pass sentence of condemnation on *Wuthering Heights*. . . . The whole atmosphere . . . is distempered, disturbed, and unnatural. . . . The emotions and the crimes are on the scale of madness. . . . Yet we have perfect confidence of powers it were perhaps impossible to estimate and mental wealth which we might vainly attempt to compute. . . .

SOURCE: from 'Ellis, Acton and Currer Bell', in *Essays in Biography and Criticism* (1857).

NOTE

1. Peter Bayne (1830–96), journalist and author, wrote at considerable length on the Brontës. In his diffusely argued later study, *Two Great Englishwomen* (1881), he expresses renewed, if even more troubled, admiration for Emily Brontë as a powerful writer, the clue to whose writings lies in her unsuccessful quest for some evidence of the existence of God.

G. H. Lewes 'Un Bête Fauve' (1857)

Emily has a singular fascination for me – probably because I have a passion for lions and savage animals, and she was un bête fauve in power, splendour and wildness. . . .

SOURCE: from a letter to Mrs Gaskell (1857).

PART THREE

Some Opinions and Criticism 1873–1949

Galaxy (New York) 'The Stamp of True Genius' (1873)

... it is more than twenty years since the first edition of Emily Brontë's works appeared, and still her poems, whose vigorous simplicity, passion, and concentration are unsurpassed ... by any poems written by a woman in this century, are a sealed book to the American public; and even in England she is known principally, as in America she is known only, through the medium of *Wuthering Heights*. This is unfortunate because, though every page of that work bears the stamp of true genius, its sombre and lurid colouring, and the gloomy and repellent qualities of its leading characters, have procured for it so decided a prejudice that it has been only once or twice candidly criticised and fairly judged. ... Indeed, its faults are too prominent to admit of either glozing or concealment. No amount of sophistry would persuade anyone that Heathcliff was a noble nature, warped by adverse circumstances; or that the elder Catherine was anything but fierce, faithless and foolish; or that such a swift succession of acts of coarse cruelty was probable or even possible in any Yorkshire manor-house, however isolated; or, finally, that an upper servant could ever have adorned a narrative with passages so eloquent and so elegant as those with which Nelly Dean not unfrequently adorns hers. But if *Wuthering Heights* admits in some respects neither of defence nor encomium, still less does it deserve the wholesale condemnation and unqualified abuse which have been heaped upon it. Though a brutal, it is not a sensual book; though coarse, it is not vulgar; though bad, it is not indecent. The passion of Heathcliff for Catherine ... is still a passion of soul for soul; and full of savage ferocity as the whole story is, it contains some exquisite pictures of childlike simplicity and innocence. Emily shared Charlotte's rare power of making the unreal vividly real to the reader. ... The grim old manor-house, with its belt of stunted firs, 'all blown aslant' by the fierce winds; the wide, gray moor stretching away into the distance on every side; the sombre interior and sombre inmates of the 'Heights' – how vividly real they are made to us! ... and how admirably is the deathless passion of Heathcliff for Catherine introduced ... as, 'believing himself to be alone', he wrenches open the lattice and stretches out hands of wild yearning to the pitiless night, with that cry of anguish: 'Cathy! oh my heart's darling! Hear me this once, Catherine, at last!' [ch. 3] ... In the absorbing intensity of this passion ... we are reminded of some of those brief but marvellous poems in which Heine ... has compressed the tragedy of a human life and ... a love godless, hopeless and desperate. ... Those few lines – 'Disturbed her? No! She has disturbed me, night and day, through eighteen years – incessantly – remorselessly – till yesterday; and yesterday night I was tranquil. *I dreamt I was sleeping the last sleep by that sleeper, with my heart stopped and my cheek frozen against hers*' [ch. 29][1] – are in themselves a dramatic poem[2] ... Emily Brontë stands alone among female poets, and, Robert Browning excepted, alone among the English poets of the present century, in ... the power of concentrating into a small space a profound psychological study ... and of expressing it with rare simplicity and strength of diction. ...

SOURCE: from 'The Life and Writings of Emily Brontë, in *Galaxy*, XV (New York, 1873).

NOTES

1. Cp. Alice Meynell in 1911 (p. 104 below).
2 Cp. G. D. Klingopulos in 1946 (p. 129 below).

T. Wemyss Reid 'A Rare and Splendid Genius' (1877)

I venture to invite the attention of my readers to this story [*Wuthering Heights*] as being in its way as marvellous a *tour de force* as *Jane Eyre* itself. It is true that as a novel it is repulsive and almost ghastly. As one reads chapter after chapter of the horrible chronicles of Heathcliff's crimes, the only literary work that can be recalled for comparison with it is the gory tragedy of *Titus Andronicus*. ... Much, however, may be said in defence of Emily Brontë's conduct in writing *Wuthering Heights*. ... She was in her twenty-eighth year when it was written. The life had been, so far as the outer world could judge, singularly barren and unproductive. Its one eventful episode was the short visit to Brussels. But Brussels had made no such impression upon Emily as it made upon Charlotte. She went back to Haworth quite unchanged; her love for the moors stronger than ever; her self-reserve only strengthened by the assaults to which it had been exposed during her residence among strangers; her whole nature still crying out for the solitary life of home, and the sustenance which she drew from the congenial society of the animals she loved and the servants she understood ... when she began to write *Wuthering Heights*, she knew nothing of the world. ... Love, except the love for nature and for her own nearest relatives, was a passion absolutely unknown to her – as anyone who cares to study the pictures of it in *Wuthering Heights* may easily perceive. Of harsh and brutal, or deliberate crime, she had no personal knowledge. She had before her, it is true, a sad instance of the results of vicious self-indulgence, and from that she drew materials for some portions of her story.[1] But so far as the great movements of human nature were concerned ... she was in absolute ignorance. ... But how vast was the intellectual greatness displayed in this juvenile work! ... From what unfathomed recesses of her intellect did this shy, nervous, untrained girl produce such characters as those which hold the foremost place in her story? Mrs Dean, the faithful domestic, we can understand; for her model was at Emily's elbow in the kitchen at Haworth. Joseph, the quaint High Calvinist ... was drawn from life. ... But Heathcliff, and the two Catherines, and Hareton Earnshaw ... come forth with all the vigour and freshness ... which can belong only to the spontaneous creations of genius. They are no copies, indeed, but living originals ... they must, I think, be counted among the greatest curiosities of literature. ... Heathcliff is the greatest villain in fiction ... We can compare him to nobody else among the creatures of fiction. We cannot even trace his literary pedigree. ... But this circumstance does not alter the fact that we accept him at once as a real being, not a merely grotesque monster. He stands as much alone as Frankenstein's creature did;[2] but we recognise within him that subtle combination of elements which gives him kinship with the human race ... Emily Brontë has succeeded ... where some of the most practised writers have failed entirely. Compare ... the fantastic horrors of Lord Lytton's 'A Strange Story' [1862], and you feel at once how much more powerful and masterly is the touch of the woman ... this haunting of Heathcliff by the ghost of his dead mistress is infinitely more terrible than if it had been accompanied either by the paraphernalia of rococo horrors which Mrs Radcliffe habitually invoked, or by those refined and subtle supernatural phenomena which Lord Lytton employs in his famous ghost story.[3]

This strict honesty which refused to allow the writer of the weirdest story in the English language to avail herself of the easiest of all the modes of stimulating a reader's terrors, is shown all through the novel. The workmanship is good from beginning to end, though the art is crude and clumsy. ... All is neatly, clearly, carefully finished off. Every date fits into its place, and so does every incident. ... [4] Differing widely in every respect from *Jane Eyre*, dealing with characters and circumstances which belong to the romance rather than the reality of life, *Wuthering Heights* is yet stamped by the same originality, the same daring, the same thoughtfulness, and the same intense individuality. Brimful of faults as it may be, that book is alone sufficient to prove that a rare and splendid genius was lost to the world when Emily Brontë died. ...

SOURCE: from *Charlotte Brontë: A Monograph* (1877).

NOTES

1. Branwell Brontë returned home July 1845 after being dismissed from his employment as a tutor at Thorp Green; he died 24 September 1848. The spectacle of his moral and physical disintegration as an important influence on Emily Brontë is emphasised by the Brontës' modern biographers, L. and E. M. Hanson, who argue that it also profoundly affected the novels of Charlotte and Anne; see *The Four Brontës* (1949), pp. 178–88. For Reid's further comments on Branwell and *Wuthering Heights*, see Mary Robinson's discussion, pp. 86–7 below.
2. Mary Shelley's *Frankenstein, or the Modern Prometheus* was published 1818.
3. Cp. Scott on the use of the supernatural, p. 157 below.
4. As C. P. Sanger demonstrates in detail in 1926 (see p. 109 below).

Mary Robinson 'A Dissenter in More Ways than One' (1883)

... Emily Brontë away from her moors, her loneliness, her poverty, her discipline, her companionship with genius, violence and degradation, would have taken another colour, as hydrangeas grow now red, now blue, according to the nature of the soil. It was not her lack of knowledge of the world that made the novel she wrote become *Wuthering Heights*, nor her inexperience, but rather her experience, limited and perverse, indeed, and specialised by a most singular temperament, yet close and very real. . . . Our surroundings affect us in two ways; subtly and permanently, tinging us through and through as wine tinges water,[1] or, by some violent neighbourhood of antipathetic force, sending us off at a tangent as far as possible from the antagonistic presence that so detestably environs us. The fact that Charlotte Brontë knew chiefly clergymen is largely responsible for *Shirley*, that satirical eulogy of the Church and apotheosis of Sunday-school teachers. But Emily, living in this same clerical evangelistic atmosphere, is revolted, forced to the other extreme; and, while sheltering her true opinions from herself under the all-embracing term 'Broad Church',[2] we find in her writings no belief so strong as the belief in the present use and glory of life; no love so great as her love for earth – earth the mother and grave; no assertion of immortality, but a deep certainty of rest. There is no note so often struck in all her work, and struck with such variety of emphasis, as this: that good for goodness' sake is desirable, evil for evil's sake detestable, and that for the just and the unjust alike there is rest in the grave.

This quiet clergyman's daughter, always hearing evil of Dissenters, has therefore from pure courage and revolted justice become a dissenter herself. A dissenter in more ways than one. Never was a nature more sensitive to the stupidities and narrowness of conventional opinion . . . and with such a nature indignation is the force that most often looses the gate of speech. . . . What, then, would this inexperienced Yorkshire parson's daughter reveal? The unlikeness of life to the authorised pictures of life; the force of evil, only conquerable by the slow-revolving process of nature which admits not the eternal duration of the perverse; the grim and fearful lessons of heredity; the sufficiency of the finite to the finite, of life to life, with no other reward than the conduct of life fulfils to him that lives; the all-penetrating kinship of living things, heather-sprig, singing lark, confident child, relentless tyrant; and, not least, not least to her already in its shadow, the sure and universal peace of death.

A strange evangel . . . but . . . evermore emphasised and deeper rooted in Emily's mind by her incapacity to acquiesce in the stiff, pragmatic teaching, the narrow prejudice, of the Calvinists of Haworth. Yet this very Calvinism influenced her ideas, this doctrine she so passionately rejected, calling herself a disciple of the tolerant and thoughtful Frederick Maurice,[3] and writing, in defiance of its flames and shriekings, the most soothing consolations to mortality that I remember in our tongue.

Nevertheless ... this antagonistic faith ... did not send her out from it before she had assimilated some of its sternest tenents. From this doctrine of reward and punishment she learned that for every unchecked evil tendency there is a fearful expiation ... not indeed in the flames of hell, but in the perverted instincts of our own children. ...

So much for the theories of life and evil that the clash of circumstance and character struck out from Emily Brontë. It happened ... that she had occasion to test these theories; and but for that she could never have written *Wuthering Heights*. ... Branwell, who sat to Anne sorrily enough for the portrait of Henry Huntingdon [in *The Tenant of Wildfell Hall*] served his sister Emily, not indeed as a model, a thing to copy, but as a chart of proportions by which to measure, and to which to refer, for correct investiture, the inspired idea. Mr Wemyss Reid ... perceives a bona fide resemblance between the character of Heathcliff and the character of Branwell Brontë as he appeared to his sister Emily. So much, bearing in mind the verse concerning the leveret,[4] I own I cannot see. ... Branwell seems to me more nearly akin to Heathcliff's miserable son than to Heathcliff. But that, in depicting Heathcliff's outrageous thwarted love for Catherine, Emily did draw upon her experience of her brother's suffering, this extract from an unpublished lecture of Mr Reid's will sufficiently reveal:

> It was in the enforced companionship of this lost and degraded man that Emily received, I am sure, many of the impressions which were subsequently conveyed to the pages of her book. Has it not been said over and over again by critics of every kind that *Wuthering Heights* reads like the dream of an opium-eater? And here we find that during the whole time of the writing of the book an habitual and avowed opium-eater was at Emily's elbow[5] ... perhaps the most striking part of *Wuthering Heights* is that which deals with the relations of Heathcliff and Catherine after she had become the wife of another. Whole pages of the story are filled with the ravings and ragings of the villain against the man whose life stands between him and the woman he loves. Similar ravings are to be found in all the letters of Branwell Brontë written at this period of his career; and we may be sure that similar ravings were always on his lips as, moody and more than half mad, he wandered about the rooms of the parsonage at Haworth. ...

So much share in *Wuthering Heights* Branwell certainly had. He was a page of the book in which his sister studied. . . .

SOURCE: from *Emily Brontë* (1883).

NOTES

1. Echoing Catherine's speech to Nelly Dean, 'I've dreamt in my life dreams that have stayed with me ever after, and changed my ideas: they've gone through and through me like wine through water, and altered the colour of my mind' (ch. 9).

2. Perhaps inferred from remarks made by Ellen Nussey, who supplied Mary Robinson with material for her biography of Emily. The single recorded comment by Emily Brontë on religious belief is preserved by Charlotte's friend Mary Taylor, 'One time [during a visit to Haworth Parsonage] . . . I mentioned that someone had asked me what religion I was of . . . I said that that was between God and me; – Emily (who was lying on the hearthrug) exclaimed 'That's right'. This was all I ever heard Emily say on religious subjects' (*Life and Letters*, 1, 137).

3. No evidence exists to support this statement. A somewhat strained attempt to establish a link between Emily Brontë and F. D. Maurice through the Haworth curate James Bradley is made by Eanne Aram in her 'Emily and F. D. Maurice: some parallels of thought' – *Brontë Society Transactions*, part 67 (1957), pp. 131–40. Maurice (1815–72) would have been known in Emily's lifetime chiefly from his early work *The Kingdom of Christ* (1842).

4. See 'Well some may hate, and some may scorn . . .' (*The Complete Poems of Emily Jane Brontë*, ed. C. W. Hatfield (1941), p. 132–3), stanzas 4–5,

> Do I despise the timid deer
> Because his limbs are fleet with fear?
>
> Or would I mock the wolf's death-howl
> Because his form is gaunt and foul?
> Or hear with joy the leveret's cry
> Because it cannot bravely die?

5. Branwell's addiction to laudanum is discussed in Margaret Lane's *The Brontë Story* (1953), pp. 101–2.

A. C. Swinburne 'The Fresh Dark Air of Tragic Passion' (1883)

To the England of our own time, it has often enough been remarked, the novel is what the drama was to the England of Shakespeare's. The same general interest produces the same incessant demand for the same inexhaustible supply of imaginative produce, in a shape more suited to the genius of a later day and the conditions of a changed society. Assuming this simple explanation to be sufficient for the obvious fact that in the modern world of English letters the novel is everywhere and the drama is nowhere, we may remark one radical point of difference between the taste of playgoers in the age of Shakespeare and the taste of novel-readers in our own. Tragedy was then at least as popular as either romantic or realistic comedy; whereas nothing would seem to be more unpopular with the run of modern readers than the threatening shadow of tragedy projected across the whole length of a story. ... The objection to a novel in which the tragic element has an air of incongruity and caprice ... this objection seems to be thoroughly reasonable ... but the distaste for high and pure tragedy, where the close is in perfect and simple harmony with the opening, seems not less thoroughly pitiable and irrational.

A recent work ... in which the freshness of humour is as real and vital as the fervour of passion, was at once on its appearance compared with Emily Brontë's now famous story ... *Mehalah* is, as far as I know, the one other book which can bear and may challenge the comparison.[1] Its pages, for one thing, reflect the sterile glitter and desolate fascination of the salt marshes ... with the same instinctive and unlaborious accuracy which brings all the moorland before us in a breath when we open any chapter of *Wuthering Heights*. And the humour is even better ... the passion ... not less genuine. But the accumulated horrors of the close ... lack the impression of logical and moral certitude. ... Now in *Wuthering Heights* this one thing needful is as perfectly and triumphantly attained as in *King Lear* or *The Duchess of Malfi*, in *The Bride of Lammermoor*[2] or *Notre-Dame de Paris*.[3] From the first we breathe the fresh dark air of tragic passion and presage; and to the last the changing wind and flying sunlight are in keeping with the stormy promise of the dawn. There is no monotony, there is no repetition, but there is no discord. This is the first and last necessity, the foundation of all labour and the crown of all success, for a poem worthy of the name; and this it is that distinguishes the hand of Emily from the hand of Charlotte Brontë. All the works of the elder sister are rich in poetic spirit, poetic feeling, and poetic detail; but the younger sister's work is essentially and definitely a poem in the fullest and most positive sense of the term. . . .

Miss Robinson makes a little too much of the influence exercised on Emily Brontë's work by the bitter, narrow, and ignoble misery of the life which she had watched burn down into such pitiful ruin[4] . . . the intelligent reader of *Wuthering Heights* cannot fail to recognise that what he is reading is a tragedy simply because it is the work of a writer whose genius is essentially tragic. Those who believe that Heathcliff was called into existence by the accident that his creator had witnessed the agonies of a violent weakling in love and in disgrace might believe that Shakespeare wrote *King Lear* because he had witnessed the bad effects of parental indulgence, and that Æschylus wrote the 'Eumenides' because he had witnessed the uncomfortable results of matricide. The book is what it is because the author was what she was, this is the main and central fact to be remembered. . . . As an author Emily Brontë has not perhaps even yet received her full due or taken her final place. Again and again has the same obvious objection been taken to that awkwardness of construction or presentation which no reader of *Wuthering Heights* can undertake to deny. But, to judge by the vigour with which this objection is urged, it might be supposed that the rules of narrative observed by all great novelists were of an almost legal or logical strictness and exactitude with regard to probability of detail. . . . the indirect method of relation through which the story of Heathcliff is conveyed, however unlikely or clumsy it may seem from the realistic point of view, does not make this narrative more liable to the charge of actual impossibility than others of the kind. Defoe still remains the one writer of narrative in the first person who has always kept the stringent law of possibilities before the eye of his invention. Even the admirable ingenuity and the singular painstaking which distinguish the method of Mr Wilkie Collins can only give external and transient plausibility to the record of long conversations overheard or shared in by the narrator only a few hours before the supposed date of the report drawn up from memory. . . . From *Rob Roy* and *Redgauntlet*, from *David Copperfield* and *Bleak House* we might select at almost any stage of the autobiographic record some instance of detail in which the violation of plausibility, probability, or even possibility, is at least as daring and as glaring as any to be found in the narrative of Nelly Dean. Even when that narrative is removed, so to speak, yet one degree further back – even when we are supposed to be reading a minute detail of incident and dialogue transcribed by the hand of the lay figure Mr Lockwood from Nelly Dean's report of the account conveyed to her years ago by Heathcliff's fugitive wife or gadding servant, each invested for the nonce with the peculiar force and distinctive style of the author – even then we are not asked to put such an overwhelming strain on our faculty of imaginative belief as is exacted by the great writer who invites us to accept the report drawn up by Mr Pendennis[5] of everything that takes place – down even to the minutest points of dialogue, accent, and gesture – in the household of the Newcomes or the Firmins during the absence no less than in the presence of their friend the reporter. Yet all this we gladly and gratefully admit, without demur or cavil, to be thoroughly authentic and credible, because the whole matter of the report, however we get at it, is found when we do get at it to be vivid and lifelike as an actual experience of living fact. Here, if ever anywhere, the attainment of the end justifies the employment of the means.

A graver and perhaps a somewhat more plausible charge is brought against the author of *Wuthering Heights* by those who find here and there in her book the savage note or the sickly symptom of a morbid ferocity. . . . But the pervading atmosphere of the book is so high and healthy that the effect even of those 'vivid and fearful scenes' which impaired the rest of Charlotte Brontë is almost at once neutralized – we may hardly say softened, but sweetened, dispersed and transfigured – by the general impression of noble purity and passionate straight-forwardness. . . . The whole work is not more incomparable in the effect of its atmosphere or landscape than in the peculiar note of its wild and bitter pathos; but most of all is it unique in the special and distinctive character of its passion. The love which devours life itself, which devastates the present and desolates the future with unquenchable and raging fire, has nothing less pure in it than flame or sunlight. . . . this passionate and ardent chastity is . . . spontaneous and unconscious. Not till the story is ended, not till the effect of it has been thoroughly absorbed and digested, does the reader even perceive . . . any hint or suggestion of a baser alloy in the ingredients of its human emotion than in the splendour of lightning or the roll of a gathered wave. Then, as on issuing sometimes from the tumult of charging waters, he finds with something of wonder how absolutely pure and sweet was the element of living storm with which his own nature has been for a while made one. . . . As was the author's life, so is her book in all things: troubled and taintless, with little of rest in it, and nothing of reproach. It may be true that not many will ever take it to their hearts; it is certain that those who do like it will like nothing very much better in the whole world of poetry or prose.

SOURCE: from Emily Brontë, in *Athenaeum* (1883); reprinted in *Miscellanies* (1886).

NOTES

1. *Mehalah, a story of the Salt Marshes*, by Sabine Baring-Gould, 2 vols (1880).
2. On *Wuthering Heights* and Scott's *The Bride of Lammermoor* (1819) cp Appendix in Q. D. Leavis's 'A Fresh Approach to *Wuthering Heights*', see p. 238 below.
3. Victor Hugo's *Notre-Dame de Paris* was published 1831. Swinburne's enthusiasm for Hugo as a great poet is evident in much of his criticism.
4. See above, pp. 84, 86–7.
5. Thackeray's *The History of Pendennis* was published serially 1848–50.

Walter Pater 'The Spirit of Romanticism' (1889)

. . . as the term, *classical*, has been used in a too absolute, and therefore in a misleading sense, so the term, *romantic*, has been used much too vaguely, in various accidental senses. The sense in which Scott is called a romantic writer is chiefly this; that, in opposition to the literary tradition of the last century, he loved strange adventure, and sought it in the Middle Age. Much later, in a Yorkshire village, the spirit of romanticism bore a more really characteristic fruit in the work of a young girl, Emily Brontë, the romance of *Wuthering*

Heights; the figures of Hareton Earnshaw, of Catherine Linton, and of Heathcliffe [*sic*] – tearing open Catherine's grave, removing one side of her coffin, that he may really lie beside her in death – figures so passionate, yet woven on a background of delicately beautiful, moorland scenery, being typical examples of that spirit. In Germany, again, that spirit is shown less in Tieck, its professional representative, than in Meinhold, the author of Sidonia the Sorceress and the Amber-Witch. . . . [1]

SOURCE: from 'Postscript', in *Appreciations* (1889).

NOTE

1. Johan Ludwig Tieck (1773–1853), prolific German poet, novelist and critic. See p. 103n.

Leslie Stephen 'A Kind of Baseless Nightmare' (1892)

. . . Even a will directed to evil purposes has a kind of royal prerogative, and we may rightly do it homage. That seems to be the seminal thought in *Wuthering Heights*, that strange book to which we can hardly find a parallel in our literature, unless in such works as the *Revenger's Tragedy*,[1] and some other crude but startling productions of the Elizabethan dramatists. But Emily Brontë's feeble grasp of external facts makes her book a kind of baseless nightmare, which we read with wonder and with distressing curiosity, but with even more pain than pleasure or profit. . . .

SOURCE: from *Hours in a Library*, III (1892).

NOTE

1. Cyril Tourneur's *The Revenger's Tragedy* was published 1607; an edition of his plays and poems prepared by John Churton Collins appeared in 1878.

'Vernon Lee' (Violet Paget) 'A Fault of Construction' (1895)

A . . . fault of construction . . . makes the beginning of one of our greatest masterpieces of passion and romance, *Wuthering Heights*, exceedingly difficult to read. As if the step-relations and adopted relations in the story were not sufficiently puzzling, Emily Brontë gave the narrative to several different people, at several different periods, people alternating what they had been told with what they actually witnessed. This kind of construction was a fault, if not of Emily's own time, at least of the time in which many of the books which had impressed her most had been written, notably Hoffmann's, from whose *Majorat* she borrowed much for *Wuthering Heights*.[1] It is historically an old fault for the same reason which makes it a fault with beginners, namely that it is undoubtedly easier to narrate in the first person, or as an eye-witness, and that it is easier to co-ordinate three or four sides of an event by boxing them mechanically as so many stories one in the other, than to arrange the various groups of persons and acts as in real life, and to change the point of view of the reader from one to the other. These mechanical divisions also seem to give the writer courage: it is like the series of ropes which take away the fear of swimming . . . I have no doubt that most of the stories which we have all written between the ages of fifteen and twenty were either in the autobiographical or epistolary form, that they had introduction set in introduction like those of Scott, that they shifted narrator as in *Wuthering Heights*, and altogether reproduced, in their immaturity, the forms of an immature period of novel-writing. . . .

SOURCE: from 'On Literary Construction', in *Contemporary Review*, 1895; reprinted in *The Handling of Words* (1923).

NOTE

1. See above, p. 75n.

Angus M. Mackay 'Shakespeare's Younger Sister'[1] (1898)

... Emily Brontë's rank as a poet is to be measured, not by her verse, but by her single romance. The quantity as well [as] the quality of work must needs be taken into account in estimating the genius of a writer. ... But if we look only to the *quality* of the imagination displayed in *Wuthering Heights* – its power, its intensity, its absolute originality – it is scarcely too much to say of Emily that she might have been Shakespeare's younger sister. To the many, of course, this will seem merely fantastic; but the few who have really learnt to appreciate *Wuthering Heights* will see no exaggeration in the title. Putting aside the clumsiness of the framework – the only mark of the prentice-hand in the whole book – what is there comparable to this romance except the greater tragedies of Shakespeare? The single peasant in the story, Joseph, is of the kin of Shakespeare's clowns, and yet is quite distinct from them. Heathcliff ... fascinates the imagination, and in some scenes almost paralyses us with horror, and yet that subtle human touch is added which wrings from us pity and almost respect. He reminds us of Shylock and Iago ... by the sense of wonder he awakens in us at the power that could create such a being. Catherine Earnshaw, again, and Catherine Linton – are not these by their piquancy and winsomeness almost worthy of a place in Shakespeare's gallery of fair women? The whole story has something of the pathos of *King Lear* and much of the tragic force of *Macbeth*, and yet both characters and story are, perhaps, as absolutely original as any that can be named in English literature. It is not, of course, meant that Emily Brontë achieved anything comparable to Shakespeare's greatest work. ... but the material out of which the two wrought their work, the protoplasm of their creations, so to speak, was the same. ...

SOURCE: from *Westminster Review*, 1898.

NOTE

1. The article by the Reverend Angus M. Mackay from which this extract is taken forms the nucleus of his *The Brontës, Fact and Fiction* (1897),

a point-by-point rebuttal of William Wright's wildly improbable account, in *The Brontës in Ireland* (1893), of Patrick Brontë's Irish relatives. Their colourful lives are supposed by Wright to have dictated the subject-matter of the Brontë novels.

Mrs Humphry Ward 'The Grafting of a European Tradition upon a Mind already Richly Stored with English and Local Reality'[1] (1900)

I

. . . Those among us . . . who have now reached middle age can well remember that while Charlotte Brontë was a name of magic to our youth, and Mrs Gaskell's wonderful biography had stamped the stories and personalities of the two sisters upon the inmost fibres of memory and pity, *Wuthering Heights*, if we read it at all, was read in haste, and with a prior sense of repulsion, which dropped a veil between book and reader, and was in truth only the result of an all but universal tenor of opinion amongst our elders.

Indeed, Charlotte Brontë herself, in the touching and eloquent preface which she wrote for a new edition of *Wuthering Heights* in 1850, adopts a tone towards her sister's work which contains more than a shade of apology. . . .

Mrs Gaskell's comments upon *Wuthering Heights* betray a similar note of timidity. 'They might be mistaken,' she says, speaking of Emily and Anne Brontë, 'they might err in writing at all,' seeing that they could not write otherwise; but all their work, she pleads, was done in obedience to stern dictates of conscience, and under the pressure of 'hard and cruel facts'; by which are meant, of course, the facts connected with Branwell Brontë.[2] 'All I say is, that never, I believe, did women possessed of such wonderful gifts exercise them with a fuller feeling of responsibility for their use. As to mistakes, they stand now – as authors as well as women – before the judgement-seat of God.'[3]

One hears in these sentences, with their note of protesting emotion, no less than in Charlotte's tender and dignified defence, the echo of an angry public opinion, indignant in the typical English way that any young woman, and especially any clergyman's daughter, should write of such unbecoming scenes and persons as those which form the subject of *Wuthering Heights*, and determined if it could to punish the offender.

But for us, fifty years later, how irrelevant are both the attack and the defence! One might as well plead that Marlowe meant no harm by creating Tamburlaine, or Victor Hugo in imagining Quasimodo, or the fight between the *pieuvre* and Gilliatt.[4] *Wuthering Heights* lives as great imagination, of which we must take the consequences, the bad with the good; and will continue to live, whether it pleases us personally or no. Moreover, the book has much more than a mere local or personal significance. It belongs to a particular European moment, and like Charlotte's work, though not in the same way, it holds a typical and representative place in the English literature of the century. . . .

II

. . . During their eager enthusiastic youth the Brontë sisters . . . were readers of Christopher North, Hogg, De Quincey, and Maginn in *Blackwood*, of Carlyle's early essays and translations in *Fraser*, of Scott and Lockhart, no less than of Wordsworth, Southey, and Coleridge. . . . [5] There can be no question that they were 'romantic' influences, and it can be easily shown that among them were many kindling sparks from that 'unextinguished hearth'[6] of German poetry and fiction which played so large a part in English imagination during the first half of the century. . . . In *Blackwood* also, through the years when Charlotte and Emily Brontë, then at the most plastic stage of thought and imagination, were delighting in it, one may find a constant series of translations from the German, of articles on German memories and German poets, and of literary reflections and estimates, which testify abundantly to the vogue of all things Teutonic, both with men of letters and the public. In 1840, 'Maga',[7] in the inflated phrase of the time, says, indeed, that the Germans are aspiring 'to wield the literary sceptre, with as lordly a sway as ever graced the dynasty of Voltaire. No one who is even superficially acquainted with the floating literature of the day can fail to have observed how flauntingly long-despised Germanism spreads its phylacteries on every side.' In the year before (1839),

Blackwood published a translation of Tieck's *Pietro d'Abano*, a wild robber-and-magician story, of the type which spread the love of monster and vampire, witch and werewolf, through a Europe tired for the moment of eighteenth-century common-sense;[8] and, more important still, a long section, excellently rendered, from Goethe's *Dichtung und Wahrheit*.'[9] In that year Emily Brontë was alone with her father and aunt at Haworth, while her two sisters were teaching as governesses. *Blackwood* came as usual, and one may surely imagine the long, thin girl bending in the firelight over these pages from Goethe, receiving the impress of their lucidity, their charm, their sentiment and 'natural magic',[10] nourishing from them the vivid and masterly intelligence which eight years later produced *Wuthering Heights*. ... In 1842 [in Brussels] she ... learnt German diligently, and it has always been assumed, though I hardly know on what first authority, that she read a good deal of German fiction, and especially Hoffmann's tales, at Brussels.[11] Certainly, we hear of her in the following year, when she was once more at Haworth, and Charlotte was still at Brussels, as doing her household work 'with a German book open beside her',[12] though we are not told what the books were. ... It is important to realise that of the three books written simultaneously by the three sisters, Emily's alone shows genius already matured and master of its tools. ... The common, hasty, didactic note that Charlotte often strikes is never heard in *Wuthering Heights*. The artist remains hidden and self-contained; the work, however morbid and violent may be the scenes and creatures it presents, has always that distinction which belongs to high talent working solely for its own joy and satisfaction, with no thought of a spectator, or any aim but that of an ideal and imaginative whole ... no one, from the pages of *Wuthering Heights*, can guess at the small likes and dislikes, the religious or critical antipathies, the personal weaknesses of the artist who wrote it. She has that highest power – which was typically Shakespeare's power, and which in our day is typically the power of such an artist as Turgeniev[13] – the power which gives ... intensest life ... to the creatures of imagination, and ... endows them with an independence behind which the maker is forgotten. ...

Yet, at the same time, *Wuthering Heights* is a book of the later Romantic movement, betraying the influences of German Romantic imagination, as Charlotte's work betrays the influences of Victor Hugo and George Sand.[14] The Romantic tendency to invent and delight in monsters, the *exaltation du moi*, which has been said to be the secret of the whole Romantic revolt against classical models and restraints; the love of violence in speech and action, the preference for the hideous in character and the abnormal in situation – of all these there are abundant examples in *Wuthering Heights*. The dream of Mr Lockwood in Catherine's box bed. . . . Heathcliff's long and fiendish revenge on Hindley Earnshaw; the ghastly quarrel between Linton and Heathcliff in Catherine's presence after Heathcliff's return; Catherine's three days' fast, and her delirium when she 'tore the pillow with her teeth'; Heathcliff dashing his head against the trees of her garden, leaving his blood upon their bark, and 'howling, not like a man, but like a savage beast being goaded to death with knives and spears'; the fight between Heathcliff and Earnshaw after Heathcliff's marriage to Isabella; the kidnapping of the younger Catherine, and the horror rather suggested than described of Heathcliff's brutality towards his sickly son: – all these things would not have been written precisely as they were written but for the 'Germanism' of the thirties and forties, but for the translations of *Blackwood* and *Fraser*, and but for those German tales, whether of Hoffmann or others, which there is evidence that Emily Brontë read both at Brussels and after her return.

As to the 'exaltation of the Self', its claims, sensibilities and passions, in defiance of all social law and duty, there is no more vivid expression of it throughout Romantic literature than is contained in the conversation between the elder Catherine and Nelly Dean before Catherine marries Edgar Linton. And the violent, clashing egotisms of Heathcliff and Catherine in the last scene of passion before Catherine's death, are as it were an epitome of a whole *genre* in literature, and a whole phase of European feeling.

Nevertheless, horror and extravagance are not really the characteristic mark and quality of *Wuthering Heights*. . . . As in the case of Charlotte Brontë, the peculiar force of Emily's work lies in the fact that it represents the grafting of a European tradition upon a mind already richly stored with English and local reality, possessing at command a style at once strong and simple, capable both of homeliness and magnificence. The form of Romantic imagination which influenced Emily was not the same as that which influenced Charlotte; whether from a secret stubbornness and desire of difference, or no, there is not a mention of the French language, or of French books, in Emily's work, while Charlotte's abounds in a kind of display of French affinities, and French scholarship. The dithyrambs of *Shirley* and *Villette*, the 'Vision of Eve' of *Shirley*, and the description of Rachel in *Villette*,[15] would have been impossible to Emily; they come to a great extent from the reading of Victor Hugo and George Sand. But in both sisters there is a similar *fonds* of stern and simple realism; a similar faculty of observation at once shrewd, and passionate; and it is by these that they produce their ultimate literary effect. The difference between them is almost wholly in Emily's favour. The uneven, amateurish manner of so many pages in *Jane Eyre* and *Shirley*; the lack of literary reticence which is responsible for Charlotte's frequent intrusion of her own personality, and for her occasional temptations to scream and preach, which are not wholly resisted even in her masterpiece, *Villette*; the ugly, tawdry sentences which disfigure some of her noblest passages, and make quotation from her so difficult: – you will find none of these things in *Wuthering Heights*. Emily is never flurried, never self-conscious; she is master of herself at the most rushing moments of feeling or narrative; her style is simple, sensuous, adequate and varied from first to last; she has fewer purple patches than Charlotte, but at its best, her insight no less than her power of phrase is of a diviner and more exquisite quality.

III

... Its few great faults are soon enumerated. The tendency to extravagance and monstrosity may, as we have seen, be taken to some extent as belonging more to a literary fashion than to the artist. Tieck and Hoffmann are full of raving and lunatic beings who sob, shout, tear out their hair by the roots, and live in a perpetual state of personal violence both towards themselves and their neighbours. Emily Brontë probably received from them an additional impulse towards a certain wildness of manner and conception which was already natural to her Irish blood, to a woman brought up amid the solitudes of the moors and the ruggedness of Yorkshire life fifty years ago, and natural also, alas! to the sister of the opium-eater and drunkard, Branwell Brontë.

To this let us add a certain awkwardness and confusion of structure; a strain of ruthless exaggeration in the character of Heathcliff; and some absurdities and contradictions in the character of Nelly Dean. The latter criticism indeed is bound up with the first.

Nelly Dean is presented as the faithful and affectionate nurse, the only good angel both of the elder and the younger Catherine. But Nelly Dean does the most treacherous, cruel, and indefensible things, simply that the story may move. She becomes the go-between for Catherine and Heathcliff; she knowingly allows her charge Catherine, on the eve of her confinement, to fast in solitude and delirium for three days and nights, without saying a word to Edgar Linton, Catherine's affectionate husband, and her master, who was in the house all the time. It is her breach of trust which brings about Catherine's dying scene with Heathcliff, just as it is her disobedience and unfaith which really betray Catherine's child into the hands of her enemies. Without these lapses and indiscretions indeed the story could not maintain itself; but the clumsiness or carelessness of them is hardly to be denied. In the case of Heathcliff, the blemish lies rather in a certain deliberate and passionate defiance of the reader's sense of humanity and possibility; partly also in the innocence of the writer, who, in a world of sex and passion, has invented a situation charged with the full forces of both, without any true realisation of what she has done. . . . There are speeches and actions of Catherine's, moreover, contained in these central pages which have no relation to any life of men and women that the true world knows. It may be said, indeed, that the writer's very ignorance of certain facts and relations of life, combined with the force of imaginative passion which she throws into her conceptions, produces a special poetic effect – a strange and bodiless tragedy – unique in literature. And there is much truth in this; but not enough to vindicate these scenes of the book from radical weakness and falsity, nor to preserve in the reader that illusion, that inner consent, which is the final test of all imaginative effort.

IV

Nevertheless, there are whole sections of the story during which the character of Heathcliff is presented to us with a marvellous and essential truth. The scenes of childhood and youth; the up-growing of the two desolate children, drawn to each other by some strange primal sympathy . . . the gradual development of the natural distance between them, he the ill-mannered ruffianly no-man's-child, she the young lady of the house . . . Cathy's passionate discrimination, in the scene with Nelly Dean which ends as it were the first act of the play, between her affection for Linton and her identity with Heathcliff's life and being: – for the mingling of daring poetry with the easiest and most masterly command of local truth, for sharpness and felicity of phrase, for exuberance of creative force, for invention and freshness of detail, there are few things in English fiction to match it. One might almost say that the first volume of *Adam Bede* is false and mannered beside it, – the first volumes of *Waverley* or *Guy Mannering* flat and diffuse. Certainly, the first volume of *Jane Eyre*, admirable as it is, can hardly be set on the same level with the careless ease and effortless power of these first nine chapters. . . . as far as the lesser elements of style, the mere technique of writing, are concerned, one may notice the short elastic vigour of the sentences, the rightness of epithet and detail, the absence of any care for effect, and the flashes of beauty which suddenly emerge like the cistus upon the rock: [quotes from ch. 9 the conversation between Catherine and Nelly Dean: 'Nelly, do you never dream . . . frost from fire'] . . . 'The angels flung me out into the middle of the heath – where I woke sobbing for joy' – the wild words have in them the very essence and life-blood not only of Catherine but of her creator!

The inferior central scenes of the book, after Catherine's marriage, for all their teasing faults, have passages of extraordinary poetry. Take the detail of Catherine's fevered dream after she shuts herself into her room, at the close of the frightful scene between her husband and Heathcliff, or the weird realism of her half-delirious talk with Nelly Dean [ch. 12]. . . . To these may be added the charming and tender passage describing Catherine's early convalescence, and her yearnings – so true to such a child of nature and feeling – for the first flowers and first mild breathings of the spring; and the later picture of her, the wrecked and doomed Catherine, sitting in 'dreamy and melancholy softness' by the open window, listening for the sounds of the moorland, before the approach of Heathcliff and death: [quotes from ch. 15, 'Gimmerton chapel . . . steady rain'] . . .

V

. . . the third and last act of *Wuthering Heights*, which extends from the childhood of the younger Catherine to the death of Heathcliff . . . is no less masterly than the first section of the book and much more complex in plan. The key to it lies in two earlier passages – in Heathcliff's boyish vow of vengeance on Hindley Earnshaw, and in his fierce appeal to his lost love to haunt him, rather than leave him 'in this abyss where I cannot find her' [ch. 16]. The conduct of the whole 'act' is intricate and difficult; the initial awkwardness implied in Nelly Dean's function as narrator is felt now and then; but as a whole, the strength of the intention is no less clear than the deliberate and triumphant power with which the artist achieves it. . . . Not an incident, not a fragment of conversation is thrown away, and in the end the effect is complete. It is gained by that fusion of terror and beauty, of ugliness and a flying magic – 'settling unawares' – which is the characteristic note of the Brontës, and of all that is best in Romantic literature. Never for a moment do you lose hold upon the Yorkshire landscape and the Yorkshire folk . . . yet through it all the inevitable end develops, the double end which only a master could have conceived. Life and love rebel and reassert themselves in the wild slight love-story of Hareton and Cathy, which breaks the final darkness like a gleam of dawn upon the moors; and death tames and silences for ever all that remains of Heathcliff's futile cruelties and wasted fury.

But what a death! Heathcliff has tormented and oppressed Catherine's daughter; and it is Catherine's shadow that lures him to his doom, through every stage and degree of haunting feverish ecstasy, of reunion promised and delayed, of joy for ever offered and for ever withdrawn. And yet how simple the method, how true the 'vision' to the end! Around Heathcliff's last hours the farm-life flows on as usual. There is no hurry in the sentences; no blurring of the scene. Catherine's haunting presence closes upon the man who murdered her happiness and youth, interposes between him and all bodily needs, deprives him of food and drink and sleep, till the madman is dead of his 'strange happiness', straining after the phantom that slays him, dying of the love whereby alone he remains human, through which fate strikes at last – and strikes home.

'Is he a ghoul or vampire?' I mused. 'I had read of such hideous incarnate demons [ch. 34]. So says Nelly Dean just before Heathcliff's death. The remark is not hers in truth, but Emily Brontë's, and where it stands it is of great significance. It points to the world of German horror and romance . . . which . . . was congenial to her, as it was congenial to Southey, Scott and Coleridge: and it has left some ugly and disfiguring traces upon the detail of *Wuthering*

Heights. But *essentially* her imagination escaped from it and mastered it. . . . For all her crudity and inexperience, she is in the end with Goethe, rather than with Hoffmann, and thereby with all that is sane, strong, and living in literature. 'A great work requires many-sidedness, and on this rock the young author splits,' said Goethe to Eckermann, praising at the same time the art which starts from the simplest realities and the subject nearest at hand, to reach at last by a natural expansion the loftiest heights of poetry. But this was the art of Emily Brontë. It started from her own heart and life; it was nourished by the sights and sounds of a lonely yet sheltering nature; it was responsive to the art of others, yet always independent; and in the rich and tangled truth of *Wuthering Heights* it showed promise at least of a many-sidedness to which only the greatest attain. . . .

SOURCE: from the Introduction to the Haworth edition of *Wuthering Heights* (1900).

NOTES

1. Mary Augusta Ward, better known as Mrs Humphry Ward (1851–1920), was the wife of T. H. Ward and the niece of Matthew Arnold. She was a prolific novelist, her best-known work including *Robert Elsmere* (1888) and *Helbeck of Bannisdale* (1898). She was asked to write the prefaces for the Haworth edition by G. B. Smith (Charlotte's publisher) in 1898. John Sutherland's comprehensive biography, *Mrs. Humphry Ward, Eminent Victorian, Pre-eminent Edwardian*, was published in 1990.
2. See above, p. 83 and n.
3. *Life of Charlotte Brontë*, ch. 16.
4. Quasimodo appears in Victor Hugo's *Notre-Dame de Paris* (1831). 'The fight between the *pieuvre* and Gilliatt' is a reference to Gilliatt's fight with the octopus in Hugo's *Les Travailleurs de la mer* (1866).
5. See Introduction, p. 14 above.
6. Shelley's 'Ode to the West Wind' (1820) lines 66–8,

> Scatter, as from an unextinguished hearth
> Ashes and sparks, my words among mankind! . . .

7. 'Maga' was the familiar Victorian name for the monthly periodical *Blackwood's Edinburgh Magazine* (founded 1817). The quotation is taken from the lengthy commentary on Julius Weber's *Deutschland* (1834) in *Blackwood's Magazine*, XLVIII (July 1840), p. 120.
8. On Tieck, see above, p. 92n. His 'Pietro von Abano oder Petrus Apone, Zaubergeschichte' was published in 1824 and translated into English 1831 and 1839; the latter version appears in *Blackwood's Magazine*, XLVI (Aug. 1839), pp. 228–55. On the unlikelihood of the story's directly influencing Emily Brontë, see Jacques Blondel's comments (p. 162 below).

9. Goethe's *Dichtung und Wahreit* ('Poetry and Truth') was completed 1831; an English translation of the two opening books appears in *Blackwood's Magazine*, XLVI (Oct, Nov 1839), pp. 475–93, 597–613.

10. Matthew Arnold's phrase in his essay 'Maurice de Guérin', in *Essays in Criticism* (1865).

11. On Emily Brontë and Hoffmann, see above, p. 74n.

12. Mrs Gaskell's *Life of Charlotte Brontë*, ch. 8.

13. All the major works of the Russian novelist Turgenev (1818–83) had been translated into English before 1890. His popularity in England in the later nineteenth century is discussed by Gilbert Phelps in *The Russian Novel in English Fiction* (1956).

14. George Sand (Lucile-Aurore Dupin, baronne Dudevant) (1804–76), celebrated French romantic novelist, called by the critic Renan (1823–92), 'la harpe éolienne de notre temps'. Her best-known works include *Indiana* (1832), *Lélia* (1833), *Jacques* (1834), *La Mare au diable* (1846). Charlotte wrote enthusiastically about her in her letter to G. H. Lewes of 17 October 1850 (*Life and Letters*, III, 172–3).

15. *Shirley*, ch. 18; *Villette*, ch. 23. Rachel (Elisa Félix) (1821–58) was a widely admired French tragic actress; she is portrayed by Charlotte Brontë as 'Vashti' in *Villette*.

Alice Meynell 'Unparalleled Power of Imagery' (1911)

Emily Brontë seems to have a nearly unparalleled unconsciousness of the delays, the charms, the pauses and preparations of imagery. Her strength does not dally with the parenthesis, and her simplicity is ignorant of those rites. Her lesser work, therefore, is plain narrative, and her greater work is no more. On the hither side – the daily side – of imagery she is still a strong and solitary writer; on the yonder side she has written some of the most mysterious passages in all plain prose. . . .

'"Let me alone, let me alone," said Catherine. "If I've done wrong, I'm dying for it. . . . You left me too . . . I forgive you. Forgive me!" "It is hard to forgive, and to look at those eyes, and feel those wasted hands," he answered. "Kiss me again; and don't let me see your eyes! I forgive what you have done to me. I love *my* murderer – but *yours*! How can I?" They were silent, their faces hid against each other, and washed by each other's tears.' '"So much the worse for me that I am strong,"' cries Heathcliff in the same scene. '"Do I want to live? What kind of living will it be when you – Oh God, would *you* like to live with your soul in the grave?"' [ch. 15].

Charlotte Brontë's noblest passages are her own speech or the speech of one like herself acting the central part in the dreams and dramas of emotion that she had kept from her girlhood. . . . Emily had no such confessions to publish . . . her 'I' is not heard here. She lends her voice in disguise to her men and women; the first narrator of her great romance is a young man, the second a servant woman; this one or that among the actors takes up the story, and her great words sound at times in paltry mouths. It is then that for a moment her reader seems about to come into her immediate presence, but by a fiction she denies herself to him. To a somewhat trivial girl (or a girl who would be trivial in any other book, but Emily Brontë seems unable to create anything consistently meagre) – to Isabella Linton she commits one of her most memorable passages, and one which has the rare image, one of a terrifying little company of visions amid terrifying facts: 'His attention was roused, I saw, for his eyes rained down tears among the ashes. . . . The clouded windows of hell flashed for a moment towards me; the fiend which usually looked out was so dimmed and drowned' [ch. 7]. But in Heathcliff's own speech there is no veil or circumstance. 'I'm too happy; and yet I'm not happy enough. My soul's bliss kills my body, but does not satisfy itself' [ch. 34]. 'I have to remind myself to breathe, and almost to remind my heart to beat' [ch. 33]. 'Being alone, and conscious two yards of loose earth was the sole barrier between us, I said to myself; "I'll have her in my arms again. If she be cold, I'll think it is this north wind that chills me; and if she be motionless, it is sleep"' [ch. 29]. What art, moreover, what knowledge, what a fresh ear for the clash of repetition; what a chime in that phrase: 'I dreamt I was sleeping the last sleep by that sleeper, with my heart stopped, and my cheek frozen against hers. . . .' [Ibid.].

SOURCE: from *Dublin Review*, 1911; reprinted in *Hearts of Controversy* (1917).

Lascelles Abercrombie 'The Unquestionable Supremacy of Emily' (1924)

. . . the obvious thing to remark, in the way the Brontës appear to us today, is the unquestionable supremacy of Emily. The proper ground of this supremacy is, however, to be asserted precisely where Charlotte fails – and precisely where the art of the novel is most liable to fail: in its total effect, in its coherence and unity, in its form and, through that, its presiding significance. . . . I believe *Wuthering Heights* to be one of the greatest not merely of English but of European novels. As for the style of its writing, it is throughout clearly the work of a poet; and it baffles me to remember that anyone could ever have preferred Charlotte's style of writing. Charlotte is a great writer, indeed; but she never could resist the temptation to *show off*. . . . Emily never says a single thing . . . that is not absolutely just and right in its context. And she says it with all the understanding of one who knows the inmost subtlety of the power of words. Hence the apparent bare directness of her language; and hence, too, the nice and vigorous complexities of energy always electrifying her stark narrative. . . .

The book enlarges the nature of tragedy: it shows how a genuinely tragic action can be carried on past the fatality into an ending in positive happiness. But think of Heathcliff. We talk nowadays, and rightly, of the magnificence of Dostoevsky's psychology.[1] But is there anything in Russian fiction to match, for strangeness and for perfect realisation, the tortured mind of Heathcliff, the creation of this English provincial girl, who had nothing to rely on but her own genius? . . . Observation went to the making of him, no doubt; just as the Byronic tradition did. But the Byronic tradition, as well as any conceivable kind of observation, have been consumed in the fiery creative force of Emily's imagination. . . .

And yet the real greatness of Emily remains unconsidered. . . . For it is in structure, in form, in total significance that Emily's work is chiefly momentous and immortal today. The surface of the narrative is questionable, perhaps; though few narrators have made themselves so clearly felt in their words as Lockwood and Nelly Dean. Still, they are, for all their clear delineation, always a disguise of the omniscient author. . . . But it is interesting to see how successful on the whole this young girl was in 1847 with the difficult technique perfected today by Mr Joseph Conrad. . . . [2] the convention which Emily invented is one remarkably easy to accept . . . the gain of it is unmistakeable. By its means, she . . . gives her story a headlong and thrilling pace, from Lockwood's fight with the dogs to the evening quiet at the end; it enables her too to drop out all the inessentials. We never know where Heathcliff got his money from, simply because the narrators don't happen to know; and it matters nothing. It is Heathcliff himself we want. . . . And it enables Emily to call up the past as a living influence . . . into the midst of the present; and to amaze us with two . . . differing aspects of the same incident. Thus, Heathcliff's fight with Hindley Earnshaw after his vigil at Catherine's grave shows him, as we first see it, the mere demon of an insatiable revenge. But when we see it from the other side, when we understand how Heathcliff was well-nigh beside himself with the first agonies of that ghostly passion which was to madden him all the rest of his life, then we begin to understand how a man may turn into a fiend.

But the total result of all this is the important thing. At the cost of some very superficial and very excusable clumsiness, Emily succeeded in compacting her turbulent and explosive matter into lucidly shapely form: and by that means the whole book becomes the expression of one central and dominant motive. The rarest achievement in the art of the novel seems to me absolute here: *Wuthering Heights* has that perfect coherence of purpose we think of when we think of the art of Shakespeare's tragedy or Beethoven's symphony. . . . It is easy to talk of elemental passion: but here, for once in the art of the novel, we really do get the elemental passion of love . . . which consumes alike sentiment and sensuality, to which the mortal things of life are mere irrelevance, which belongs to the inward essence and takes no account of natural accidents, even when they are the brutalities of a Heathcliff. But we shall never understand Catherine and Heathcliff unless we see in them something of that which Emily so vividly expressed in 'The Prisoner'. . . .

SOURCE: from *Brontë Society Transactions*, 1924.

NOTES

1. One of the earliest attempts to relate Emily Brontë to Dostoevsky: cp. below, p. 174 and n.

2. Anticipates C. P. Sanger and David Cecil. See below p. 110, and p. 124n.

3. Quotes 'Julian M. and A. G. Rochelle', dated 9 October 1845, lines 81–8 *The Complete Poems of Emily Jane Brontë*, ed. C. W. Hatfield (1941), p. 239.

Virginia Woolf 'We the Whole Human Race' and 'You, the Eternal Powers. . .' (1916)

Wuthering Heights is a more difficult book to understand than *Jane Eyre*, because Emily was a greater poet than Charlotte. When Charlotte wrote she said with eloquence and splendour and passion 'I love', 'I hate', 'I suffer'. Her experience, though more intense, is on a level with our own. But there is no 'I' in *Wuthering Heights*. There are no governesses. There are no employers. There is love, but it is not the love of men and women. Emily was inspired by some more general conception. The impulse which urged her to create was not her own suffering or her own injuries. She looked out upon a world cleft into gigantic disorder and felt within her the power to unite it in a book. That gigantic ambition is to be felt throughout the novel – a struggle, half thwarted but of superb conviction, to say something through the mouths of her characters which is not merely 'I love' or 'I hate', but 'we, the whole human race' and 'you, the eternal powers. . .' the sentence remains unfinished. It is not strange that it should be so; rather it is astonishing that she can make us feel what she had it in her to say at all. It surges up in the half-articulate words of Catherine Earnshaw, 'If all else perished and *he* remained, I should still continue to be; and if all else remained and he were annihilated, the universe would turn to a mighty stranger; I should not seem part of it' [ch. 9]. It breaks out again in the presence of the dead. 'I see a repose that neither earth nor hell can break, and I feel an assurance of the endless and shadowless hereafter – the eternity they have entered – where life is boundless in its duration, and love is sympathy and joy in its fulness' [ch. 16]. It is this suggestion of power underlying the apparitions of human nature and lifting them up into the presence of greatness that gives the book its huge stature among other novels. But it was not enough for Emily Brontë to write a few lyrics, to utter a cry, to express a creed. In her poems she did this once and for all, and her poems will perhaps outlast her novel. But she was novelist as well as poet. She must take upon herself a more laborious and a more ungrateful task. She must face the fact of other existences, grapple with the mechanism of external things, build up, in recognisable shape, farms and houses and report the speeches of men and women who existed independently of herself. And so we reach these summits of emotion not by rant or rhapsody but by hearing a girl sing old songs to herself as she rocks in the branches of a tree; by watching the moor sheep crop the turf; by listening to the soft wind breathing through the grass. The life at the farm with all its absurdities and its improbability is laid open to us. We are given every opportunity of comparing *Wuthering Heights* with a real farm and Heathcliff with a real man. How, we are allowed to ask, can there be truth or insight or the finer shades of emotion in men and women who so little resemble what we have seen ourselves? But even as we ask it we see in Heathcliff the brother that a sister of genius might have seen; he is impossible we say, but nevertheless no boy in literature has a more vivid existence than his. So it is with the two Catherines; never could women feel as they do or act in their manner, we say. All the same, they are the most lovable women in English fiction. It is as if she could tear up all that we know human beings by, and fill these unrecognisable transparences with such a gust of life that they transcend reality. Hers, then, is the rarest of all powers. She could free life from its dependence on facts; with a few touches indicate the spirit of a face so that it needs no body; by speaking of the moor make the wind blow and the thunder roar.

SOURCE: from '*Jane Eyre* and *Wuthering Heights*' (written 1916), reprinted in *The Common Reader* (1925).

C. P. Sanger 'Remarkable Symmetry in a Tempestuous Book' (1926)

. . . The most obvious thing about the structure of the story which deals with three generations is the symmetry of the pedigree. Mr and

Mrs Earnshaw at Wuthering Heights and Mr and Mrs Linton at Thrushcross Grange each have one son and one daughter. Mr Linton's son marries Mr Earnshaw's daughter, and their only child Catherine marries successively her two cousins – Mr Linton's grandson and Mr Earnshaw's grandson. See the following pedigree [opposite].

In actual life I have never come across a pedigree of such absolute symmetry. I shall have to refer to this pedigree again later. It is a remarkable piece of symmetry in a tempestuous book.

The method adopted to arouse the reader's interest and to give vividness and reality to the tale is one which has been used with great success by Joseph Conrad.[1] But it requires great skill . . . during the major part of the book Mr Lockwood is telling us what Ellen Dean told him, but sometimes, also, what Ellen Dean told him that someone else – for instance, Isabella – had told her. Only a small part, perhaps one-tenth of the book, consists of direct narrative by Lockwood from his own knowledge. But such a scheme may be confusing, and it is easy to muddle the time. Did Emily Brontë realise and let us know the dates when each event happened? She did, but not by giving them directly. Look again at the pedigree. The dates there have all been derived from the book, yet only one is directly stated. What first brought me to study the book more closely was when I noticed that the first word in the book was a date – 1801. I thought this must have some significance. Similarly, the first word of chapter 32 is 1802. Apart from this, only one other date is given directly. In the last sentence of chapter 7, Ellen Dean says, 'I will be content to pass on to the next summer – the summer of 1778, that is, nearly twenty-three years ago.' This gives no further information, as 1801 is twenty-three years after 1778, but in the first sentence of the next chapter she tells us that Hareton was born in June. This is how I get June 1778 for Hareton's birth in the pedigree. But what about the rest of the dates, not only those in the pedigree but of all the incidents in the story? There are a considerable number (perhaps nearly a hundred) indications of various kinds to help us – intervals of time, ages of characters, the months, the harvest moon, the last grouse, and so forth, and we learn, incidentally, that the younger Catherine's birthday was on 20 March. Sometimes, too, we know the day of the week – thus Ellen Dean will remember something which happened on a Sunday, or on a Christmas Eve. Taking all these indications, it is, I think, possible to ascertain the year, and, in

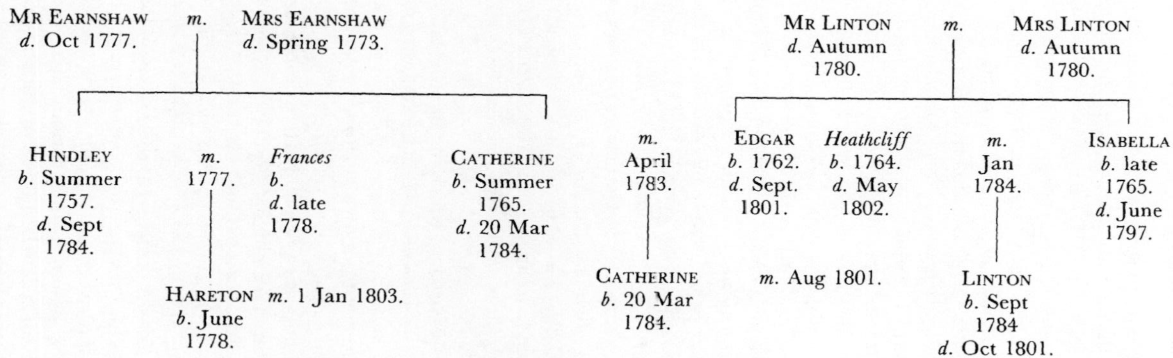

Mr Earnshaw
d. Oct 1777.
m.
Mrs Earnshaw
d. Spring 1773.
Mr Linton
d. Autumn
1780.
m.
Mrs Linton
d. Autumn
1780.
Hindley
b. Summer
1757.
d. Sept
1784.
m.
1777.
Frances
b.
d. late
1778.
Catherine
b. Summer
1765.
d. 20 Mar
1784.
m.
April
1783.
Edgar
b. 1762.
d. Sept.
1801.
Heathcliff
b. 1764.
d. May
1802.
m.
Jan
1784.
Isabella
b. late
1765.
d. June
1797.
Hareton
b. June
1778.
m. 1 Jan 1803.
Catherine
b. 20 Mar
1784.
m. Aug 1801.
Linton
b. Sept
1784
d. Oct 1801.

most cases, the month of the year in which every event takes place – also the ages of the various characters, except, naturally, there is a slight doubt as to Heathcliff, because no one knows his exact age when he was found by Mr Earnshaw. But one has to go warily and consider all the indications together, for there is a curious subtlety that sometimes the characters are described as *looking* some ages which are not exact. Thus Lockwood when he first describes them says that Heathcliff was about forty and Catherine did not look seventeen. In fact, Catherine was seventeen and three-quarters and Heathcliff cannot have been more than thirty-eight. It would be too tedious to state the process by which I have discovered each date. . . . But I will give one or two illustrations. We already know that Hareton was born in June 1778; we are told that he was nearly five when Catherine Earnshaw married Edgar Linton, so that the marriage was before June 1783. But Heathcliff returned in September after they had been happily married for six months. Thus the marriage was in April 1783. We are told that the scene that led to Catherine's death was a Sunday in the March after Heathcliff's return, and that her daughter, Catherine, was born about midnight, and the mother died two hours after. Later on we learn that Catherine's birthday was the twentieth (and that this was also treated as the day of her mother's death). Hence Catherine died at 2 a.m. on Monday, 20 March 1784.

I will give only one other instance. Lockwood begins his account in 1801; it is snowy weather, which might be in January or February or in November or December. But he returns in 1802 before his year's tenancy is out. Hence the story begins at the end of 1801. A Michaelmas tenancy begins on 10 October – not on 20 September – because when the calendar was reformed eleven days were left out. Therefore, the story begins after 10 October 1801. Now after Lockwood has been ill three weeks Heathcliff sends him some grouse, the last of the season. Since the Game Act, 1831, grouse may not be shot after 10 December, so we may take this as about the date for the last grouse. Thus the story begins about the middle of November, and this fits pretty well with the later indications. That is sufficient to illustrate the process. Sometimes it is only by fitting together several indications, each rather vague, that one can find the month. There is, however, one curious fact. We can ascertain Hindley's age. Now Ellen Dean was of the same age. She was his foster sister, and the doctor also refers to her as being of the same age as Hindley. Yet she makes two mistakes about her own age. Middle-aged people do, of course, make mistakes about their age, and these slips may have been intentional on the part of Emily Brontë, but, if so, it seems to me a little over-subtle.

The topography is equally precise. On going from Thrushcross Grange to the village of Gimmerton a highway branches off to the moor on the left. There is a stone pillar there. Thrushcross Grange lies to the south-west, Gimmerton to the east, and Wuthering Heights to the north. The distance from Thrushcross Grange to Wuthering Heights is four miles, and Penistone Crags lie a mile and a half farther on. It was half an hour from Gimmerton to Thrushcross Grange.

The botany is sure to be correct. Emily Brontë loved the country. I was a little surprised to find an ash tree in bud as early as 20 March, but then I realised that it was not on the moor but in the park at Thrushcross Grange, which lay low and was no doubt sheltered.

I now come to the final problem. Heathcliff schemed to get all the property of both the Earnshaws and the Lintons. How did he do it? Emily Brontë clearly had a considerable knowledge of the law. We know the source of George Eliot's use of a base fee for the plot of *Felix Holt.*[2] We do not know the source of Jane Austen's unerring grasp of the law of real property; but she lived among people who had settled estates and could easily have obtained it. But how Emily Brontë acquired her knowledge I cannot guess. There is also this difficulty. *Wuthering Heights* was written in the eighteen-forties. It was published in 1847. But the period of the tale is from 1771 to 1803. The Inheritance Act of 1834, the Wills Act of 1837, and, I think, the Game Act of 1831, had changed the law. Did Emily Brontë apply the law at the time she wrote or that at the period of the tale? In one case, as we shall see, she used the earlier law.

Novelists sometimes make their plots depend on the law and use legal terms. But they frequently make mistakes and sometimes are absurd as Trollope is in *Orley Farm.* What is remarkable about *Wuthering Heights* is that the ten or twelve legal references are, I think, sufficient to enable us to ascertain the various legal processes by which Heathcliff obtained the property. It is not a simple matter. There was a fundamental difference between the law of land (real property) and that of money and goods (personal property).

Let us begin with Wuthering Heights. The Earnshaws were

farmers and not likely to have their estate settled. The property had been in their family since 1500. We may take it then that Mr Earnshaw was owner in fee-simple, that is in effect absolute owner of Wuthering Heights, and was not likely to have possessed any investments. It is more likely that there was a mortgage on the house and farm. On Mr Earnshaw's death the land descended to Hindley as his heir-at-law. There is no mention of a will. The personal property, which, probably, was only the farming stock and the furniture, would go equally to his children, Hindley and Catherine, subject to the payment of his debts out of it. On Catherine's marriage Edgar would have become entitled to her personal property. Now Hindley drinks and gambles away all he has, and at his death the property is mortgaged up to the hilt. Heathcliff we find is the mortgagee. The personal property would also be liable to the debts. So that Heathcliff is mortgagee in possession and, for practical purposes, owner of all the Earnshaw property except any personalty that had gone to Catherine. This is all fairly simple; but it is more difficult when we come to the Linton property. They were landed gentry; they had a park, they had tenants. Mr Linton, and Edgar after him, was a magistrate. Such people, generally, had a settlement of their land, and we find, in fact, that Mr Linton had settled it by his will. To understand what happens it is necessary to go into the intricacies of real property law and to look at the pedigree.

I must explain very shortly the law of entails. What is called an estate tail is an estate which descends according to the following rules: (1) Males are preferred to females; (2) males take in order according to seniority of birth, but females take equally; (3) descendants represent their ancestor. In case of a conflict between them, rule (3) prevails. A tenant in tail of full age in possession could by means of a fictitious action (for which a deed was substituted by the Fines and Recoveries Act, 1833) bar the entail and obtain the fee-simple, which practically amounts to absolute ownership. By his will a testator could settle his land on living persons for life, but could not give life estates to the children of such persons who were not alive at the testator's death. Consequently, if he wanted to tie up his estate as long as possible, he gave life estates to such of his descendants as were living at his death, followed by estates tail to their children.

Now the settlement made by Mr Linton's will must have been as follows: The estate was devised to Edgar, his only son, for life, then to Edgar's sons in tail; Edgar's daughters were passed over in favour of Mr Linton's daughter, Isabella, who, presumably, had a life interest with remainder to her sons in tail. This is the usual form. Thus on Edgar Linton's death, Linton Heathcliff became tenant in tail in possession during the few weeks he survived his uncle. As a minor he could not bar the entail. It is most improbable that he had an estate in fee-simple; that would have been too unusual. Isabella might have had an estate tail instead of a life interest. This is most improbable, but if she did, her son, Linton Heathcliff, would have become tenant in tail by descent, so the result is the same. Heathcliff claims the property – by what right? Ellen Dean says that he claimed and kept the Thrushcross Grange estate in his wife's right and in his son's also. She adds: 'I suppose, legally at any rate, Catherine, destitute of cash and friends, cannot disturb his possession' [ch. 30]. She is quite right in her suspicions. Even if Isabella had had an estate tail, or even an estate in fee-simple, Heathcliff would not have had any right as husband to an estate for life – the estate known as an estate by courtesy – because Isabella was never in possession. And even if, which to my mind is not possible, Linton Heathcliff had had an estate in fee-simple, his father would not have been his heir before the Inheritance Act, 1833, because it was considered unnatural that an inheritance should ascend directly; and, as Ellen Dean knows and states, Linton Heathcliff as a minor could not dispose of his land by will. There is no difficulty as to the personal property. Whatever Isabella had Heathcliff got by marrying her. There was no Married Women's Property Act in these days. They eloped, so there was no question of a marriage settlement. Edgar Linton had saved out of his rents to make a provision for his daughter, Catherine. When dying he decides, in order to prevent Heathcliff getting at them, to alter his will so as to settle them on Catherine for life and then for her children. The attorney for whom he sends is, however, kept from going by Heathcliff, and Edgar dies before his will is altered, so the money passes to Catherine and then to her husband, Linton. He, though a minor, could (before the year 1838) make a will of personalty. He is induced or forced to do so, and leaves it all to Heathcliff.

Thus, at Heathcliff's death, the position seems to be that he has acquired all the personal property of both families: he is mortgagee in possession of Wuthering Heights, and is, though wrongfully, in possession of Thrushcross Grange, which he has let to Lockwood.

He thinks of making a will but does not do so. What then happens on his death? He has no relations, so that his real property will escheat, and his personal property will go to the Crown as *bona vacantia*. What then bcomes of Hareton and Catherine who, when the tale ends, are to be happily married on New Year's Day, 1803? At one time I thought this was the climax of the tragedy. These young people, ill-educated and incompetent, were to be left destitute. But that would be going too far. Catherine, as you will see from the pedigree, is the sole living descendant of Mr Linton. In some way or other, I need not go through the various alternatives, she must have become entitled to Thrushcross Grange, which is plainly by far the most valuable property. Heathcliff had been mortgagee in possession of Wuthering Heights for eighteen years, but this was not long enough to obtain an absolute title by adverse possession. Hareton, as Hindley's heir, would be entitled to the equity of redemption. Now if Heathcliff, who managed well, properly accounted for his profits during the eighteen years as he could be made to do, it may well be that they were sufficient, if he was charged a proper occupation rent, to pay off the mortgage. So that Hareton would get the house and land unincumbered or, at any rate, only slightly burdened. The personal property was comparatively unimportant, and we can only hope that the Crown did not insist on its rights, if it knew of them, or that if it did insist, the happy couple could buy out the Crown's claim out of the rent which Lockwood, as we know, paid.

There is, so far as I know, no other novel in the world which it is possible to subject to an analysis of the kind I have tried to make. This in itself makes the book very unusual. Did the authoress carry all the dates in her head, or did she work with a calendar? Was 20 March 1784, for example, on a Monday? According to my calculations it was not, it was a Saturday, but I should like to have this confirmed by some competent chronologist; for if I am right, it shows that Emily Brontë did not use a calendar, and that nothing will be gained by finding out, for instance, the date of Easter in 1803.

However dull and technical the above details may be, they do, I believe, throw a light on the character of Emily Brontë and her book. German romances can hardly have been the source of her knowledge of English law. A great critic has spoken of the passionate chastity of the book; but the extreme care in realising the ages of the characters at the time of each incident which is described seems to me a more unusual characteristic of a novel. It demonstrates the vividness of the author's imagination.

SOURCE: from *The Structure of Wuthering Heights* (1926).

NOTES

1. See above, p. 107n.
2. George Eliot consulted Frederic Harrison about laws of entail ('base fee' is tenure which is terminated on the fulfilment of a certain contingent qualification or limitation) [O.E.D.].

E. M. Forster 'Prophecy' (1927)

Prophecy – in our sense – is a tone of voice. It may imply any of the faiths that have haunted humanity – Christianity, Buddhism, dualism, Satanism, or the mere raising of human love and hatred to such a power that their normal receptacles no longer contain them. . . . Why should *Wuthering Heights* come into this enquiry? It is a story about human beings, it contains no view of the universe.

My answer is that the emotions of Heathcliff and Catherine Earnshaw function differently to other emotions in fiction. Instead of inhabiting the characters, they surround them like thunder clouds, and generate the explosions that fill the novel from the moment when Lockwood dreams of the hand at the window down to the moment when Heathcliff, with the same window open, is discovered dead. *Wuthering Heights* is filled with sound – storm and rushing wind – a sound more important than words and thoughts. Great as the novel is, one cannot afterwards remember anything in it but Heathcliff and the elder Catherine. They cause the action by their separation: they close it by their union after death. No wonder they 'walk': what else could such beings do? even when they were alive their love and hate transcended them.

Emily Brontë had in some ways a literal and careful mind. She constructed her novel on a time chart even more elaborate than Miss Austen's, and she arranged the Linton and Earnshaw families symmetrically, and she had a clear idea of the various legal steps by which Heathcliff gained possession of their two properties.[1] Then why did she deliberately introduce muddle, chaos, tempest? Because in our sense of the word she was a prophetess: because what is implied is more important to her than what is said; and only in confusion could the figures of Heathcliff and Catherine externalize their passion till it streamed through the house and over the moors. *Wuthering Heights* has no mythology beyond what these two characters provide: no great book is more cut off from the universals of Heaven and Hell. It is local, like the spirits it engenders, and whereas we may meet Moby Dick in any pond, we shall only encounter them among the harebells and limestone of their own county.

SOURCE: from *Aspects of the Novel* (1927).

NOTE

1. See C. P. Sanger's analysis above.

H. W. Garrod 'An Insufficient Acquaintance with the Craft of Fiction' (1930)

The faults of *Wuthering Heights* proceed, not from defective knowledge of human nature, but from inferior technique, from an insufficient acquaintance with the craft of fiction. The story is in general ill constructed, and in its detail often complicated and obscure. In parts it is uncertainly conceived, the pattern of it haunted by bad example – the 'novel of edification' and the 'Tale of Terror' both lend to it vicious elements. Out of these defects the book is redeemed, first, by its strong instinct for a living scene – nowhere else, perhaps, save in *Lear*, are the scene and the actors to the same degree a single tragical effect; – secondly, by its power in the depiction of manners – in part a historical talent, for we are too apt to forget that the time of *Wuthering Heights* is as remote as the place: Mr Earnshaw's death must be placed in 1777; and thirdly, by the fact that, with the single exception of Mr Lockwood, every character in the book is a living person, whose fortunes are the object to us of pity or fear. . . .

SOURCE: from the introduction to the World's Classics edition of *Wuthering Heights* (1930).

Q. D. Leavis 'Not an Instrument of Wish-fulfilment' (1932)

Wuthering Heights is not and never has been a popular novel (except in the sense that it is now an accepted classic and so on the shelves of the educated). Though there is evidence enough in the novel that Emily shared her sister's disabilities, *Wuthering Heights* is not an instrument of wish-fulfilment. It proceeds from a stronger mind, a sensibility that has triumphed over starvation and is not at its mercy. The cries of hunger and desire that ring through the book do not distress by a personal overtone, the reader is not made to feel embarrassed by the proximity of an author's face. The emotion exhibited in *Wuthering Heights*, unlike the emotion exhibited in *Jane Eyre*, has a frame round it; it is at least as poignant but it is controlled and directed, how deliberately the bare bones of the novel (admirably dissected by C. P. S[anger] in *The Structure of Wuthering Heights*) show: *Wuthering Heights* is the best example in Victorian fiction of a total response novel. . . .

SOURCE: from *Fiction and the Reading Public* (1932).[1]

NOTE

1. Mrs Leavis's later views on *Wuthering Heights* appear in her 'A Fresh Approach to *Wuthering Heights*', *Lectures in America* (1969), pp. 85–152; see Introduction, pp. 28, 29 above.

David Cecil Emily Brontë and *Wuthering Heights* (1934)[1]

The Theme of *Wuthering Heights*

... if this extraordinary story is what it is generally assumed to be, an orthodox Victorian tale of ordinary human beings, involving conflict between the heroes, Edgar Linton and Hareton, on the one hand, and the villain, Heathcliff, on the other, and ending in the discomfiture of the villain and a happy marriage, it is certainly a terrible muddle. It is fantastically improbable for one thing with its ghost and disappearances and sudden, timely deaths. And for another, it is very badly constructed. Why have two heroes and one villain for one drama? Why kill off half the characters in the middle of the book and start again with a new batch who play much the same role in the action as the first? Why work up the story to a tragic climax and then in the last few chapters contrive a happy ending by so grotesque a device as a ghost, the sight of which drives a man to self-starvation? Besides, the characters do not fill their roles properly. Edgar, the first hero, is a poor creature – one can well understand Catherine's preference for Heathcliff – Hareton, the second, is a sketch: neither is a proper counterpart for the tremendous Heathcliff. Alike in form and detail Emily Brontë fails consistently to make her book conform to the model she is assumed to have chosen.

However, a closer examination of it conclusively shows that she did not choose such a model at all. Elements in the story, clearly of the first importance, make any such hypothesis impossible. The character of the first Catherine, for one thing: what role can she be supposed to play in a conventional conflict between heroes and villain? She is all the way through on the side of the villain, and dies committed to him and alienated from her husband. Yet she feels no remorse for this; nor does her creator seem to blame her. Again, the conclusion of a conflict between good and evil, if it is to be happy, should entail either the discomfiture of the villain or his repentance. In *Wuthering Heights* neither happens. Heathcliff is not discomfited: the love between Hareton and Catherine, which gives the book its happy ending, is made possible only by his own tacit relinquishment of his plans. Yet this is due to no change of heart on his part. He never shows a sign of regret for his wrongdoing; he only stops tormenting Catherine and Hareton because he is otherwise occupied. Finally – and oddest of all – after his death it is he who is rewarded by spiritual union with the first Catherine; not Edgar, her lawful husband and the supposed hero of the story.

Nor, wild as the plot may be by conventional standards, does careful examination of it support the view that this wildness is unintentional. It is not a clumsy improvisation, like the plot of *Bleak House*. The author calling himself 'C. P. S[anger]' in his remarkable essay, *The Structure of Wuthering Heights*, has shown how carefully the concrete facts with which the action deals are worked out and documented; the accuracy of its elaborate legal processes, its intricate family relationships, its complex time system. It is impossible to believe that an author so careful of the factual structure of her story as Emily Brontë shows herself to be, should be careless of its artistic structure. And, indeed, if we can manage to read her book with a mind unprejudiced by preconceived ideas, we do not feel it to be carelessly constructed. . . .

If *Wuthering Heights* gives a confused impression the confusion lies only in our own minds – and not Emily Brontë's. We are trying to see it in the wrong focus. When we shift our focus to reconsider *Wuthering Heights* in the light of her particular vision, its apparent confusion vanishes. From a murky tangle lit by inexplicable flashes, it falls into a coherent order.

The setting is a microcosm of the universal scheme as Emily Brontë conceived it. On the one hand, we have Wuthering Heights, the land of storm; high on the barren moorland, naked to the shock of the elements, the natural home of the Earnshaw family, fiery, untamed children of the storm. On the other, sheltered in the leafy valley below, stands Thrushcross Grange, the appropriate home of the children of calm, the gentle, passive timid Lintons. Together each group, following its own nature in its own sphere, combines to compose a cosmic harmony. It is the destruction and re-establishment of this harmony which is the theme of the story.[1] It opens with the arrival at Wuthering Heights of an extraneous element – Heathcliff. He, too, is a child of the storm; and the affinity between him and Catherine Earnshaw makes them fall in love with each other. But since he is an extraneous element, he is a source of discord, inevitably disrupting the working of the natural order. He drives the father, Earnshaw, into conflict with the son, Hindley, and as a result Hindley into conflict with himself, Heathcliff. The order is still further dislocated by Catherine, who is seduced into uniting herself in an 'unnatural' marriage with Linton, the child of calm. The shock of her infidelity and Hindley's ill-treatment of him now, in its turn, disturbs the natural harmony of Heathcliff's nature, and turns him from an alien element in the established order, into a force active for its destruction. He is not therefore, as usually supposed, a wicked man voluntarily yielding to his wicked impulses. Like all Emily Brontë's characters, he is a manifestation of natural forces acting involuntarily under the pressure of his own nature. But he is a natural force which has been frustrated of its natural outlet, so that it inevitably becomes destructive; like a mountain torrent diverted from its channel, which flows out on the surrounding country, laying waste whatever may happen to lie in its way. Nor can it stop doing so, until the obstacles which kept it from its natural channel are removed.

Heathcliff's first destructive act is to drive Hindley to death. Secondly, as a counterblast to Catherine's marriage, and actuated not by love, but by hatred of the Lintons, he himself makes another 'unnatural' marriage with Isabella. This, coupled with the conflict induced in her by her own violation of her nature, is too much for Catherine; and she dies. Heathcliff, further maddened by the loss of his life's object, becomes yet more destructive, and proceeds to wreak his revenge on the next generation, Hareton Earnshaw, Catherine Linton and Linton Heathcliff. These – for Hindley, like Heathcliff and Catherine, had married a child of calm – cannot be divided as their parents were into children of calm or storm; they are the offspring of both and partake of both natures. But there is a difference between them. Hareton and Catherine are the children of love, and so combine the positive 'good' qualities of their respective parents: the kindness and constancy of calm, the strength and courage of storm. Linton, on the other hand, is a child of hate, and combines the negative 'bad' qualities of his two parents – the cowardice and weakness of calm, the cruelty and ruthlessness of storm.[2] Heathcliff obtains power over all three children. Catherine is married to her natural antipathy, Linton; so that her own nature, diverted from its purpose, grows antagonistic to her natural affinity – Hareton. The natural order is for the time being wholly subverted: the destructive principle reigns supreme. But at this, its high-water mark, the tide turns. From this moment the single purpose that directs the universe begins to re-assert itself, to impose order once more. First of all Linton Heathcliff dies. Negative as his nature is, it has not the seed of life within it. Then, freed from the incubus of his presence, the affinity between Hareton and Catherine begins to override the superficial antagonism that Heathcliff's actions have raised between them; they fall in love. The only obstacle left to the re-establishment of harmony is Heathcliff's antagonism; finally this, too, changes. His nature could never find fulfilment in destruction; for it was not – as we have seen – primarily destructive, and has become so only because it was frustrated of its true fulfilment – union with its affinity, Catherine Earnshaw. Heathcliff's desire for this union never ceased to torment him. Even at his most destructive, her magnetic power dragged at his heart, depriving him of any sense of satisfaction his revenge might have obtained for him. Now it grows so strong that it breaks through the veil of mortality to manifest itself to his physical eye in the shape of her ghost. The actual sight of her gives him strength at last to defeat the forces that had upset his equilibrium: with a prodigious effort the stream breaks through the obstacles that had so long stood in its way, and flows at last in a torrent down its rightful channel. He forgets his rage, he forgets even to satisfy the wants of physical nature; he wants only to unite himself with Catherine. Within two days his wish is satisfied. He dies. His death removes the last impediment to the re-establishment of harmony. Hareton and Catherine settle down happy and united at Thrushcross Grange. Wuthering Heights is left to its rightful possessors, the spirits of Heathcliff and the first Catherine. The wheel has come full circle; at length the alien element that has so long disturbed it has been assimilated to the body of nature; the cosmic order has been established once more.

This analysis is enough to show how wide of the mark the usual criticisms of *Wuthering Heights* are. It is not incoherent. On the contrary, its general outline is as logical as that of a fugue. Nor is it an improbable story. On the plane on which it is composed its every incident is the inevitable outcome of the situation. Still less is it remote from the central issues of human life. It may seem so, because it presents the world from an angle in which the aspects which bulk biggest to most novelists are hidden from its view. But those aspects with which it is concerned are nearer to the heart of life than those explored by any other Victorian novelist. Even the varied world-panorama of *Vanity Fair* seems trivial beside this picture of a sparsely-populated country village, revealed as it is against the background of the eternal verities.

The structure of *Wuthering Heights*

... *Wuthering Heights* is usually considered as artistically confused, just as it is considered intellectually confused. But it is no more the one than it is the other. Its form fits the subject like a glove. There is not a loose thread in it. So far from being crude, it is far more sophisticated than the narrative method employed by Dickens and Trollope. To find anything so complex we must go forward eight years, to Henry James and Conrad. As a matter of fact, the form of *Wuthering Heights* is very like that of a Conrad novel.[3] Just as in *Lord Jim*, the story is shown to us through the eyes of a character; and a character not involved in its central drama – so in *Wuthering Heights* it is told partly by Nelly Dean, the servant of the Lintons, and partly by Mr Lockwood, who takes Thrushcross Grange after Edgar Linton's death. Such a method serves two objects. First, it ensures that we see the drama in all the fresh reality in which it would have shown itself to its spectators: and secondly, since these spectators are detached and normal, we see it as it really was, undistorted by the emotions of those actors who were involved in it.

Again as in *Lord Jim*, Emily Brontë begins her story in the middle. The book opens with Mr Lockwood's first visit to Wuthering Heights at the climax of Heathcliff's revenge, when he has at last obtained complete power over Catherine and Hareton, before the forces of harmony have begun to make themselves felt. Mr Lockwood sees Heathcliff triumphant, Catherine and Hareton miserable: beleaguered for the night by a storm, he is kept awake by the first Catherine's spirit calling at the window. Such an opening serves three purposes.

To begin with it introduces us in the best way possible to the scene and the characters. We see Heathcliff and Wuthering Heights for the first time in all the fresh vivid detail in which they would appear to the curious stranger. In the second place it enables Emily Brontë to set the story from the first in its right perspective, to put the reader in a place of vantage where his eye is directed to the contrast on which the interest of the action turns, the contrast between a world of discord and a world of harmony. Straight away we are shown a 'close-up' of the discord at its height; so that our interest is immediately directed to learn whence it arises and how it is to be resolved.

Such an opening, finally, strikes the right emotional key. This is very important. For the plot of *Wuthering Heights* is so remote from our ordinary experience that unless we approach it from the start with a mind tuned to its key, we are bound to find it unconvincing. If Emily Brontë had started off with the relatively credible incidents of Heathcliff's and Catherine's childhood, she would have found it very hard to maintain the reader's belief in the story when the time came to tell him of its extraordinary catastrophe. But with supreme daring she storms the very citadel of the reader's scepticism at the outset. She begins straight away with ghosts and infernal passions: and this induces in us a heightened, inflamed mood of the imagination that makes us accept without any difficulty the most sensational events of its climax.

Having set the stage, Emily Brontë now goes back twenty years, and in the person of Nelly Dean tells the story of the beginning. She continues until she has reached that point in the plot to which we are introduced in the first chapter. Then once more darkness descends on the story for a period; and when it dissipates Mr Lockwood, not Nelly Dean, is the narrator. He has returned after nine months' absence to find Wuthering Heights steeped in an evening peace. He asks Nelly Dean what has happened: she resumes and finishes the story: Mr Lockwood takes a last look at the place, and leaves.

This second break in the narrative is also carefully calculated to reinvigorate the reader's interest. More important, like the opening, it sets the story in a perspective from which its essential significant trend is visible. As at first we are shown a 'close-up' of Wuthering Heights at the climax of discord, so now we are shown a 'close-up' of it in the fullness of harmony; and, as before, with the added actuality which would invest it in the eyes of a stranger from the outside world. The artistic scheme of the book is worked out with the same rigid symmetry as is the intellectual. . . .

SOURCE: from *Early Victorian Novelists* (1934).

NOTES

1. See Introduction, pp. 27–9 above.
2. Cecil notes, 'Of course, this is true only in a broad sense. Emily Brontë

has too great a sense of reality to create unmitigated villains or impeccable heroes. Moreover, all three children, springing as they do from "unnatural" unions are not perfectly homogeneous characters. Hareton can be surly, Catherine wilful. And Linton – for his mother loved his father at first, if only with a physical passion – is touched at times with a redeeming gleam of pathos.'

3. Cecil's comparison was anticipated by Lascelles Abercrombie and C. P. Sanger (pp. 107, 110 above). There are, of course, wide differences between Conrad's indirect narrative method and Emily Brontë's but see Introduction, pp. 17–18 above.

Irene Cooper Willis Vigour and Directness of Style in *Wuthering Heights* (1936)

. . . Writing, as Vernon Lee pointed out in her *Handling of Words*, is an art of substitution of effects. The writer has to find a substitute in words for the movement which in the real scene is going on all the time but which he cannot continually be reiterating. In watching a real scene, the observer is not, of course, aware of how his eye shifts from one point to another; this fact, however, can soon be discovered by experiment . . . innumerable examples [are] to be found in *Wuthering Heights* of a very direct method of introducing movement by means of extra accent upon certain focusing words.[1] . . .

Each sentence goes straight as a dart to the impression sought to be conveyed. Going back to the first chapter, consider this paragraph:

> Wuthering Heights is the name of Mr Heathcliff's dwelling. 'Wuthering' being a significant provincial adjective, descriptive of the atmospheric tumult to which its station is exposed in stormy weather. Pure, bracing ventilation they must have up there at all times, indeed: one may guess the power of the north wind blowing over the edge, by the excessive slant of a few stunted firs at the end of the house; and by a range of gaunt thorns all stretching their limbs one way, as if craving alms of the sun. Happily, the architect had foresight to build it strong: the narrow windows are deeply set in the wall, and the corners defended by large jutting stones.

'*Wuthering Heights is the name of Mr Heathcliff's dwelling.*' The name, with all that it means to the author and is going to mean to us, comes first. 'The name of Mr Heathcliff's dwelling is Wuthering

Heights,' a sentence which contains the same information as the other, would not strike the same note. Then comes a parenthesis – '"Wuthering" being a significant provincial adjective, descriptive of the atmospheric tumult', etc. Strictly before this and after 'dwelling', there should be a comma instead of the full stop; nevertheless, the slip serves to give the remark the appearance of an 'aside' leading up to what follows, when its full force is exposed. 'Pure, bracing ventilation . . . up there, at all times, indeed' – the writer puts an exclamatory turn into the phrase, besides introducing a feeling of windiness by the use of the word 'ventilation', which is much more suggestive of activity than 'air'. It may be only my fancy, but the next sentence seems to me to give the direction as well as the power of that 'north wind blowing over the edge'; it is an extended sentence and seems in the actual line of the drive of the gales which wrought that 'excessive slant of a few stunted firs at the end of the house' and swept onward to that 'range of gaunt thorns all stretching their limbs one way, as if craving alms of the sun'. Fancy or not, however, there is no denying a vivid impression of the way the wind blows up on those heights, and the assurance, which the writer hastens to give, as to the strength of the house, is welcome and restoring to our sense of shaken equilibrium.

Now take the indoors scene and notice how the paint, so to speak, is put on there: [quotes from ch. 1, 'One step . . . other recesses'] . . .

Observe the straightness of the direction of the first sentence – 'One step brought us into the family sitting-room' – it marches exactly with the action it describes. Again, see how verbs of movement are used about things which in themselves are motionless, and how, by a change of mood of the verb, from active to passive, variety of movement and also spatial dimension are suggested. 'The kitchen is *forced to retreat*' – 'one or two heavy black ones [chairs] *lurking* in the shade' – 'ranks of immense pewter dishes . . . *towering*.' The roof is given personality; its anatomy is spoken of. Another substantial effect is produced upon the reader by direct emphasis upon Lockwood's visual and audible impressions, 'a chatter of tongues'; 'a clatter of culinary utensils'; 'light and heat from ranks of immense pewter dishes'. All this is astonishingly dramatic, yet it does not affect us astonishingly, until we come to examine the structure; in reading it in the ordinary way, we feel merely that we are in close contact with the scene. The technique is as effective as the craft of the stage-furniture maker, who has to cut all decorative detail much more deeply than it would be cut for everyday use, in order that it may be seen at a distance from the front of the stage – where it merely looks like ordinary furniture.

Equally effective is the way in which, in the scene of the disturbance when Lockwood is set upon by the dogs and has to be rescued by the cook, we are made to realize his discomfort and gradual return to composure. [quotes from ch. 1, 'I took a seat ... humour took that turn'] ...

From the moment when Lockwood flung the bitch back and roused the whole hive against him, his almost defenceless attitude is registered by a noticeable change in the orientation of the sentences. Either the passive mood of a verb or a semi-passive form of expression is used for describing Lockwood: '*I felt* my *heels and coat-laps* peculiar subjects of attack'; '*I was constrained* to demand, aloud, assistance.' Upon the entrance of the cook and her magical subdual of the storm, we lose sight of Lockwood altogether, as is natural, and when he reappears, it is in keeping with his rather inglorious position that he is made to speak of himself in the accusative case. '"What the devil is the matter?" he [Heathcliff] asked, eyeing *me*.' The interval between his fright and feeling that it would be foolish to sit sulking is well indicated by Lockwood's answers, 'No, thank you'; 'If I had been, I would have set my signet on the biter,' being set down on the page without the usual accompanying 'I said' or 'I replied'. This not only suggests curtness but it marks an alteration of temper, the rage of 'I muttered' quietening down through a midway sort of indifference to a resumption of good manners: 'I bowed and returned the pledge.'...

The technique throughout is the same as that so far examined; if the reader doubts this statement, he should pursue the analysis and in particular study the passage, in chapter 3, beginning: 'This time, I remembered I was lying in the oak closet, and I heard distinctly the gusty wind, and the driving of the snow.' Therein he will find, as indeed he will find in whatever passage he turns to, the same telling accent upon centres of movement and the same direct impressionism, which I have compared, and not without reason, to the stage-furniture maker's craft. The author of *Wuthering Heights* was first and foremost a spectator of events, an observer of drama from the outside. Even when the drama was psychological, it came more natural to that author to relate it as observed by someone than as occurring straightforwardly. Hence, in the history of Heathcliff's and Catherine's passion for one another, destructive of themselves and of much else besides, we get Mrs Dean, who tells the tale, interposed between us and the characters of the book, and Mrs Dean's occasional understudies, Zillah and Isabella, and finally Lockwood, in the role of a reporter of Mrs Dean's own words. This interposition of an eye-witness, and, be it noted, an eye-witness not of present happening but of events long past, somewhat differentiates the technique of the main part of the book from that of the opening chapters, but does not alter it essentially. The interposition is itself a device, though a primitive and clumsy one,[2] for enhancing the reality of the story. 'I was there'; 'I saw it with my own eyes'; 'I heard that very conversation,' a narrative in the first person singular carries all these assurances with it and so helps to build up certainty in the mind of the reader. . . .

SOURCE: from *The Authorship of Wuthering Heights* (1936).

NOTES

1. References throughout are to the text of 1847 as edited by H. W. Garrod for the 1930 World's Classics edition.
2. Cp. Mrs Ward and H. W. Garrod on narrative clumsiness (pp. 99, 118 above).

G. D. Klingopulos *Wuthering Heights* as Dramatic Poem (1946–7)

If *Wuthering Heights* does not represent the coherence of a *Macbeth*, it is important to remember that the novel is the first in English which invites the same kind of attention that we give to *Macbeth*. It has a similar complexity, makes the same claim as poetry. Not only because the novelist's method is dramatic; but because the status of the language, the seriousness of the purposes for which it is used are those of poetry. As an Elizabethan play stands or falls by the quality of the poetry at its crises of meaning, so *Wuthering Heights* may be said to justify itself by the quality of some half-dozen or so speeches of Catherine's and Heathcliff's which are as direct and as highly organized in word and rhythm as poetry. In such speeches the novel establishes the reality of its subject matter. And the subject matter of *Wuthering Heights* is a way of feeling about man's place in the universe. This is also the subject matter of *Cold in the earth.*[1]

One can read *Wuthering Heights,* as one reads *Cold in the earth,* without questioning the seriousness of situations so poignantly and strongly presented. The quality of achievement from chapter to chapter is so consistent that it establishes as much unity and interconnection as the common reader requires. We are reminded repeatedly of that fine control of feeling which distinguishes Emily Brontë's best known poem.

> 'Come in! Come in!' he sobbed. 'Cathy, do come. Oh do – *once* more! Oh! my heart's darling! hear me *this* time, Catherine, at last!'

Her italics, far from being obtrusive, are usually as much in place as the stress in a line of poetry, and suggest a vivid exactness in what she wishes to do. There are not many things in the book which one reads with reservations and those are a few passages in which the intensity and repetition are felt to be static, adjectival and insistent rather than an enrichment, felt to be rather mechanical.

> 'You talk of her mind being unsettled. How the devil could it be otherwise in her frightful isolation? And that insipid, paltry creature attending her from duty and humanity! From pity and charity! He might as well plant an oak in a flower-pot and expect it to thrive, as imagine he can restore her to vigour in the soil of his shallow cares.'

There is more mere raillery in this than was probably intended: the analogy is literary and too deliberate. So too, the whole speech in chapter XV which contains the following syllogism: 'I have not broken your heart: you have broken it, and in breaking it you have broken mine'. And in one of the key passages in the novel, Catherine's 'I *am* Heathcliff!' is an assertion that needs the rest of the book to justify it or at least to make it acceptable. For, again, that speech has more resonance, more overtone, than (one must surmise) was intended.[2] It balances between the passionate assertion of love, and an attempt to state the meaning of living. Catherine's attitude to Heathcliff is, indeed, the main subject of the book, and it is an exceedingly complex knot of feelings, of attachments, of loyalties, of intensities – and Heathcliff is plainly not an adequate object for them all. After Catherine's death, Heathcliff has to be made to explain and to represent his own significance, and his declarations of feeling towards the vanished Catherine are usually closer to those of a mere lover. The feelings of Catherine towards Heathcliff are different from his towards her; and her feelings are more than feelings towards him. They are feelings towards life and death, Wuthering Heights, the universe. On her deathbed she cries:

> 'That is not *my* Heathcliff. I shall love mine yet: and take him with me: he's in my soul. And' she added musingly, 'the thing that irks me most is this shattered prison, after all. I'm tired of being enclosed here. I'm wearying to escape into that glorious world, and to be always there: not seeing it dimly through tears and yearning for it through the walls of an aching heart; but really with it and in it.'

Recent accounts of the novel have tended to smooth over many of the difficulties, to make it more of a work of art than it is, to make more completely separate than they were, the woman who suffered and the woman who created. She appears to have striven to make as clear an object as she could, and there are few more impersonal novels in English. Yet the 'I' is present: not in omniscient comment, but in a phrase, a rhythm, that is 'deeper' than 'work of art' suggests. There is a serious idiosyncrasy in the point of view as in the word 'solid' in the line 'Oh that this too too solid flesh would melt'. It represents another level of sincerity than that of the staple prose.

This is partly the explanation of much dislike of the novel. Another cause of misunderstanding is the absence of anything one could confidently name a moral. The 'structure' of the novel is firmly there as one reads. But it is not a moral tale. The author's preferences are not shown,[3] do not reveal themselves unambiguously even to analysis. . . .

The reticence of the novelist in the last pages of her work, her reluctance to underline, to perorate, should make its interpretation exceptionally tentative. And we are not helped, as in reading an Elizabethan play, by a recognition of the interaction of the poetry and Elizabethan ethics, by a sense of 'relevant intensity'. The value of such words as 'You sure and firmset earth' or 'Good morning to the day! And next – my gold' is rich yet definite because they combine with other coherent ideas and feelings in Elizabethan language and in the plays themselves. But there are places in *Wuthering Heights*, especially in the account of the Hindley–Heathcliff struggle, where the force and precision are great, yet the amount of meaning is disproportionately slight.

> The charge exploded, and the knife, in springing back, closed into its owner's wrist. Heathcliff pulled it away by main force, slitting up the flesh as it passed on and thrust it dripping into his pocket. He then took a stone,

struck down the division between two windows, and sprang in. His adversary had fallen senseless with excessive pain and the flow of blood that gushed from an artery or a large vein. The ruffian kicked and trampled on him and dashed his head repeatedly against the flags.

Particularity, vividness and insistence in language are a sign that special meaning is being given. The force of 'gushed' 'slit up the flesh' 'dripping' 'dashed' is greater than the amount of meaning created by the situation. To consider the scene as merely another demonstration of Heathcliff's ruthlessness seems inadequate; yet that is probably all that the author intended. The excess of vividness must therefore be taken either as a symptom of immaturity, of insufficiently understood intensity; or as an error of judgment on the author's part, a failure to recognize that the physical violence and ruthlessness of Heathcliff had already been established without the insistence on the 'gushing' and 'slitting'.

Yet it is the particularity which makes the novel and carries us over those passages where we might be inclined to demur. The feelings of Catherine towards Edgar and Heathcliff are finally convincing and they are the most important theme in the book. It is after her death that Heathcliff tends to lose three-dimensional value, to become a type of ruthlessness and relentless hatred. His ferocity towards Hindley lacks the meaning of his antipathy to the Lintons: neither the value of his forbearance towards Cathy and Hareton, nor the significance of the survival of the lovers is made unambiguously clear. To have made these things clear would have meant sentimentalizing the whole book, and Heathcliff violently repulses the idea that he might be won by 'love'. 'How the devil can you dream of fawning on me!' The Heights are left empty. The view that the young lovers are a necessary compromise between the Linton and the Heathcliff levels is almost certainly a sentimental one. For if Emily Brontë has been careful about anything, she has been most careful not to qualify whatever the Catherine and Heathcliff themes may be taken to mean. For Catherine and Heathcliff are what she set out to say. . . .

When it has acknowledged that *Wuthering Heights* does not possess the coherence of a *Macbeth*, criticism is freed to enjoy what is indestructible and rare and heroic in Emily Brontë's achievement. For she has been more ambitious than Shakespeare, has shown a 'gigantic ambition' of the order which the quotation from Virginia Woolf's essay splendidly suggests. Her world is emptier than

Shakespeare's and her view less reassuring. 'Nobody knew what ailed her but me,' wrote Charlotte. 'I felt in my heart she would die if she did not go home.' Her novel touches a level of experience which does not often come into the world of letters. It is a quality of suffering: it has anonymity. It is not complete. Perhaps some ballads represent it in English, but it seldom appears in the main stream, and few writers are in touch with it. It is a quality of experience the expression of which is at once an act of despair and an act of recognition or of worship. It is the recognition of an absolute hierarchy. This is also the feeling in Aeschylus. It is found amongst genuine peasants and is a great strength. Developing in places which yield only the permanent essentials of existence, it is undistracted and universal. It is behind Tolstoy and Conrad, in whom it is 'transferred' to the sea. It is not strongly present in English life. It enriches the mind of Europe with a layer of unembittered asceticism.

Emily Brontë works in that level, in prose and in some poems. There she finds her recurrent theme. She was not a philosophic novelist. The value of her novel is in the vitality of the feelings, the steady unwillingness to make a pattern to simplify the experience of her young life.

* * * *

'The Elizabethan morality was an important convention . . . it hindered no feeling' (T. S. Eliot, *Selected Essays*). The status of a literary form, the seriousness of the purposes for which it is used, varies from age to age, and from country to country. The Elizabethan drama was remarkable in that, although it was 'public', it could be on occasion a vehicle for the most serious feelings of the greatest dramatists – could justify the use of poetry. *Wuthering Heights* is the first English novel to aim at a comparable seriousness.

The thorough dramatization of this novel is not necessarily to be taken as showing a dissatisfaction with the novel form. Emily Brontë could not have written as an omniscient author without being compelled to adopt an omniscient attitude, to distance by her tone and comment, to explain what she could not explain. She aimed at the maximum of statement with the minimum of explanation. It is her method which gives her language its consistent immediacy. The absence of *parti pris* (or decorum or agreement between writer and reader) in her language is another reason why her novel is disliked. She probably had no reading public in mind.

Perhaps *Wuthering Heights* does demonstrate how incapable the novel is of replacing the drama. The protagonist in a Greek play represents the maximum of communal affirmation and seriousness; and the play's tragic universality is greater than that of any Elizabethan tragedy because the point of departure and return (i.e., the chorus) represents nothing as comforting as Elizabethan morality. The chorus in Greek tragedy represents merely a possible hypothesis. This too is the tone at the end of *Wuthering Heights*.

SOURCE: from 'The Novel as Dramatic Poem (11)', *Scrutiny*, XIV (CUP, 1946–7).

NOTES

1. The Gondal poem, dated 3 March 1845, which celebrates undying passion and begins, 'Cold in the earth, and the deep snow piled above thee! . . .' Contrast Homans on the poems, pp. 216–23 below.
2. The author draws attention to the 'similar resonance' and the 'echo "cease to be"' in Emily Brontë's poem, 'No coward soul is mine' (see ll. 21–4).
3. The author notes, 'Even Linton Heathcliff is not a complete wretch'; he links him with 'an idea of Moira not irrelevant to the main themes of the novel', and quotes from ch. 24, 'You are so much happier . . . spoke the truth.'

Mark Schorer 'Metaphors Color all her Diction' (1949)

To exalt the power of human feeling, Emily Brontë roots her analogies in the fierce life of animals and in the relentless life of the elements – fire, wind, water. 'Wuthering', we are told, is 'a significant provincial adjective, descriptive of the atmospheric tumult to which its station is exposed in stormy weather', and, immediately after, that 'one may guess the power of the north wind blowing over the edge, by the excessive slant of a few stunted firs at the end of the house; and by a range of gaunt thorns all stretching their limbs one way, as if craving alms of the sun'. The application of this landscape to the characters is made explicit in the second half of the novel when Heathcliff says, 'Now, my bonny lad, you are *mine*! And we'll see if one tree won't grow as crooked as another, with the same wind to twist it!' This analogy provides at least half of the metaphorical base of the novel.

Human conditions are like the activities of the landscape, where rains *flood*, blasts *wail*, and the snow and wind *whirl wildly* and *blow* out lights. A serving woman *heaves* 'like a sea after a high wind'; a preacher '*poured* forth his zeal in a *shower*'; Mrs Dean *rushes* to welcome Lockwood, 'exclaiming *tumultuously*'; spirits are 'at high-water mark'; Linton's soul is as different from Heathcliff's 'as a moonbeam from lightning, or frost from fire'; abuse is *lavished* in a *torrent*, or *pours forth* in a *deluge*; illnesses are '*weathered* . . . through'; 'sensations' are felt in a *gush*; 'your veins are *full* of *ice water*; but mine are *boiling*'; hair *flies*, bodies *toss* or *tremble* like reeds, tears *stream* or *rain down* among ashes; discord and distress arise in a *tumult*; Catherine Linton 'was *struck* during a *tempest* of passion with a kind of fit' and '*flew off* in the *height* of it'.

Faces, too, are like landscapes: 'a *cloud* of meditation' hangs over Nelly Dean's '*ruddy* countenance'; Catherine had 'a suddenly *clouded* brow; her humor was a mere *vane* for constantly varying caprices'; 'the surface of' the boy Heathcliff's 'face and hands was dismally *beclouded*' with dirt; later, his face '*brightened* for a moment; then it was *overcast* afresh'. 'His forehead . . . *shaded* over with a heavy *cloud*'; and 'the *clouded* windows of hell', his eyes, '*flashed*'. Hareton, likewise, grows 'black as a *thunder-cloud*'; or *darkens* with a frown. The older Catherine experienced whole '*seasons* of gloom', and the younger Catherine's 'heart was *clouded* . . . in double *darkness*'. Her 'face was just like the *landscape* – *shadows* and *sunshine* flitting over it in rapid succession; but the *shadows* rested longer, and the *sunshine* was more transient'. Sometimes 'her eyes are *radiant* with *cloudless* pleasure', and at the end, Hareton shakes off 'the *clouds* of ignorance and degradation', and his '*brightening* mind *brightened* his features'.

Quite as important as the imagery of wind and cloud and water is the imagery of fire. In every interior, the fire on the hearth is the centre of pictorial interest, and the characters sit '*burning* their eyes out before the fire'. Eyes *burn* with anguish but do not *melt*; they always *flash* and *sparkle*. Fury *kindles*, temper *kindles*, a '*spark* of spirit' *kindles*. Catherine has a *fiery* disposition, but so do objects and states: words *brand*, shame is *burning*, merriment *expires* quickly, fevers *consume* life; hot coffee and basins *smoke*, they do not steam; and Isabella shrieks 'as if witches were running *red-hot* needles into her'. Sometimes fire is identified with other elements, as when a servant urges '*flakes* of *flame* up the chimney', or when Isabella complains that the fire causes the wound on her neck, first stopped by the icy cold, to stream and smart.

Metaphors of earth – earth takes more solid and durable forms than the other elements – are interestingly few. Twice Heathcliff is likened to 'an arid wilderness of *furze* and *whinstone*'; there is a reference to his '*flinty* gratification'; and once he speaks scornfully of 'the *soil* of' Linton's 'shallow cares'. Earth and vegetation sometimes result in a happy juxtaposition of the vast or the violent and the little or the homely, as when Heathcliff says of Linton that 'He might as well plant *an oak in a flower-pot*', or when he threatens to 'crush his ribs in like *a rotten hazel-nut*', which is like his saying that Catherine's passion could be as readily encompassed by Linton as '*the sea* could be . . . contained in that *horse-trough*'.

Most of the animals are wild. Hareton's 'whiskers encroached *bearishly* over his cheeks', and Heathcliff denies the paternity of 'that bear'. Hareton had been 'cast out like an unfledged *dunnock*', and Heathcliff is a 'fierce, pitiless, *wolfish* man'. He is also 'a *bird* of bad omen' and 'an evil *beast*' prowling between a 'stray *sheep*' 'and the fold, waiting his time to spring and destroy'. He has a 'ferocious gaze' and a *savage* utterance; he *grows* and *howls* 'like a beast', and is many times named 'a brute', 'a beast', 'a brute beast'. He struggles like a *bear*, he has *sharp cannibal teeth* which *gleam* 'through the dark', and '*basilisk* eyes . . . *quenched* by sleeplessness'. He *gnashes* his teeth and *foams* like a *mad dog*. He is 'like a *bull*' to Linton's '*lamb*', and only at the very end, the exhausted end, 'he breathed as fast as a *cat*'.

For the domestic and the gentler animals are generally used for purposes of harsh satire or vilification. Edgar, 'the soft thing', 'possessed the power to depart, as much as a *cat* possesses the power to leave a *mouse* half killed, or a *bird* half eaten'. He is 'not a *lamb*' but 'a sucking *leveret*', and his sister is a 'pitiful, slavish, mean-minded *brach*', she is among those *worms*, who, 'the more they writhe, the more' Heathcliff yearns 'to crush out their entrails'. Hindley dies in a stupor, 'snorting like a *horse*'; 'flaying and scalping' would not have roused him, and when the doctor arrives, 'the *beast* has changed to *carrion*'. Hareton is 'an infernal *calf*', and young Linton is a '*puling chicken*' and a '*whelp*'. Like a dying dog, he 'slowly *trailed* himself off, and lay down', or, like a cold one, he '*shrank* closer to the fire'. He 'had *shrunk* into a corner of the settle, as quiet as a *mouse*'; he is called 'a little perishing *monkey*'; and he 'achieved his exit exactly as a *spaniel* might'. He is also 'an abject *reptile*' and 'a *cockatrice*'. Hareton, who is capable on occasion of gathering '*venom* with reflection', is once called a '*magpie*', and once said to be 'obstinate as a *mule*' – one of the few kindly animal references in the novel. To be sure, Isabella describes herself as though she were a deer: 'I *bounded, leaped* and *flew* down the steep road; then . . . *shot* direct across the moor, *rolling* over banks, and *wading* through marshes.' And Catherine, on the whole, is not abused. She is a 'cunning little *fox*' and she runs 'like a *mouse*', but chiefly she is 'soft and mild as a *dove*'.

Emily Brontë's metaphors color all her diction. As her epithets are charged with passion – 'jealous guardianship', 'vexatious phlegm', 'importunate branch' – so her verbs are verbs of violent movement and conflict. . . .

SOURCE: from 'Fiction and the Matrix of Analogy', in the *Kenyon Review*, 1949, reprinted in *The World We Imagine* (1968).

PART FOUR

Modern Approaches 1949–1989

Derek Traversi *Wuthering Heights* After a Hundred Years (1949)

. . . Almost from the first publication of the novel exactly a century ago, the book has been variously regarded as a finished literary creation and as a crude and clumsy melodrama; some readers have found in it the deepest spiritual content and others a perverse conception in which the exaltation of brutality and hatred borders on the repulsive. In the formation of both these conceptions the element of distraction introduced by excessive concentration upon the romantic antecedents of the plot on the one hand, and upon the legendary circumstances of the family life of the Brontë sisters, on the other, has played a great part in obscuring a true understanding of the book . . . neither in isolation produces an intelligible picture of *Wuthering Heights* as a work of art, and neither illuminates sufficiently the extraordinary mixture of personal inspiration and romantic commonplace, of spiritual exaltation and primitive emotion which is the true substance of the novel and upon a definition of which any true estimate of its value must inevitably rest. . . .

To trace a literary creation to its formal origins is not necessarily to define the true character of the impulse which produced it. A melodramatic plot may, under certain conditions, produce the subject for a great work of art; the case of *Hamlet*, the theme of which is at least as crude and improbable as that of Emily Brontë's novel, proves this conclusively. What is truly important in *Wuthering Heights*, as in *Hamlet*, is not the story itself, which is clearly derivative in many of its aspects, but the transformation which it undergoes under the operation of an emotion sufficiently strong to mould it into a highly individual creation. Given the circumstances of Emily Brontë's life it was natural, and indeed inevitable, that the commonplaces of romantic inspiration should play a great part in her novel, but an examination of the *writing*, the treatment of the subject, proves conclusively that its true significance lies not in its obvious romanticism, but in the transformation of this romanticism through the operation of an intensely personal imaginative power. . . .

The qualities by which the book is differentiated from the

commonplaces of romantic sensibility are ... apparent ... in the opening description of Heathcliff's house and its surroundings. Wuthering Heights is described, as Mr Lockwood sees it, in a series of vivid and exact touches. The exposition, careful, orderly, and even slightly pedantic, as befits the speaker, rises almost imperceptibly to the deeply poetic reference to 'the range of gaunt thorns all stretching their limbs one way, as if craving alms of the sun' [ch. 1], so that this evocation does not strike the reader as in any way unjustified or merely a poetic intrusion. Above all, the temptation to exploit the poetic note thus introduced, and so to diminish its effectiveness, is firmly resisted and the description of the interior of the house which follows, as precise in detail as it is appreciative in tone and careful to stress the normality of the setting ('The apartment and furniture would have been nothing extraordinary as belonging to a homely northern farmer' [ch. 1]), reveals a type of writing diametrically opposed to the romantic sensationalism which the authoress might so easily have derived from her natural models. The same firm grasp of the concrete detail is apparent a few pages further on even in Mr Lockwood's account of his highly theatrical dream, where if anywhere we might have expected the strained romantic note to impose a suitable lack of precision, but where in fact the illusion of reality is conveyed with an immediate sense of physical pain that borders on the intolerable: 'Terror made me cruel; and, finding it useless to attempt shaking the creature off, *I pulled its wrist on to the broken pane, and rubbed it to and fro* till the blood ran and soaked the bedclothes' [ch. 3]. In such a passage the peculiar intensity of Emily Brontë's romanticism – if we may use the word for lack of a better – even though working on conventional material achieves its effect through a remarkable and characteristic concreteness. It was the capacity to ... unite the immediate and concrete with the intensity of feeling proper to poetry that enabled her to raise a melodramatic theme to the level of a profoundly personal creation.

To understand the true inspiration of *Wuthering Heights* we need, in fact, to set aside the romantic machinery of passion and revenge and to consider ... the two central themes of the book. These themes, which we might call respectively its 'personal' and 'social' aspects, stand in the closest relationship to one another. Both are direct reflections of an intensely individual creative faculty. The first or 'personal' theme, by which the whole book is illuminated, concerns the love of Catherine Earnshaw for Heathcliff, and of Heathcliff in turn for Catherine. The relationship between these two is based, no doubt, on the familiar romantic conception of irresistible passion. Like so many pairs of romantic lovers, Catherine and Heathcliff are, so to speak, consecrated one to another, each feeling his or her passion as the consuming reality of existence. What is undeniably personal, however, in the manner of their love is the peculiar, almost religious intensity with which it is expressed and which perhaps finds its most significant manifestation in Catherine's attempt to explain her feelings to Nelly Dean [quotes from ch. 9, 'I cannot express . . . separation again'] . . .

The phrasing of Catherine's outburst, far from reflecting the common romantic purpose of diffusing emotion, focuses the whole weight of feeling upon a relationship almost entirely stripped of the accidents of personality. The whole speech leads up to the simple and comprehensive affirmation 'I *am* Heathcliff', which is clearly the statement of a necessity based upon the true being, the essential nature of the speaker, rather than upon any transitory impulse of desire. Whatever may be our reaction to the kind of experience which Catherine's words reflect we must recognise in them the presence of a true and genuine emotion whose remoteness from the mere contingencies of romantic passion is reflected in the extraordinary keenness and power of the expression. False or sentimental emotions are invariably involved in verbiage to make them appear greater and more genuine than they really are; but here the statement of passion is presented in all its bareness, expressed with a sharp, defined clarity that is its own guarantee of truth. The speaker of these words, judge her as we may choose, is concerned with essentials in a way that admits of no distraction or irrelevance; and it is only in the light of a similar concern that the reader of *Wuthering Heights* can usefully attempt to pass judgement on her. . . .

The outstanding characteristic of romantic sentimentality is its self-centredness, we might even say its egoism. For the romantic, emotion tends to be its own justification and the intense kindling of sentiment a sufficient guarantee of spiritual value. With Catherine, however, this is not so. She bases the defence of her attitude to Heathcliff upon a recognition that the individual is not sufficient to himself, that his or her experience thirsts for completion through a vivifying contact with another existence which can only satisfy what is in effect an essentially spiritual craving in so far as it is situated beyond the self: 'What were the use of my creation, if I were entirely contained here?' The emphasis so placed upon the idea of creation, and upon that of the *end* of our existence, is profoundly typical. The nature of Emily Brontë's experience of life, here expressed perhaps more directly than in any other part of the novel, was essentially religious in type: religious not merely in the sense of the rather indefinite 'mysticism' which has often been conceded to her on the strength of isolated passages in her poems, but in an awareness, at once more clear-cut and more open to intellectual definition, of the necessary incompleteness of all the elements that go to make up human nature in its time-conditioned state. It is upon this awareness and not upon phrases which, taken in isolation, may mean everything or nothing, that any estimate of the religious significance of Emily Brontë's work must rest. In the light of it that significance strikes us less, perhaps, as an experience than as an intense recognition of a need. The spirit in which *Wuthering Heights* was conceived, though absolutely distinct from that of Christian mysticism, can none the less only be interpreted as a thirst for religious experience. From a profound sense of the finite and dependent nature of man ('surely you and everybody have a notion that there is or should be an existence of yours beyond you') there arises the desire to make contact with a reality which is beyond the self and by which the self may be completed. In the light of this desire the world of mere external presentation – in so far as it remains merely external, unrelated to the spiritual intuition born of this consuming metaphysical passion – appears empty, and the very sense of this emptiness acquires a significance which can properly be related to the experience of religious desolation: 'If all else perished, and *he* remained *I* should still continue to be; and if all else remained, and he were annihilated, the universe would turn to a mighty stranger: I should not seem a part of it.'

If we accept . . . the religious nature of the emotion expressed through the words of Catherine, we shall not be surprised to find that its consequences extend to the moral order. Her love for Heathcliff explicitly transcends all that is petty, vulgar or sentimental. The contrast between Catherine's feelings for Heathcliff and her attitude to Linton, an attitude which we must also regard as genuine in its own sphere, as having a part to play in what may be called the symbolic structure of the novel, is highly important in this respect. The figure of Linton may be held, in a certain sense, to symbolize the superficial graces of civilised life, in which Heathcliff is totally lacking. It is perfectly natural that Catherine should feel herself attracted to Linton. Courtesy, charm and urbanity are all qualities worthy of admiration, and it is on account of them that she is, at a certain level of her nature, impelled to respond to Linton's affection; but, as she herself recognises, it is not the deepest part of her nature which is thus involved: 'My love for Linton is like the foliage in the woods: time will change it, I'm well aware, as winter changes the trees. My love for Heathcliff resembles the eternal rocks beneath: a source of little visible delight, but *necessary*.' Once more the conflict between two types of feeling that are regarded as mutually exclusive is stated with a simplicity that is fundamentally intellectual in its sense of definition and emphasizes the absence behind it of all purely transitory or sentimental considerations. In the contrast between the *agreeable* and the *necessary*, between emotions which serve at best to adorn life and others whose absence is equivalent to spiritual death, we can observe once more the peculiar inspiration of the book, and our judgement of it as a whole is likely to depend upon our reaction to these words. ...

... behind such passionate utterances ... there lies a moral problem of the utmost seriousness. ... We feel its presence perhaps more clearly when we follow, through the eyes of Nelly Dean, the process of reasoning by which Catherine is urged to abandon Heathcliff, a process which ends only by producing ... her passionate statement of the inevitability of that love. ... Nelly, guided by her inherent good nature and by her long if not particularly imaginative experience of life, maintains that Edgar is a good match for Catherine, that he is socially speaking acceptable and likely to bring her to normal domestic happiness, whereas – she implies – her devotion to Heathcliff can only end in disaster and degradation.[1] All this is undoubtedly true, but the impressive simplicity of Catherine's reply, by which the whole issue is raised from the practical to what we can only call the spiritual plane, is in itself sufficient evidence that it is not all the truth. 'He' (Heathcliff) 'is more myself than I am. Whatever our souls are made of, his and mine are the same; and Linton's is as different as a moonbeam from lightning, or frost from fire.' Confronted with this assertion of necessary affinity the arguments of common sense are reduced to irrelevance.

Catherine's retort, indeed, is the expression of a spiritual concentration as deep and genuine as it is unquestionably disturbing. The emphasis is upon souls and their elemental substance, upon affinities which precede choice and conscious attraction rather than upon the pleasing accidents of personality. It is from this emphasis that the moral problem of the novel derives. For many readers of *Wuthering Heights*, as for Nelly, the strange intensity which breathes through Catherine's words will be disagreeable, and in that case it is unlikely that they will be attracted to the novel. . . . We need to recognise at once, as I have already indicated, that there is in the inspiration of *Wuthering Heights* nothing that we can call properly Christian. The book, as it stands, might equally have been written if Christianity had never existed; but the peculiar religious impulse which went to its making was not without consequences that are undeniably moral. The force with which the contrast between the 'agreeable' and the 'necessary' is driven home derives, in fact, from an attitude to life which, expressed though it be in terms that may strike us as unusual, challenges a moral judgement. If the speaker brushes aside the accidental pleasures, and even the normal social intimacies of life, it is because she is taken up in a consuming experience that leaves no place for them. That this attitude is open to proper criticism of a certain kind may be agreed. There can be no doubt that the peculiar intensity with which it is expressed is due in part to its limitations, to the absence behind it of a philosophy sufficiently ample to embrace it and at the same time to relate it to a wider sphere of realities. Concentration rather than maturity is the distinctive quality of *Wuthering Heights*. . . . Like her sister Charlotte, but to an even greater degree, Emily seems to have combined the intensity and concentration of purpose which are generally associated with maturity with a remarkably infantile simplicity of vision. Doubtless this most unusual combination emphasized in her a certain remoteness from the world of contemporary culture and social activity, but equally certainly it produced, when applied with inflexible logic to the contemplation of certain aspects of human passion, the desire, constantly present in *Wuthering Heights*, to transcend the purely personal and temporal elements in experience. Hardly anywhere else in the nineteenth century are the fundamental human passions so simply, unadornedly portrayed. Many of the great English novelists who were Emily Brontë's contemporaries – Dickens, Thackeray, George Eliot – show moral preoccupations and social interests more explicit than those revealed in *Wuthering Heights*. No doubt the range of these writers is wider, their points of contact with the human scene more extensive; but it is doubtful whether in any of them the sense of a dominating creative impulse is as sustained as in Emily Brontë or whether they reveal an attempt equally consistent to interpret life in terms of something so similar to religious experience.

Considered in the light of this central passion it becomes easier to understand the second main theme of the novel: the contrast between the two houses, Wuthering Heights and Thrushcross Grange. Wuthering Heights clearly reflects the character of Heathcliff, who owns it; we might, indeed, describe Heathcliff as its human incarnation. Severe, gloomy and brutal in its atmosphere (so at least it appears to such an observer as Mr Lockwood), there is no place in it for the strictly necessary. Firmly rooted though it is in local tradition and in local custom, it lacks the civilised adornments of existence and is a suitable background for the life of bare and primitive passion which is characteristic of its owner. Thrushcross Grange, the home of the Lintons, is in every respect completely different. It reflects a conception of life which appears at first sight altogether more agreeable, but which when closely observed shows clear signs of decadence. Like Wuthering Heights, though with very different results, Thrushcross Grange reflects the character of its owners. Judged from a superficial standpoint, after the manner of Nelly Dean, the Lintons seem to possess refinement, kindness, amiability; but a closer inspection shows that this is by no means all the truth. Beneath the surface of refinement there exist moral flaws which play a part of the utmost importance in the development of the story.

There is at the beginning of the novel a most significant moment in which the house and those who dwell in it are seen . . . from the standpoint of external and critical observers. . . . Heathcliff and Catherine, still young children, climb up . . . to look into the illuminated windows of Thrushcross Grange. . . . [quotes from ch. 6, 'And now, guess . . . despise them'] . . . The contempt apparent in Heathcliff's words is undoubtedly a direct reflection of Emily Brontë's opinion.[2] It is the contempt felt by a primitive soul, in whom the fundamental passions are still intensely alive, and associated with an equally genuine and primitive moral seriousness, for a world which claims to be superior but which is in reality trivial, selfish and empty. Throughout the book there is evidence that it was part of Emily Brontë's intention to relate the spiritual conflict which was the main theme of her book to the deliberate presentation of a social contrast. The emphasis laid upon the soft and clinging luxury in which the Lintons live, protected by bull-dogs and obsequious servants from the intrusion of the children of the inferior world outside, is deliberately calculated to produce an impression of excessive sweetness and decay: 'We saw – ah! it was beautiful – a splendid place carpeted with crimson, and crimson-covered chairs and tables, and a pure white ceiling bordered by gold, a shower of glass-drops hanging in silver chains from the centre, and shimmering with little soft tapers' [ch. 6]. The sight of so much unsuspected luxury certainly strikes the two children from outside as 'beautiful'; but it also, more subtly, rouses in them a feeling of repudiation which is only intensified by the behaviour of the dwellers in this 'paradise'. The 'gold', the crimson carpets and chair-coverings which serve to deaden, to mollify the impact of life, the slightly unreal prettiness of the 'shower of glass-drops hanging in silver chains', and the scene of barely defined exquisite decadence in the reference to the 'little *soft* tapers': all these, seen through the eyes of the children outside, point to a highly significant contrast. The contrast is, indeed, an essential part of the main story. When Catherine, now a grown woman, brings Edgar Linton (whom, in her superficial attraction for exactly this kind of luxury, she has married) the news of the return of Heathcliff – now, be it noted, 'a tall, athletic, well-formed man', 'much older in expression and decision of feature than Mr Linton', 'intelligent' in countenance and 'dignified' in manner – and asks if she is to bring him up into the parlour, he looks 'vexed' and suggests 'the kitchen as a more suitable place for him'; to which Catherine, responding to the promptings of her deeper nature, replies by instructing Nelly to prepare two tables, 'one for your master and Miss Isabella, being gentry; the other for Heathcliff and myself, being of the lower orders' [ch. 10]. To the social distinction thus stressed by the Lintons, and clearly regarded by Catherine and her creator as being irrelevant, corresponds a number of findings in the moral order which are part of the book's very substance. 'Pettish', 'silly', 'whining', 'envious' are the adjectives characteristically applied to Edgar Linton by Catherine; and Emily Brontë is at some pains to relate them to the world of pampered luxury in which the family live. It is no accident that the child who was protected by bull-dogs from the intrusion of two harmless children into the family property later calls upon his servants, after attempting to retire himself, to eject his hated rival from his house. As we come to know the Lintons better, we find beneath their sickly and essentially unformed character refinement undoubtedly, but also selfishness, meanness, and even a cruelty, which, although very different from Heathcliff's brutality, is certainly not less inhuman. And it is in part his reaction against the debased civilization represented by the Linton world that induces Heathcliff to embark upon the destructive activity which finally brings him to his death.

To desire to see in *Wuthering Heights* no more than a contrast between civilized decadence and primitive vitality would, however, be too simple. If Catherine's love for Heathcliff is undoubtedly of consuming importance for her, it is also true that there is beneath that love a genuine conflict. The more superficial part of her character is sufficiently attracted by the agreeable aspect of life in the society of the Lintons for her to marry Edgar and come to form part of the family. Indeed, Catherine herself never refuses to give the name of 'love' to her feeling for Edgar Linton. Yet this love – and here we return once more to what might be called the deeper, more personal content of the novel – satisfies only the more superficial part of her nature. All that is permanent in her character and emotions is not satisfied with Linton, impels her to return to Heathcliff; through the whole of her story we are faced with the contrast between the changing 'foliage' and the 'eternal rocks' beneath. Yet the foliage, although in no sense fundamental, represents nonetheless a reality which cannot be ignored without simplifying unduly the issues upon which the novel turns. For *Wuthering Heights* represents, not the statement of a 'naturalist' thesis, but a genuine clash of ideals; and it is the clash, not the thesis, that gives the novel its character and greatness. This clash can be seen, indeed, in one of the most surprising and beautiful passages of the whole book. In it Cathy, daughter of Catherine and Edgar Linton and therefore heiress to two conflicting outlooks, describes a discussion between herself and the sickly son of Heathcliff and Isabella Linton [quotes from ch. 24, 'One time, however . . . very snappish'] . . . Here once more we may detect something of the nature of the peculiar spiritual emotion which Emily Brontë imparted to her characters. The emotion is of the same type, indeed, as we find in the most directly personal of her poems. It is characteristic of the essentially religious nature of her inspiration that what begins as a discussion of the best way of passing a hot day in July turns rapidly into a comparison between two contrasted ideas of the nature of celestial happiness.'...

What is really at stake here, as well as two different reactions to natural beauty, is a clash between two opposed conceptions of life, each of which gives, by contrast, added meaning to its opposite. For Linton Heathcliff, life is peace, calm passivity; for Cathy, it consists in active identifications with the surrounding world. Yet the fact that Catherine's emotion is so powerful as to sweep aside the impression of passivity left by Linton cannot alter our realisation that both emotions formed a part of Emily Brontë's intuition of life, that Catherine's identification with the forces of universal motion tended as its end towards a peace and quiescence which, if not that of Linton Heathcliff, is nonetheless implied in the type of emotion which inspired *Wuthering Heights*. That she felt *both* emotions, that her own creative impulse depended upon the balance, the continual tension set up between them, is sufficiently clear from this passage and from others in the book. If her characteristic reaction to nature was one of eager and active acceptance, it is also true that she sought through and beyond this acceptance an intuition of permanence which was essentially contemplative. The impulse to unite these two necessities of her nature is the true source of the inspiration of the novel.

We have by now said enough to show that this extraordinary novel is essentially religious, though not Christian, in character. We might compare it to a work of pagan inspiration, whose characters are seen less as persons than as great figures simplified and dominated by a single passion; they are in reality and at their most convincing moments passions purged of all that is accidental, trivial and secondary by the very intensity with which they are conceived. It is not surprising to find, on analysing *Wuthering Heights*, that emotions considered in this light do not always lend themselves readily to become the subject of a novel. The novel as an artistic form is above all concerned with the analysis of character through the unfolding of events, but the persons who dominate Emily Brontë's book are too simple, too elemental, to lend themselves to analysis of this kind. In *Wuthering Heights* each of the protagonists, rather than a person, is in reality a passion purged of all accidental qualities. For this reason they are too simply conceived to play their part with complete conviction in a novel the spirit of which approaches rather the severe simplicity of the pagan tragedies of ancient Greece. ...

. . . the key to an understanding of *Wuthering Heights* has to be sought in the transformation of romantic passion into pagan feeling, of a definite if peculiar religious character. To complete our analysis of the novel we need only to point to another element present in it which is profoundly characteristic: the tendency to see human life and individual passions in the shadow of death. The presence of death is felt intensely in *Wuthering Heights*, sometimes as something against which the passionate protagonists react with all the force of their vitality, and sometimes as a profound intuition of peace. The two attitudes need to be seen in relation to one another if we are not to simplify excessively the true nature of the emotion which the novel conveys. The death of Mr Earnshaw and the final lingering of the narrator over the graves of the sleepers 'in that *quiet* earth', characteristic as they are of Emily Brontë,[3] no doubt owe part of their inspiration to an attraction for the idea of peace which can be associated with adolescent emotion. They do not, however, stand alone. For a full understanding of them we need to remember other and closely associated phrases which point to emotions of a more complex kind. When Nelly Dean, after Mr Earnshaw's death, hears the children comforting each other she makes, indeed, her own sentimental comment – 'no parson in the world ever pictured heaven so beautifully as they did in their innocent talk'; but the comment is not the last word and the next sentence comes as the intrusion of a more real and more truly tragic experience, as unexpected as it is profound in its simplicity: 'while I sobbed and listened, I could not help wishing we were all there *safe* together' [ch. 5]. The end of Heathcliff, too, stands in the closest relationship to his tragedy. If he appears at the end of the novel to have found a kind of peace in death, one of his last phrases recalls once more that his was no simple slipping into unconsciousness or craving for fictitious repose: 'My soul's bliss kills my body, but does not satisfy itself' [ch. 34]. The phrase is Emily Brontë's, but the spirit of metaphysical passion which animates it, the consuming desire for a completeness unattainable in time but implied by temporal experience, is not – when due allowance has been made for the world of theological differences which separated her from Christian belief – altogether remote from that of a St John of the Cross.

SOURCE: *Dublin Review* (1949).

NOTES

1. In fact, Nelly at first deplores Catherine's scheme because it seems to involve deserting Heathcliff ('As soon as you become Mrs Linton, he loses friend, and love, and all!'). When she understands it better she deplores it because it involves Catherine's 'wicked and unprincipled' exploitation of her future husband in order to further Heathcliff's interests. This means that Nelly Dean's arguments are based on a stronger moral foundation than the mere practical common sense attributed to her.

2. But it is worth noticing the irony which makes the speaker himself the cause of dissension between a brother and sister.

3. The passage, however, is attributed to Lockwood, a fact which draws attention to the ambiguity surrounding the conclusion of the novel.

Dorothy Van Ghent Dark 'Otherness' in *Wuthering Heights* (1953)

Significantly, our first real contact with the Catherine–Heathcliff drama is established through a dream – Lockwood's dream of the ghost-child at the window. Lockwood is motivated to dream the dream by the most easily convincing circumstances; he has fallen asleep while reading Catherine's diary, and during his sleep a tempest-blown branch is scratching on the windowpane. But why should Lockwood, the well-mannered urbanite, dream *this*? 'I pulled its wrist on to the broken plane, and rubbed it to and fro till the blood ran down and soaked the bedclothes' [ch. 3]. The image is probably the most cruel one in the book. Hareton's hanging puppies, Heathcliff's hanging the springer spaniel, Hindley's forcing a knife between Nelly's teeth or throwing his baby over the staircase, Catherine's leaving the blue print of her nails on Isabella's arm, Heathcliff stamping on Hindley's face – these images and others like them imply savagery or revengefulness or drunkenness or hysteria, but always a motivating set of emotional circumstances. But this is the punctilious Lockwood – whose antecedents and psychology are so insipid that we care little about them – who scrapes the dream-waif's wrist back and forth on broken glass till the blood runs down and soaks the bedclothes. The cruelty of the dream is the gratuitousness of the violence wrought on a child by an emotionally unmotivated vacationer from the city, dreaming in a strange bed. The bed is an old-fashioned closet bed ('a large oak case . . . it formed a little closet' with a window set in it): its panelled sides Lockwood has 'pulled together' before going to sleep. The bed is like a coffin (at the end of the book, Heathcliff dies in it, behind its closed panels); it had been Catherine's bed, and the movable panels themselves suggest the coffin in which she is laid, whose 'panels' Heathcliff bribes the sexton to remove at one side. Psychologically, Lockwood's dream has only the most perfunctory determinations, and nothing at all of result for the dreamer himself, except to put him uncomfortably out of bed. But poetically the dream has its reasons, compacted into the image of the daemonic child scratching at the pane, trying to get from the 'outside' 'in', and of the dreamer in a bed like a coffin, released by that deathly privacy to indiscriminate violence. The coffin-like bed shuts off any interference with the wild deterioration of the psyche. Had the dream used any other agent than the effete, almost epicene Lockwood, it would have lost this symbolic force; for Lockwood, more successfully than anyone else in the book, has shut out the powers of darkness (the pun in his name is obvious in this context); and his lack of any dramatically thorough motivation for dreaming the cruel dream suggests those powers as existing autonomously, not only in the 'outsideness' of external nature, beyond the physical windowpane, but also within, even in the soul least prone to passionate excursion.

The window-pane is the medium, treacherously transparent, separating the 'inside' from the 'outside', the 'human' from the alien and terrible 'other'. Immediately after the incident of the dream, the time of the narrative is displaced into the childhood of Heathcliff and Catherine, and we see the two children looking through the window of the Lintons' drawing-room.

> Both of us were able to look in by standing on the basement, and clinging to the ledge, and we saw – ah! it was beautiful – a splendid place carpeted with crimson, and crimson-covered chairs and tables, and a pure white ceiling bordered by gold, a shower of glass-drops hanging in silver chains from the centre, and shimmering with little soft tapers. Old Mr and Mrs Linton were not there; Edgar and his sister had it entirely to themselves. Shouldn't they have been happy? We should have thought ourselves in heaven! [ch.6].

Here the two unregenerate waifs look *in* from the night on the heavenly vision of the refinements and securities of the most privileged human estate. But Heathcliff rejects the vision: seeing the

Linton children blubbering and bored there (*they* cannot get *out*!), he senses the menace of its limitation;[1] while Catherine is fatally tempted. She is taken in by the Lintons, and now it is Heathcliff alone outside looking through the window.

The curtains were still looped up at one corner, and I resumed my station as a spy; because, if Catherine had wished to return, I intended shattering their great glass panes to a million of fragments, unless they let her out. She sat on the sofa quietly ... the woman-servant brought a basin of warm water, and washed her feet; and Mr Linton mixed a tumbler of negus, and Isabella emptied a plateful of cakes into her lap ... Afterwards, they dried and combed her beautiful hair ... [ch. 6].

Thus the first snare is laid by which Catherine will be held for a human destiny – her feet washed, cakes and wine for her delectation, her beautiful hair combed (the motifs here are limpid as those of fairy tale, where the changeling in the 'otherworld' is held there mysteriously by bathing and by the strange new food he has been given to eat). By her marriage to Edgar Linton, Catherine yields to that destiny; later she resists it tormentedly and finds her way out of it by death. Literally she 'catches her death' by throwing open the window.

'Open the window again wide: fasten it open! Quick, why don't you move?' [she says to Nelly].

'Because I won't give you your death of cold,' I answered.

'You won't give me a chance of life, you mean,' she said ... [ch. 12].

In her delirium, she opens the window, leans out into the winter wind, and calls across the moors to Heathcliff, 'Heathcliff, if I dare you now, will you venture? ... Find a way, then! ... You are slow! ... you always followed me!' [ch. 12]. On the night after her burial, unable to follow her (though he digs up her grave in order to lie beside her in the coffin from which the side panels have been removed), he returns to the Heights *through the window* – for Hindley has barred the door – to wreak on the living the fury of his frustration. It is years later that Lockwood arrives at the Heights and spends his uncomfortable night there. Lockwood's outcry in his dream brings Heathcliff *to the window*, Heathcliff who has been caught ineluctably in the human to grapple with its interdictions long after Catherine has broken through them. The treachery of the window is that Catherine, lost now in the 'other', can look through the transparent membrane that separates her from humanity, can scratch on the pane, but cannot get 'in', while Heathcliff, though he forces the window open and howls into the night, cannot get 'out'. When he dies, Nelly Dean discovers the window swinging open, the window of that old-fashioned coffin-like bed where Lockwood had had the dream. Rain has been pouring in during the night, drenching the dead man. Nelly says,

> I hasped the window; I combed his black long hair from his forehead; I tried to close his eyes: to extinguish, if possible, that frightful, lifelike gaze of exultation before any one else beheld it. They would not shut: they seemed to sneer at my attempts . . . [ch. 34].

Earlier, Heathcliff's eyes have been spoken of as 'the clouded windows of hell' from which a 'fiend' looks out [ch. 17]. All the other uses of the 'window' that we have spoken of here are not figurative but perfectly naturalistic uses, though their symbolic value is inescapable. But the fact that Heathcliff's eyes refuse to close in death suggests the symbol in a metaphorical form (the 'fiend' has now got 'out', leaving the window open), elucidating with simplicity the meaning of the 'window' as a separation between the daemonic depths of the soul and the limited and limiting lucidities of consciousness, a separation between the soul's 'otherness' and its humanness.

There is still the difficulty of defining, with any precision, the quality of the daemonic that is realized most vividly in the conception of Heathcliff, a difficulty that is mainly due to our tendency always to give the 'daemonic' some ethical status – that is, to relate it to an ethical hierarchy. Heathcliff's is an archetypal figure, untraceably ancient in mythological thought – an imaged recognition of that part of nature which is 'other' than the human soul (the world of the elements and the animals) and of that part of the soul itself which is 'other' than the conscious part . . . this archetype has had in modern mythology, constantly a status in relation to ethical thought. The exception is Heathcliff. Heathcliff is no more ethically relevant than is flood or earthquake or whirlwind. It is as impossible to speak of him in terms of 'sin' and 'guilt' as it is to speak in this way of the natural elements or the creatures of the animal world. In him, the type reverts to a more ancient mythology and to an earlier symbolism. *Wuthering Heights* so baffles and confounds the ethical sense because it is not informed with that sense at all: it is profoundly informed with the attitudes of 'animism', by which the natural world – that world which is 'other' than and 'outside of' the consciously individualized human – *appears* to act with an energy similar to the energies of the soul; to be permeated with soul energy but of a mysterious and alien kind that the conscious human soul, bent on securing itself through civilization, cannot identify itself with as to purpose: an energy that can be propitiated, that can at times be canalized into humanly purposeful channels, that *must* be given religious recognition both for its enormous fertility and its enormous potential destructiveness. But Heathcliff does have human shape and human relationships; he is, so to speak, 'caught in' the human; two kinds of reality intersect in him – as they do, with a somewhat different balance, in Catherine; as they do, indeed, in the other characters. Each entertains, in some degree, the powers of darkness – from Hindley, with his passion for self-destruction (he, too, wants to get 'out'), to Nelly Dean, who in a sense 'propitiates' those powers with the casuistry of her actions, and even to Lockwood, with his sadistic dream. Even in the weakest of these souls there is an intimation of the dark Otherness, by which the soul is related psychologically to the inhuman world of pure energy, for it carries within itself an 'otherness' of its own, that inhabits below consciousness. . . .[2]

SOURCE: *The English Novel, Form and Function* (1953).

NOTES

1. See above, p. 152n. 2
2. For arguments against 'attributing to Catherine and Heathcliff a unique metaphysical status', see John Hagan's 'The Control of Sympathy in *Wuthering Heights*': 'They are said to be not merely human beings . . . but the embodiment of special cosmic 'forces', 'energies' or 'principles'. . . . In Lord David Cecil's . . . interpretation . . . Catherine and Heathcliff are said at one moment to incarnate a 'spiritual principle' . . . and at another to be 'a manifestation of natural forces'. . . . Similarly Mrs Van Ghent seems undecided whether [their] strange 'otherness' is 'the raw, inhuman reality of anonymous natural energies' . . . the unconscious mind . . . or some literal demonism . . . these different forces and principles cannot be regarded as identical . . . they are . . . the inevitably confused results of trying to discover in the novel more metaphysical concreteness than it can yield . . .' *Nineteenth-Century Fiction*, xx (1966), pp. 288–9. See further, Select Bibliography, p. 237 below.

Jacques Blondel Literary Influences on *Wuthering Heights* (1955)

Walter Scott

... 'For fiction – read Scott alone', Charlotte advised Ellen Nussey in the year that she wrote *The Spell* [1834].[1] His reputation in the parsonage was unassailed; to Emily he was a master of style and a guide for her sensibility and imagination. ... He was himself indebted to the Gothic novel, of which so many traces are apparent in so many of his novels. But he did not fully approve the romantic ideas peculiar to Lewis[2] and Mrs Radcliffe. The latter, like the author of *The Monk* (1796), creates supernatural effects which are abruptly explained away by natural causes. ... The essential weakness of the 'Gothic' supernatural lies in its dependence on a trick, which is revealed once the reader's feelings have been wound up to their highest pitch ... the emotions aroused are merely a false alarm administered to the reader's sensibility. ... Scott's approach was different. He disapproved of Maturin's method in *The Fatal Revenge*,[3] which ensured that the conflict would be resolved by rational means; he was severely disposed to the entire Gothic school ... [he] believed in the marvellous and refused to be tricked by crude contrivances.[4] ... The influence of his own work on Emily Brontë, apart from that of his literary criticism, is clear ... [and] has been discussed in a short study by Florence Dry [*The Sources of Wuthering Heights*, 1937]. ... Emily Brontë's general narrative style clearly indicates her familiarity with Scott's novels. In *Wuthering Heights*, as in *Old Mortality*, events unfold within each chapter with a sobriety and discipline which tax to its furthest limits the reality that the interpolated narrator wishes to depict. Moreover local dialect is used as it is in Scott.

Florence Dry points out various influences deriving from *The Black Dwarf* [1816], *The Heart of Midlothian* [1818] and *Guy Mannering* [1815]. The first story is the shortest and the most illuminating here. Some of the deformed dwarf's utterances when the young Earnscliff meets him near his hut diffusely resemble Heathcliff's general style of expression.

> 'Were there a man who had annihilated my Soul's dearest hope . . . I would not dash him to atoms thus —' (He flung the vessel with fury against the wall). 'No!' (he spoke more composedly, but with utmost bitterness), 'I would pamper him with wealth and power to inflame his evil passions and to fulfil his evil designs; he should lack no means of vice and villainy; he should be the centre of a whirlpool that should know neither rest nor peace, but boil with unceasing fury, while it wrecked every goodly ship that approached its limits! He should be an earthquake capable of shaking the very land in which he dwelt, and rendering all its inhabitants friendless, outcast and miserable – as I am!' [*The Black Dwarf,* ch. 4]

Here, in effect, is an elder brother to the Heathcliff who dedicates himself to the destruction of a human soul while being, like Scott's dwarf, 'in league with the invisible world'. . . . the hero of Scott's story is called Earnscliff and the 'villain' Ellieslaw. The dwarf saves an Isabella from a hasty marriage; he, on his side, falls victim to Ellieslaw, who elopes with his bride. But these exhaust the possible parallels, which Florence Dry pursues somewhat too far. [A short summary follows of parallels, principally in matters of incidental detail, with *The Heart of Midlothian* and *Guy Mannering*.][5]

The Gothic Novel

. . . there is no evidence that the works of Mrs Radcliffe or Maturin were known at the parsonage . . . elements in *Wuthering Heights* recalling one feature or another of the Gothic novel . . . can be reduced principally to a matter of atmosphere, since none of the individual details appear to have been the result of a direct borrowing. The themes of vengeance unfolded by the Irish priest Maturin, in novels from which there burst forth violent explosions of extreme feeling, throw into lurid relief the desperate necessity to surrender an innocent victim, body and soul, to the Faustian charms of Melmoth.[6] . . . the salvation of the soul merely serves as the pretext for a drama in which the novelist's imagination excludes any moral purpose and feeds an appetite for sensation at the expense of verisimilitude. . . . She may have rediscovered in these indifferently written pages the appeal of a particular kind of experience, which strengthened other, earlier, impressions associated with the sometimes troubling adventures encountered in the stories which she had read in Miss Branwell's religious magazines.[7] ... in her memory the 'villains' of fiction and those of local history could have lodged easily enough side by side. ... If she read *The Mysteries of Udolpho*,[8] she may also have learnt from it the art of suggesting a sense of anguished expectancy. Lockwood's dream at the beginning of the book and the strangeness which grips him before listening to Mrs Dean are of this order, and so too is the latter's anxiety when she has a presentiment of a fatal event [ch. 11]; the hand which knocks on the window-pane in the room where Lockwood sleeps certainly recalls the one which seizes Adeline's hand in *The Romance of the Forest*.[9] The habit of associating events with a particular landscape is also noticeable here and there [in Mrs Radcliffe's novels], as it is in Scott. But one can speak only of an influence of method, not of an influence of feeling. Mrs Radcliffe's themes do not lend themselves to any poetic or psychological development, since reason and common sense are at hand to lull the reader, and no element of the metaphysical is permitted to intrude.

Wuthering Heights presents a further minor parallel with the Gothic novel: we find the same schematic simplification in the casting of characters. On the one side, sympathetic figures, victims of the 'villain's' wickedness, and, on the other side, a set of unappealing figures; these confront each other in Mrs Radcliffe's novels. Emily Brontë employs an equally simple structure, situating at the centre of her novel the 'dark' character, a descendant of the traditional 'traitor' who is set outside all social conventions. But it is important to recognise Heathcliff's originality; if he seems like a brother to so many of the 'villains' of the Gothic novel, he differs from them in essentials ... it is only external details which compel us to make these comparisons. ... Here is an example ...

> An habitual gloom and severity prevailed over the deep lines of his countenance and his eyes were so piercing that they seemed to penetrate at a single glance into the hearts of men and to read their most secret thoughts. [Mrs Radcliffe, *The Italian*, 1797, ch. 11]

It is in keeping with the traditions of this genre that the evil-doer should be distinguished in appearance and physically robust. ... Heathcliff is tough physically and sober in his habits. He tells Mrs Dean, 'With my hard constitution and temperate mode of living, and unperilous occupations I ought to, and probably shall, remain above ground till there is scarcely a black hair on my head ...' [ch. 33].

Still closer to the 'villain' of the Gothic novel is Mrs Dean's description of his appearance [quotes from ch.7, 'Do you mark . . . devil's spies?'].

Byron

In this way, Heathcliff is identified with a still continuing tradition, and furthermore reveals his affinity with the Byronic hero. Yet here, too, the likenesses are principally external, for the motivation of the character is different. We know that Heathcliff 'from childhood . . . had a delight in dwelling on dark things and entertaining odd fancies . . .' [ch. 33], and it is asked of Byron's Lara, 'Why slept he not when others were at rest?'[10] Heathcliff is a child of darkness, darkness which protects his flight, his return, and the accomplishing of his schemes. Weighing upon him is a doom which we have already seen working in the Gondal characters, but the principal impulse behind his actions is not that he feels himself to be on the fringe of a society which condemns him, and so needs to find a pose through which he can assert his will to power; Heathcliff has the looks of a Byronic hero, but his pride places him on a different level. He is conscious of his own frustration and, like Milton's Satan, wishes to become destructive. . . . He does not love his frustration for the delight which he finds in it, but rather for the suffering which it allows him to inflict on his victims, as if on the agents of his destiny. In him . . . melancholy is neither the sickness of the Byronic soul, nor is it connected with the need to feel set apart from others; he does not foster in himself that cult of 'separateness' which distinguishes Childe Harold and Manfred; nor does he resort to a pose in order to protect himself from the threat of disintegration which circumstances have brought his way. Without Bryon, he could not have been conceived, but he goes further than the Byronic hero in his romantic rebellion. . . .[11]

Hoffmann's Das Majorat

. . . Some have suggested a conscious source in Hoffmann's tale *Das Majorat*', which Emily Brontë could have read in German while she was in Brussels in 1842.[12] In the first place, we have to remember that Hoffmann was not much of a success in England. Scott, whose reservations concerning the Gothic novel we already know, pronounced against fantastic literature; and Hoffmann's reputation seems not to have survived beyond 1832. ... it is unlikely that *Das Majorat* could have had the decisive influence claimed for it by A. L. Wells and Romer Wilson.[13] [An account of the story follows.] Certainly there are some disconcerting parallels ... in *Das Majorat*: a similarly wintry setting ... a similar interest in the supernatural, communicating this through two characters who, like Lockwood, are ignorant of the story; and it employs a similarly indirect narrative method, which incorporates concise references to dates. But all this amounts to very little. The localities in the story do not have the same bewitching power linking the characters together whether they will or not. The supernatural is of a different order; it does not illuminate the psychology of the characters, who completely lack Heathcliff's and Catherine's metaphysical dimensions, nor does it represent at once a threat to their existence and a hope of their liberation from the imprisoning body. Love has no decisive part to play in Hubert's frustration. The sentimental Séraphine cannot possibly be compared with any of Emily Brontë's characters. Daniel is merely a pawn; he is not a baleful, unforgettably vivid presence like Joseph. Again, the story is set in a distant, indeterminate period, while Emily Brontë, who is careful to preserve a remarkably precise chronological sequence, situates her novel in the recent past and founds it on lifelike situations derived from local history. Lastly, *Wuthering Heights* adumbrates the triumph of a naturally good order over the forces of evil while *Das Majorat* is a moralising tale concerned with a particular injustice and its far-reaching consequences.

Tales in Blackwood's Magazine

... This periodical regularly published stories from the original German. ... Here is a passage from 'The Brothers', which appeared in February 1834:[14]

> A man dressed with elegance ... who treated libertinism as though it were a science and discussed the various devices of sensual depravity with as much cool precision as readiness. 'He pleased the ear' while he disgusted the moral sense ...'

The 'villain' once more is blackened and appears here as a sadistic creature, some of whose attributes resemble Heathcliff's. The theme of calculated cruelty is discovered, as we know, in Charlotte Brontë's 'The Foundling' as early as 1833. On the other hand, Emily wrote a French essay in Brussels entitled 'Lettre d'un frère à un frère', which deals with the memory of a fratricidal hatred.[15] The reading of *Blackwood's* left permanent traces, and this particular recollection is still evident in *Wuthering Heights*.

The stories in *Blackwood's* used similar themes and subjects: the curse ('The Headsman, A Tale of Doom', February 1830; 'A Father's Curse', November 1833[16]), and the 'Gothic' supernatural ('The Bracelets: a sketch from the German', January 1832). Added to these were poems translated from [Ludwig] Uhland and Frederick Rückhert (March and May 1836). However, it is wrong to exaggerate these German influences on Emily Brontë in the period from 1830 to 1840 ... for it was not solely to these that she owed her taste for violence and the supernatural ... Mrs Humphry Ward ... makes too much of the part played by them, even calling attention to a story by Tieck, 'Pietro D'Abano', published by the same magazine in August 1839.[17] [An account of the story follows.] ... One fails to see any resemblances here to *Wuthering Heights* apart from the terrifying atmosphere, which is common to both stories, the part played by dreams, and the fascination of the supernatural. But in each of these areas the differences are profound. ... 'Pietro d'Abano' must be placed beside the many other pieces in *Blackwood's Magazine* which could have interested Emily Brontë and her sisters without our therefore necessarily having to conclude that they exercised a decisive influence on her work.

In November, 1840, however, the same magazine published 'The Bridegroom of Barna', a story to which Leicester Bradner has already drawn attention.[18] It is an Irish tale about the marriage of Hugh Lawlor and Ellen Nugent. ... the construction of the plot in no way foreshadows Emily Brontë's novel, though it is difficult to avoid comparing Heathcliff with Hugh Lawlor, who is a foundling and takes his name from the 'thicket or wood' where he was discovered.[19] But it is in the closing stages of the story that we find a striking parallel. When Hugh is betrayed, and realises that he has been deceived, Ellen, to whom he has given shelter for the night, falls into delirium and dies of grief. Hugh then embarks on a funeral ritual which will at once seem familiar to readers of *Wuthering Heights*.

By the side of Ellen Nugent's newmade grave sat the murderer Lawlor, enclosing in his arms the form that had once comprised all earth's love and beauty for him and which, like a miser, with wild and maniac affection he had unburied once more to clasp and contemplate. The shroud had fallen from the upper part of the body upon which decay had as yet made slight impression.

The wan face turned up to him as if it still could thrill to the mad kisses in which he steeped it, while he had twined one of the white arms frantically about his neck. 'Ellen', he said, 'speak to your murderer . . .'

It is true that Lawlor is repentant, and that his murderous act is directed against his rival, while Edgar in *Wuthering Heights* is spared . . . but the effect of this macabre scene on the events in chapter 29 of Emily Brontë's novel should not be overlooked. In *Wuthering Heights*, however, it is enriched with fresh details, transfigured by a sense of the supernatural, which is absent from 'The Bridegroom of Barna', and indeed purged by this of the sense of crudity that mars the close of that dark tale . . .[20]

So it is the primacy of her own creative imagination, so far as the use of elements borrowed from various sources is concerned, which urges us to place the influence of the Gothic novel – and in particular of the stories published in *Blackwood's Magazine* – in this fresh perspective. Emily Brontë derived from these some encouragement to write a story of her own . . . but her care for truth over-rides any mere desire to arouse violent emotions in the reader . . . familiarity with *Blackwood's* informed her about public taste, but so far from alienating her from reality, confirmed in her the need to make what she knew of life play its part in her literary creation.

The Gothic novel may also . . . be seen as providing the best method of concealing the author's personality from the reader. . . . Emily Brontë could share in the illusion created while at the same time detaching herself from it. . . . She found thus a disguise which was even more likely to throw a reader off the scent than her identity as 'Ellis Bell'. . . .

The Gothic novel, then, was to the evolution of *Wuthering Heights* what the Gondal poems were to Emily Brontë's personal emotions; in the former, she profited from the literary framework and the exceptionally high register of feeling, in the latter from the myth and the poetical form – these helped her to achieve a certain aesthetic distance when recreating experience in a work of imagination.

Shakespeare

The emotions aroused by this familiarity with romantic literature only partly explain the genesis of *Wuthering Heights*. ... [Emily Brontë] longed to express in a work of the creative imagination ... her compulsive desire to exercise sovereignty over a vast universe of metaphysical proportions. In investing *Wuthering Heights* with the same interior impulse which had found expression in her Gondal epic, Emily Brontë looks once again towards Shakespearian drama. What she found there was not merely a 'catalogue of the passions', but an image of life as she conceived it.

... *King Lear*, to which Lockwood makes a passing reference, and also *Macbeth*, could well have played a significant part in the novel's composition. ... there are certain minor analogies linking the novel with these two tragedies: the division of the world into two camps of the weak and the wicked; the preoccupation with the urge to destroy in order to possess; the acceptance of destiny. We might remember, too, the scenes of sadistic cruelty in *King Lear* and Heathcliff's passion for destruction, which he shares with the bastard Edmund, who cries, 'Legitimate Edgar, I must have your land ...' [*King Lear*, I ii 16]. Further, Heathcliff knows the bitterness of failure, and life for him will never be anything other than 'a tale told by an idiot, full of sound and fury. ...' ... Heathcliff and Edmund. ... work to destroy their victims because their private dreams are frustrated and because they are deprived of what they consider to be their rights. Both feel that they are unloved. ... Both men experience at the end ... some glimmering of moral feeling, which does not take them quite as far as repentance, at any rate not in Heathcliff's case. ... Emily Brontë, seeming to draw her 'villain' down the steep slope which brings Richard III to grief, shows him to be even more perverse than Edmund. ... Finally the drama is enacted on a wide expanse of space, where, as before in *King Lear*, men have the freedom to upset, for a short space, the established order of things. The power notwithstanding to overcome the gulf between life and death, through some kind of visionary power, is vouchsafed to Emily's lovers: we think of the death of Antony, for whom 'All length is torture ...' [*Antony and Cleopatra*, IV xii 46]; so when Heathcliff dies, his soul's happiness kills his body ['I'm too happy; and yet I am not happy enough. My soul's bliss kills my body, but does not satisfy itself ...', ch. 34].

These similarities . . . are not more than reminiscences, certainly, but they seem important for our understanding of the author's depth of purpose.[21] Emily Brontë found in Shakespearian tragedy a poetic vision of the world and an inspiration which in order to be given fresh life and form had to be combined with new elements derived from romantic literature and from her own experience. Without this emotional bond between Emily Brontë and Shakespeare, *Wuthering Heights* could have been a daring achievement, but not a poem in which all human destiny is subjected to scrutiny.

SOURCE: *Emily Brontë: expérience spirituelle at création poétique* (Paris, 1955).

NOTES

1. See Introduction, p. 14n above.
2. Matthew Gregory Lewis (1775–1818), remembered as the author of *The Monk* (1796), also wrote various dramas; his verses had some influence on Scott's earlier poetry.
3. Charles Robert Maturin (1782–1824), celebrated for his 'Gothic' novels, was educated at Trinity College, Dublin, took orders and for a time kept a school. His *The Fatal Revenge, or the Family of Montorio* (1807) is discussed by Scott in the *Quarterly Review*, 1810 (see Scott's *Miscellaneous Prose Works*, 1853 ed., vol. II, pp. 157–72).
4. '. . . we disapprove of the mode introduced by Mrs Radcliff[e], and followed by Mr Murphy [Charles Maturin] and her other imitators, by winding up their story with a solution by which all the incidents, appearing to partake of the mystic and marvellous, are resolved by very simple and natural causes' (Scott, cited in n. above, p. 166).
5. Mrs Leavis argues for the probable additional influence of Scott's *The Bride of Lammermoor* (1819) in her recent study (see below, p. 238 and p. 91n. above).
6. Maturin's *Melmoth the Wanderer* was published 1820.
7. Charlotte Brontë recollects her aunt's copies of the *Methodist Magazine* in *Shirley*, 'mad Methodist Magazines, full of miracles and apparitions of preternatural warnings, ominous dreams and frenzied fanaticism' [ch. 22].
8. Mrs Radcliffe's *The Mysteries of Udolpho*, published 1794.
9. Mrs Radcliffe's *The Romance of the Forest*, published 1791.
10. *Lara* (1814) I ix 147.
11. For other discussions of Emily Brontë and Byron, see Helen Brown, 'The Influence of Byron on Emily Brontë, in *Modern Language Review*, XXXIV (1939); Margiad Evans, 'Byron and Emily Brontë, in *Life and Letters To-day*, LVII (1948); Ann Lapraik Livermore, 'Byron and Emily Brontë', in *Quarterly Review*, CCC (1962).
12. On Emily Brontë and Hoffmann, see above, p. 74 and n.
13. A. L. Wells in *Les Sœurs Brontë et l'étranger* (Paris, 1937); Romer

Wilson in *All Alone: the life and private history of Emily Jane Brontë* (1928) (see Introduction p. 23).

14. *Blackwood's Magazine*, XXXV (Feb. 1834), pp. 191–203.

15. The brothers in the *Blackwood's Magazine* story are not, however, at enmity with each other. An English translation of Emily's essay by L. W. Nagel is printed in *Brontë Society Transactions*, XI (1950), pp. 339–40.

16. Thomas Aird's pedestrian 'A Father's Curse' is a narrative in verse, *Blackwood's Magazine*, XXXIV (Nov. 1833), pp. 814–19.

17. See above, pp. 96–7.

18. In his pioneering study, 'The Growth of *Wuthering Heights*', in *PMLA*, XLVIII (1933), pp. 129–46.

19. It is not Lawlor, but Tom Bush, Lawlor's betrayer, who is the 'foundling'; see *Blackwood's Magazine*, XLVIII (Nov. 1840), pp. 680–704, esp. 685.

20. It should be added that there is a striking similarity between the treatment of Ellen Nugent's last tranquil hours by her window at 'the close of a sweet evening in July' and Emily's handling of Catherine's last hours in *Wuthering Heights*, ch. 15: in both cases calm is broken by the violent intrusion of the lover, an impassioned dialogue follows, and the outcome of the meeting is tragic.

21. For a further discussion of the Shakespearian echoes in Emily's novel, see Lew Girdler, '*Wuthering Heights* and Shakespeare', in *Huntington Library Quarterly*, XIX (Aug. 1956), pp. 385–92.

Miriam Allott The Rejection of Heathcliff? (1958)[1]

I

The influence of Lord David Cecil's analysis of *Wuthering Heights* in *Early Victorian Novelists* (1934) . . . does not necessarily imply a simple approval of the total meaning he ascribes to the book. . . .

Cecil's main contentions about the principles of storm and calm and their relationship to each other in the novel are the following. First, they are 'not conflicting': they are to be thought of either as separate aspects of a pervading spirit or as component parts of a harmony. Second, they are not in themselves destructive. If in life they become so, it is because 'in the cramped condition of their earthly incarnation these principles are diverted from following the course that their nature indicates . . . the calm becomes a source of weakness . . . the storm a source not of fruitful vigour but disturbance . . . even in this world their discords are transitory . . .' Third, the system composed of the balance of these opposites can only be subject to temporary interruptions because it is self-righting. It operates to restore the equilibrium which is momentarily lost. Of the stormy Earnshaws and the Linton 'children of calm', Cecil asserts, 'Together each group, following its own sphere, combines to compose as cosmic harmony. It is the destruction and the re-establishment of this harmony which is the theme of the story.' These are the conclusions drawn by Cecil from his study of the novel. . . . If they are accepted as self-evident, an interpretation of *Wuthering Heights* can be made which does justice to many elements of Emily Brontë's art, but at the same time the pattern of the novel suffers distortion, and much has to be overlooked. . . .

Indeed the whole structure of the novel suggests a deeper and more compulsive concern with the elements of 'storm' than this reading allows for. As everyone has noticed, Emily Brontë extends her themes into the story of a second generation of Earnshaws and Lintons; Cecil himself comments on the way in which she uses her two generations to illustrate contrasts between 'calm' and 'storm', and to reveal the workings of inherited characteristics. But . . . most remarkable about the second generation story is the effort it makes to modify the 'storm-calm' opposition in such a way as to eliminate the most violent and troubling elements that give the first generation story its peculiar intensity. . . . She substitutes for the violent Cathy–Edgar–Heathcliff relationships of the first part the milder Catherine–Linton–Hareton relationships of the second; and she alters the earlier savage Hindley–Heathcliff relationship (of victimiser and embittered victim) into the more temperate Heathcliff–Hareton relationship (where the tyrant has some feeling for his victim, while the victim himself remains loving and unembittered). . . . Hindley's savage and destructive grief for his wife, Frances, and Heathcliff's frenzy at Cathy's death, reappear as Edgar's deep but quiet grief for the same Cathy, and has Hareton's 'strong grief' for Heathcliff – a grief 'which springs naturally from a generous heart, though it be tough as tempered steel'. Again, while Emily Brontë replaces the wildness of the first-generation story by a quality of energy in the second generation which is more normal and human, she also shows us in the second generation a demoralizing extreme of calm. Thus Heathcliff, the epitome of 'storm', fathers Linton, who takes 'Linton' qualities, inherited from Isabella, to their furthest point of lethargic inaction.

Seen in this way, the book ... describes two nearly symmetrical 'arcs'. The first bears us on through the violence of Catherine's and Heathcliff's obsessional feelings for each other, and through the stress of their relationships with the Lintons, to end in a mood of doubtful equipoise (for the spirits, apparently united and at rest, lie near the bare moors, and in the rain and darkness they still 'walk'). The other 'arc', also passing through stress, ends in the quiet of the valley. ...The two arcs suggest that the novel is an effort to explore and, *if possible*, to reconcile conflicting 'attractions'. ... In the story of the first generation the clash of these opposites is worked out in terms of a strong emotional commitment to the values of storm. What does such a commitment in all its furthest implications really entail? – this is the question Emily Brontë, with her unsentimental honesty, seems to ask. The answer is troubling. The second part of the novel examines an alternative commitment and poses another question: if storm-values are dangerous or undesirable, what is the nature of the calm that one must try to accept in the place of storm? For example, are we to accept calm if it implies a universe like Linton's, in which men and women are only 'half alive'?

The book's extraordinary power derives at least in part, then, from an attempt to do justice to the conflicting demands of heart and head. Powerful emotions lie with Heathcliff (or 'storm', or 'earth in its harsher aspects' – whichever of these labels one prefers). But Heathcliff is ultimately a dark and troubling image. ... Everything ... suggests that so far from 'union ... with its affinity' being, as Lord David Cecil suggests, a means to harmony, such a union is, in fact, an ominous conception, generating images of 'darkness' and 'storm' from the first, and gathering increasingly disquieting associations the more it is contemplated. ... Here one must add that [Emily Brontë] would probably have rejected Lord David Cecil's comment that her outlook concerned itself 'not with moral standards, but with those conditioning forces of life in which the naïve erections of the human mind that we call moral standards are built up'. They were certainly not 'naïve erections' to her. ... Indeed the second generation story seems to result from a ruthlessly determined effort to supersede Heathcliff and everything identified with the harsher, more destructive aspects of 'storm' – we learn from Charlotte how strong Emily's will could be,[2] and head would have had no success in the conflict of heart and head if her will had been weak or vacillating. I am stressing here that this is the direction in which the second generation story moves, but also that it finds no permanent solution of the conflict. . . . The rights of feeling, however dark and troubling, are safeguarded, for Heathcliff, defeated in one way, is triumphant in another. Even though he can no longer prevent the happiness of Hareton Earnshaw and the younger Catherine, he 'retains' the deserted Earnshaw property that he has usurped, inhabiting Wuthering Heights and the bare moorland with the elder Catherine.

At the end, then, a certain balance has been achieved. But it is not, as Lord David Cecil claims, an inevitable harmony following Heathcliff's posthumous union with his affinity, Catherine, nor the re-establishment of the balance of forces at the beginning of the book when Lintons and Earnshaws existed harmoniously but in separation. It is, in fact, a balance effected by a new combination of Earnshaws and Lintons, with Earnshaw energy modified by Linton calm. Heathcliff obsessions are excluded. Moreover, in order to achieve the new alliance, the Earnshaws at last abandon their old house; the significance of this departure is stressed by Emily Brontë's emphasis on the inscription over the old door, which Lockwood notices early in the first chapter – 'among a wilderness of crumbling griffins and shameless little boys, I detected the date "1500", and the name of "Hareton Earnshaw"' – and which the dispossessed Hareton is so pleased to be able to read for himself in chapter 24. After three hundred years the Earnshaws withdraw from Wuthering Heights and come down to Thrushcross Grange, bringing to the valley some of their own energy but also in their turn being modified by the values it represents. The situation at the end of the novel, therefore, is vastly different from the situation at its beginning. The management of the narrative suggests how important the establishment of a balanced relationship between Lintons and Earnshaws was for the novel's bringing about at least a partial resolution of opposites. Through Lockwood's narrative we are brought to the threshold of the first meeting between the two families in chapter 3, we are carried up to this point again in chapter 6, when Nelly Dean speaks portentously of the consequences of the meeting ('there will more come of this business than you reckon on'), and we look back to its effects in the scenes of Catherine's delirium in chapters 11 and 12. Perhaps the one clear assertion is that for the purposes of ordinary life – and given the special Earnshaw nature – Lintons are better for Earnshaws than Heathcliff is. To that extent, Emily Brontë's novel makes a moral judgement: but whether there is a final commitment to the rejection of Heathcliff is another matter.

The reading here suggested is, I believe, forced on us by the book's structure, but the evidence from structure may be strengthened by noting the different texture of the writing in different parts of the novel. The emotional quality of the first part of the book is quite different from that of the second, and to a great extent it is the compulsive nature of the imagery in the first generation story that contributes to this effect. The prevailing images in the first part of the book are sombre and troubling, those of the second part not only carry less disturbing associations, but in many cases they appear to be frankly contrived, though they remain the product of a creative sensibility which still makes them fresh, vivid, genuinely apt. . . .

II

What this sensibility tried to free itself from when seeking an alternative to Heathcliff . . . is suggested by certain recurrent *motifs* that accompany and emphasise the stormy 'Heathcliff feelings' described in the earlier part of the book. These *motifs* appear at moments of great emotional pressure and bring with them overtones of violence and the supernatural. Heathcliff is inseparably associated with discord and distress from his first arrival. Because Mr Earnshaw carries the child Heathcliff in his arms all the way from Liverpool, his own children are deprived of the toys he has promised them – Cathy's whip is lost, Hindley's fiddle crushed – and they immediately set up a clamour and turn against the newcomer. The same early chapter (4) gives us other details that underline the discordant elements in Heathcliff's nature, and it ends with the savage little incident of the two ponies, which drives Heathcliff and Hindley even further apart. Very early in the novel certain images are linked with the farouche figure of Heathcliff. These tend to recur at crucial phases of the story when Catherine's passion for him is most violently felt.

The recurrent image-pattern first appears in chapter 3, where we are still in the 'present' of 1801. Lockwood, lying in the first Catherine's oak-panelled bed at Wuthering Heights – the bed which is itself a part of the pattern – reads her account of the 'awful Sunday' back in 1777, when, as we learn later (on our return from the 'present' of Lockwood to the past of Nelly Dean's narrative in chapter 6), she and Heathcliff, driven out by Hindley, first came into contact with the Lintons. Lockwood falls into a fitful sleep, disturbed by 'the branch of a firtree that touched my lattice, as the blast wailed by, and rattled its dry cones against the panes...' [ch. 3]. In his dream he is made to recall his surroundings: 'I was lying in the oak closet, and I heard distinctly the gusty wind, and the driving of snow; I heard, also, the fir-bough repeat its tearing sound . . . and, I thought, I rose and endeavoured to unhasp the casement . . . [ch. 3]. But the hook is 'soldered into the staple' and he has to smash the glass in order to try to reach 'the importunate branch'. As he does so, his fingers close on the fingers of 'a little ice-cold hand!' [quotes from ch. 3, 'The intense horror . . . "let me in"']. This 'pattern', then, has physical and mental elements: it includes objects such as the oak-panelled bed, the opened window letting in ice-cold wind from the moors, the fir-tree and its tapping cones, but it also includes sensations, feelings and attitudes linked with them – sensations of pain, feelings of savagery and supernatural awe, notions of exile and imprisonment (which are persistent themes of Emily Brontë's poems). The pattern recurs at important moments in the story when 'Heathcliff' feelings are intensified. It is only once associated with the second Catherine – when she escapes from Wuthering Heights and from Heathcliff through her mother's window and with the help of the fir branch (chapter 38). But the first Catherine's connection with the pattern is very different. At the height of her Linton–Heathcliff torment in chapter 12 Catherine lies delirious on the floor at the Grange. She dreams that she is back in her own old bed at Wuthering Heights, and that she is 'enclosed in the oak-panelled bed at home, and my heart ached with some great grief . . . my misery arose from the separation that Hindley had ordered between me and Heathcliff. I was laid alone for the first time . . .' In the dream we are back once more in 1777, the period Lockwood reads about in Catherine's 'diary', and of which Nelly Dean tells him once more in chapter 6. Catherine is remembering the time when she and Heathcliff, already separated by Hindley, are on the point of being driven even further apart by the Lintons. Still dreaming, she tries to push back the panels of the oak bed, only to find herself touching the table and the carpet at the Grange: 'my late anguish was swallowed in a paroxysm of despair. I cannot say why I was so wildly wretched ...' Her attempted explanation of this despair, beginning '... supposing at twelve years' old I had been wrenched from the Heights ...', with its associations of exile and longing, recalls the dream she has already recounted in chapter 9, where she imagines herself in heaven, breaking her heart 'with weeping to come back to earth'. The feelings are identical. She tries to conjure up the freedom and atmosphere of Wuthering Heights: 'I'm sure I should be myself were I once among the heather in those hills. Open the window wide ...' Most of this chapter is taken up with the account of Catherine's delirious fantasies – 'she alternatively raves and remains in a half-dream', Nelly Dean tells Dr Kenneth – and her dreams are 'appalling': 'I dread sleeping: my dreams appal me,' she declares. With her dreaming is combined an intense desire to hear and feel once more the cutting north-east wind off the moors. Three times we are confronted with such longings:

> 'Oh, if I were but in my own bed – in the old house!' she went on bitterly, wringing her hands. 'Do let me feel it – it comes straight down the moor – do let me have one breath!'
> To pacify her, I held the casement ajar a few seconds. A cold blast rushed through: I closed it and returned to my post. She lay still now, her face bathed in tears. Exhaustion of spirit had entirely subdued her spirit: and fiery Catherine was no better than a wailing child.

The echo of Lockwood's nightmare is unmistakable, particularly in the final phrase. In the third of these passionate outbursts, Catherine not only recalls the earlier appearances of the image-pattern, but also anticipates its final emergence at the end of the book. Struggling to the window to let in the wind once more, she imagines she sees the old house (we are told both here and in chapter 10 that Wuthering Heights is 'not visible' from the Grange):

> Look! ... that's my room with the candle in it, and the trees swaying before it ... It's a rough journey, and a sad heart to travel it; and we must pass by Gimmerton Kirk, to go that journey! We've braved its ghosts often together, and dared each other to stand among the graves and ask them to come. But Heathcliff, if I dare you now, will you venture? If you do, I'll keep you. I'll not lie there by myself: they may bury me twelve feet deep, and throw the church down over me, but I won't rest till you are with me. I never will!'

And it is because Heathcliff believes that she does indeed 'walk' that he answers her call at last. ... Years later ... exhausted by his self-inflicted fast and spent with watching for her ghost, Heathcliff finally dies in Catherine's oak-panelled bed, where he lay in anguish after Lockwood's dream at the beginning of the novel (which, it should be remembered, refers to a period not long before the date we finally reach at the end of the story). The window is wide open, and it is now his hand, and not that of the wailing child-ghost, that the lattice has grazed: 'his face and throat were washed with rain; the bedclothes dripped, and he was perfectly still. The lattice, flapping to and fro, had grazed the hand that rested on the sill; no blood trickled from the broken skin . . .' [ch. 34].

When we consider the emotional quality of these scenes, and the nature of the obsession which they indicate, it does not seem difficult to understand why, in spite of a tremendous pull the other way, Emily Brontë attempted a final rejection of 'Heathcliff' by constructing a new order from her judicious combination of 'Lintons' and 'Earnshaws'. Passion for sombre earth – which is identified with Heathcliff, and is the same 'earth' for which in her poem, 'I see around me tombstones grey,' Emily Brontë declares she will not exchange the brightest heaven – leads ultimately, it would seem, to the wildness and strangeness of an unhallowed after-life. Obviously no real compromise is possible with this darkly compelling image: its effects are too strong, acting – to use one of the elder Catherine's metaphors – like 'wine in water' and permanently altering the colour of the mind.

The 'wine in water' metaphor occurs in the strange passage leading up to the account of Catherine's dream about heaven in chapter 9. . . . She has just agreed to marry Edgar Linton, but, believing herself to be alone with Nelly Dean and the infant Hareton, she tries to explain her uneasiness about this decision. . . . Nelly Dean, in attempting to elicit from Catherine the real reason for her uneasiness at accepting Edgar, says:

'. . . you will escape from a disorderly, comfortless home into a wealthy, respectable one; and you love Edgar, and Edgar loves you. All seems smooth and easy: where is the obstacle?'

'*Here and here!*' replied Catherine, striking one hand on her forehead, and the other on her breast: 'in whichever place the soul lives. In my soul and in my heart, I'm convinced I'm wrong!'

The abnormality of Catherine's feelings is stressed by Nelly's comment, 'That's very strange! I can't make it out,' and by Catherine's reply, 'It's my secret,' and her statement that she cannot 'explain' it 'distinctly', but will try to give Nelly 'a feeling of how I feel'. The atmosphere becomes increasingly tense as Catherine, about to recount her dream, grows 'sadder and graver'. . . . Finally, a 'dream' is told – but Catherine's mood has changed . . . 'I was only going to say that heaven did not seem to be my home; and I broke my heart with weeping to come back to earth; and the angels were so angry that they flung me out into the middle of the heath on the top of Wuthering Heights; where I woke sobbing for joy.' The emotional ambiguity is emphasised when Catherine adds: 'That will do to explain my secret as well as the other.' What the 'other' dream was, or even what her 'secret' is, we are never really told. The implication is, of course, that the untold dream is too strange, too terrible or too startling to tell, but one must suppose that the substituted dream gives a real clue to its nature. If this is so, the strangeness and the horror seem to accumulate round the idea of Catherine's becoming aware that she is a predestined being – that the deepest bent of her nature announces her destiny, since she cannot even desire heaven or feel that it is her home. Her secret – with its 'consolation' – is that her destiny cannot be separated from Heathcliff's: she will be doing wrong in marrying Edgar because this is an attempted evasion of what is already determined. Whatever Catherine meant, a range of emotions and fearful imaginings is suggested for which frustrated union with a natural affinity is too simple an explanation. There is at least a kind of cosmic outlawry, and perhaps this explains why Heathcliff should sometimes remind us of Byron's Manfred or Cain.[3] . . .

III

The altered emphasis in the second part of the book is apparent at once from the nature imagery, which is one of Emily Brontë's most important pieces of dramatic apparatus. The predominantly sombre nature imagery expressive of the elder Catherine's love for Heathcliff now gives place to the brighter images of summer landscape and summer heather which surround the younger Catherine.[4] The conflict eventually destroying the first Catherine . . . is presented figuratively in a whole series of contrasted alternatives; 'a bleak hilly coal country' or 'a beautiful fertile valley' [ch. 8]; moonbeam or lightning; frost or fire [ch. 9]. Catherine's love for Linton, 'like foliage in the woods: time will change it . . . as winter changes the trees', is set against her love for Heathcliff, which 'resembles the eternal rocks beneath: a source of little visible delight but necesary' [ch. 9]. Again, Heathcliff is 'an unreclaimed creature, without refinement, without cultivation'; and if Isabella Linton marries him it will be like putting a little canary into the park on a winter's day' [ch. 10]. The opposition that these contrasts present to us is a direct one between the extremes of 'storm' and 'calm', between 'Earth' in her dark guise and 'Earth' in her fairer aspect, and the complication arises because Catherine identifies herself with the darker element while allying herself with the fairer one.

The way in which this opposition is modified in the second generation story is perhaps best illustrated by the account of the younger Catherine's quarrel with Linton in chapter 24. Catherine has fallen in love with her young and sickly cousin, Heathcliff's child by Isabella Linton, and she steals away from the 'valley' and Thrushcross Grange in order to be with him as often as she can. But Linton is peevish, irritable and mortally ill, and their relationship is not harmonious [quotes 'One time, however . . . very snappish']. The energetic literary qualities of this passage help to strengthen the point it is trying to make. It is a vivid restatement in fresh terms and with a different emphasis of the conflict expressed in the elder Catherine's dream in chapter 9. Emily Brontë's intention, almost certainly, is that we should recall this dream now when the child of the first Catherine and the child of Heathcliff in their turn discuss ideas of 'heaven's happiness'. It is only one of the many oblique comments that this passage makes on the first generation story that the whole incident should be entirely free from the more troubled feelings that accompany the account of the elder Catherine's dream; the 'quarrel' is a brief one – 'and then we kissed each other, and were friends'. More importantly, the passage shows that whereas for the elder Catherine the bare hard moor is 'heaven's happiness', for her daughter that happiness is identified with a bright animated landscape in which the moors are 'seen at a distance'. Moreover, the brilliant sunlit moors in which Linton lies in his 'ecstasy of peace' have nothing to do with the bleak moors in which his father ran wild when he was young. In fact we now find qualities earlier associated with the 'valley' imposed on the Heights, and *vice versa*. Each quality is modified in transit: 'storm' retains its energy but sheds its destructiveness; 'calm', losing its positive qualities, is a delicious but languorous inactivity (the attitude of the first Lintons to the elder Catherine had involved much more passiveness – 'the honeysuckles embracing the thorn' as Nelly Dean says in chapter 10).

In using this passage as part of her commentary on the first generation story, the author also uses her nature imagery to sharpen and contrast the characters of her two Catherines. The younger Catherine's ideal landscape includes larks, thrushes, blackbirds, linnets and cuckoos, all 'pouring out music on every side'. Her description recalls the delirious fantasies of chapter 12, where her mother, the elder Catherine, tears her pillow in a frenzy, and then pulls out the feathers, arranging them in groups and remembering the creatures to whom they once belonged. It is in keeping with the differences in texture in the two parts of the story that the elder Catherine's birds (she mentions lapwings, moorcocks and wild duck) should not only be more identifiable with a northern, moorland countryside but should also bring with them ideas of violence, vanished childhood, winter and death – ideas which are associated with 'Heathcliff' feelings, and have no comparable urgency in the story of the younger Catherine. The younger Catherine's birds, on the contrary, suggest notions of summer and sunshine and happy vitality.

Determination to prognosticate a brighter future for the new Linton-Earnshaws is revealed in the good-weather imagery lavished on the account of the younger Catherine's childhood and adolescence. One of the earliest Gondal poems, 'Will the day be bright or cloudy', is concerned with weather omens presiding over a child's birth: the poem sketches three alternative kinds of destiny, tranquil, troubled or vitally active, according to the omens, and these alternatives more or less anticipate the differences between Linton and the two Catherines. Now, in her novel, Emily Brontë stresses the fact that for the younger Catherine – and also for Hareton, whom she will marry – the weather omens are favourable. Both children are born in fine weather, the one in spring, the other in the hay-making season. They are both children of love, and it is established that Catherine was conceived in the 'calm' period of Edgar's and the first Catherine's 'deep and growing happiness' before Heathcliff's return (the predominant mood of the six months since their marriage is suggested by Nelly Dean in chapter 10 when she tells Lockwood about Heathcliff's sudden return). Though the second Catherine is 'puny' and unwelcome to begin with (her mother dies in giving birth to her), her first morning is 'bright and cheerful out of doors': and this fine weather lasts throughout the week. There is a resurgence of first generation violence in chapter

17, when the first Catherine is buried on the Friday, and so enters her 'glorious world' of the moors: 'That Friday made the last of our fine days for a month . . . the wind shifted and brought rain first, and then sleet and snow.' This intervening chapter of storm marks Heathcliff's violent emotional reaction to her death and underlines the supernatural element (explained later, in the 'flashback' of chapter 29, when Heathcliff tells Nelly Dean that he was prevented from opening Catherine's coffin by the sense that her spirit was already standing beside him in the darkness). From the beginning of the next chapter [ch. 18], however, when we are led steadily on into the second generation story, all this violence dies away. Spring and summer images indicate the untroubled years of Catherine's childhood in the valley – her first twelve years are described by Nelly Dean as 'the happiest of my life'. In these years she is almost as secure from the troubling associations of Wuthering Heights as a princess in an enchanted castle, and Penistone Crags in the distance are 'golden rocks', even though Nelly Dean had to explain 'that they were bare masses of stone, with hardly enough earth in their clefts to nourish a stunted tree' [ch. 18]. Catherine's sixteenth birthday is 'a beautiful spring day' [quotes from ch. 21, 'She bounded before me . . . content']. On other occasions she climbs trees, 'swinging twenty feet above the ground' and 'lying from dinner to tea in her breeze-rocked cradle', singing. (Much of this reminds us of Ellen Nussey's account of the Brontë girls out on the moors.)

. . . the importance of Hareton's birth is stressed by the break in Nelly Dean's narrative at the end of chapter 7, when she takes up the story again at his birthday in 'the summer of 1778, that is nearly twenty-three years ago', and her next words, placed prominently at the opening of chapter 8, suggest the auspiciousness . . . attending the arrival of this latest member of the ancient Earnshaw family:

> On the morning of a fine Sunday, my first bonny nursling, and the last of the Earnshaw stock was born. We were busy with the hay in a far-away field, and the girl that usually brought out breakfasts came running out an hour too soon, across the meadow and up the lane, calling as she ran: 'Oh, such a grand bairn,' she panted out. 'The finest lad that ever breathed. . .'

And in almost all the scenes in which Hareton appears in the second generation story his connection with the fertile earth and gentleness with living things are kept before our eyes. Nelly Dean, seeing him for the first time after his many years with Heathcliff (in ch. 18), detects 'evidence of a wealthy soil, that might yield luxuriant crops under other and favourable circumstances'.

. . . the characters in the second generation story have to contend with Heathcliff's animosity, but their 'dark' scenes of conflict are quite unlike those of the first generation story. In the earlier part of the book storm images establish the prevailing emotional atmosphere. . . . There is no comparable 'stormy' weather in the later story: the 'dark' scenes are not so much different in degree as in kind, their final effect no more sombre than clouds passing over a sunny landscape, an idea suggested more than once by Nelly Dean's descriptions of the second Catherine.

What, then, becomes of the storm-centre, Heathcliff himself, in this second half of the book? Our attention is turned to him once more when he traps Catherine into staying at Wuthering Heights. . . . He inveigles Catherine into the marriage with Linton, he prevents her from joining her dying father, he makes her nurse the mortally sick Linton unaided, he secures her property once Linton is dead, he treats her with systematic harshness. Yet this behaviour seems hardly more sinister than a stage villain's. The strongest emotion Heathcliff arouses throughout the greater part of the later narrative is a kind of angry exasperation at his injustice. He is still capable of making ferocious remarks:

> . . . what a savage feeling I have to anything that seems afraid of me! Had I been born where laws are less strict and tastes less dainty, I should treat myself to a slow vivisection of those two, as an evening's amusement. . .

but this lacks the resonance of such passionate outbursts as his speech to 'Cathy' before her death [quotes from ch. 15, 'You deserve this . . . in the grave']. Angry exasperation is an emotion on too small a scale to suit this earlier Heathcliff. On the other hand, the portrayal of Heathcliff still communicates the kind of sympathy which makes the earlier story so remarkable – it is a story, after all, which not only depicts the 'heroine' and the 'villain' falling in love with each other, but describes their passion with a sympathetic power so intense that it makes nonsense of the more usual responses to such a situation and upsets conventional value judgements. This sympathy is now partly suggested through Nelly Dean – whose function for Heathcliff is rather more than that of *confidante* – and partly through such mitigating circumstances as Hareton's persistent love for him, a feeling that is not unreturned (we also remember that Heathcliff saved Hareton's life in ch. 9). Again, the bad effect on us of Heathcliff's callousness to his son is complicated by the fact that Linton is a sorry mixture of peevishness and irritability. . . .

But at the very point where his need for vengeance dies, Heathcliff does in fact fully revive . . . as the powerfully compelling and complex figure of the first part of the story. Hitherto, in the second half of the book, Emily Brontë has concentrated on her 'calm' figures, who represent alternatives to Heathcliff and to everything that he stands for, and as long as she makes him serve as a foil to these figures he is merely their vindictive enemy. But when she turns to look directly and exclusively at him again, we see and feel what we saw and felt earlier. . . . This happens with the monologue she gives him late in the story (in ch. 29), when he tells Nelly Dean about his two attempts to open the first Catherine's coffin – once on the night of her funeral, and a second time, successfully, when – years later – Edgar's grave is being prepared beside hers, and, with the help of the sexton, he at last sees her dead face ('It is hers still'). As he watches the growing alliance between the second Catherine and Hareton (the latter resembling the first Catherine in appearance more and more, 'because his senses were alert, and his mental faculties wakened to unwanted activity'), Heathcliff senses the 'strange change approaching', and in another outburst to Nelly Dean, in chapter 33, he resumes much of the intensity and passion of his earlier appearances:

> . . . In every cloud, in every tree – filling the air at night, and caught by glimpses in every object by day – I am surrounded with her image! The most ordinary faces of men and wmen – my own features – mock me with a resemblance. The entire world is a dreadful collection of memoranda that she did exist, and that I have lost her! Well, Hareton's aspect was the ghost of my immortal love; of my wild endeavours to hold my right, my degradation, my pride, my happiness and my anguish —.

Later still, when the tale is nearly at its end and Catherine's ghost seems to walk once more, the old feelings are fully revived, the obsessional pattern of *motifs* reappears, and Nelly Dean, finding Heathcliff lying motionless and soaking wet in the oak bed, his eyes staring, his wrist grazed by the open lattice, cries, 'I could not think him dead', and tries 'to extinguish, if possible, that frightful life-like gaze of exultation'.

It is now that the first of the story's two 'arcs' approaches its final point of rest. It reaches this point, moreover, at the same moment that the second generation story is coming to its own conclusion, and this 'coincidence' draws attention to ambiguities in the attempted resolution of conflict . . . within the space of a single page, we turn from the phantoms of Heathcliff and the elder Catherine restlessly walking the Heights in rain and thunder . . . to contemplate those other 'ramblers' on the moors, Hareton and the younger Catherine, who halt on the threshold of the old house to take 'a last look at the moon – or, more correctly, at each other by her light'. The closing passage of the book might suggest to an unwary reader that the final victory is to them. It is possible to mistake this last comment of Lockwood's, indicating 'calm' after 'storm', for a statement of calm's ultimate triumph. But such a reading overlooks the departure of Hareton and the younger Catherine to the valley, and their abandonment of the old house to the spirits of the still restless Heathcliff and the elder Catherine. There is, after all, no escaping the compulsive emotional charge identified with Heathcliff; there can only be an intellectual judgement that for the purposes of ordinary life he will not do. It is the artist's business, Tchekov tells us, to set questions, not solve them. . . . It is an indication of the urgency of internal conflict that the tones of an authorial voice can be heard even through the controlled 'oblique and indirect view' of Catherine's and Heathcliff's fated alliance. The tones are those of someone aware that conflicting claims remain unreconciled, and that though moral judgement might desire otherwise no ultimate closure is possible.

SOURCE: *Essays in Criticism* (1958).

NOTES

1. See Introduction, p. 29 above.
2. For example, in her letters of September to December 1848 and in her letter to Miss Wooler, 30 January 1846 (*Life and Letters*, II, 76).
3. And perhaps also why Albert Camus finds it possible to discuss Heathcliff's passion for Catherine in the same context as Ivan Karamazov's 'metaphysical rebellion' in *L'Homme revolté* (1951) ch. 1. On the differences between Heathcliff and the Byronic hero, see Jacques Blondel's discussion (p. 160 above).
4. Jacques Blondel also notes in his comments on this part of the essay the importance of Emily Brontë's use of the adjective 'mellow' ('Emily Brontë, récentes explorations', in *Études anglaises*, XI (1958), p. 328 n).

Mary Visick The Genesis of *Wuthering Heights* (1958)

. . . It is well known that Emily Brontë lived a great part of her adult life with a dream-world which she constructed with her sister Anne and called Gondal. They peopled it with wild and elemental characters whose stories they recorded in a series of prose 'books', which have not survived (they may have been destroyed by Charlotte or by her husband, by Emily herself or by Anne after Emily's death). The complications of the Gondal references occasionally make Emily Brontë's poetry appear freakish and even childish; but, tempting though it is to see in her work a progressive emancipation from Gondal, it remains true that the fantasy produced some beautifully wrought poetry, much of which, recording as it does lyric moments in the Gondal saga, can be valued for its own sake. Such are the exquisite double lyric which Charlotte called 'The Two Children', the famous lament 'Cold in the Earth', and 'The Prisoner'. Emily Brontë is not justly estimated if she is known only as the author of half a dozen familiar pieces; her collected poems reveal her as a fine craftsman, and each poem is 'made' with deliberation. . . .

Miss Fannie E. Ratchford has assembled nearly all Emily Brontë's poems, including those to which the author gave no specific Gondal context, into a consecutive narrative which she has called *Gondal's Queen* [1955]. . . . Miss Ratchford has most ingeniously compelled the poems to tell a story, but the story they tell will not bear much scrutiny. . . . Nevertheless, the material assembled in *Gondal's Queen* comes to have a different significance if we can see in it a starting point for *Wuthering Heights*. For if the novel is a reworking of Gondal we find ourselves watching the creative imagination in the act not of scrapping but of totally re-forming the material on which it has so far worked. To say this, of course, is not to deny the independent value of the poems, especially, but not exclusively, those which their author did not relate to the Gondal saga.

That *Wuthering Heights* is an extraordinarily powerful achievement is hardly to be questioned. . . . It is the work of a poet who wants to write a novel. The wildly un-naturalistic theme of a woman who betrays her deepest self and so destroys herself, and of a man who in his turn dies simply for love of her, is not played down or apologised for, or explained away; rather, it is reinforced by a sane narrator, Nelly Dean, and a commonplace listener, Lockwood. It commands assent of the kind we accord to tragedy. It is a commonplace to call it 'poetic' but the judgement is sometimes qualified by expressions of doubt whether it is a novel at all – Dr Leavis has called it 'a kind of sport'.[1] But if an ear for the actual speech of men and women, an eye for personal idiosyncrasy and a power to present the slow unconscious growth of complex interrelationships between people, and between them and their environment, be the gifts of a novelist, Emily Brontë was surely a novelist . . . one example out of many, the scene of Heathcliff's return to Thrushcross Grange, his ecstatic welcome by Catherine and her husband's lack of enthusiasm, will illustrate the solidity and economy we associate with the greatest novelists. Heathcliff is speaking:

> 'You were really sorry for me, were you? Well, there was cause. I've fought through a bitter life since I last heard your voice; and you must forgive me, for I struggled only for you.'
>
> 'Catherine, unless we are to have cold tea, please to come to the table,' interrupted Linton, striving to preserve his ordinary tone, and a due measure of politeness. 'Mr Heathcliff will have a long walk, wherever he may lodge tonight; and I'm thirsty.' [ch. 10]

It is in such settings, and in contrast to the cadences of ordinary speech, that the great lyric outbursts of Heathcliff and Catherine are to be read. We cannot think that Emily Brontë did not know what she was doing when she lifted their speech to the level of poetry, as in Catherine's confession to Nelly, or in the last interview between her and Heathcliff. . . .

While she was at work on *Wuthering Heights* Emily Brontë wrote the poem which has been wrongly taken as a death-bed utterance, 'No coward soul is mine. . .':[2]

> . . . O God within my breast
> Almighty ever-present Deity
> Life, that in me hast rest
> As I Undying Life, have power in Thee. . .
>
> Though Earth and moon were gone
> And suns and universes ceased to be
> And thou wert left alone
> Every Existence would exist in thee. . .

Catherine Earnshaw says of Heathcliff:

'I cannot express it; but surely you and everybody have a notion that there is or should be an existence of yours beyond you. What were the use of my creation, if I were entirely contained here? My great miseries in the world have been Heathcliff's miseries, and I watched and felt each from the beginning: my great thought in living is himself. If all else perished and *he* remained, I should still continue to be; and if all else remained, and he were annihilated, the universe would turn to a mighty stranger: I should not seem a part of it . . . Nelly, I *am* Heathcliff! He's always, always in my mind: not as a pleasure, any more than I am always a pleasure to myself, but as my own being . . . [ch. 9]

If we set these two passages side by side we see what *Wuthering Heights* is 'about'. Catherine betrays what amounts to a mystical vocation, for social position and romantic love. But the betrayal is not the end. Catherine's daughter marries Heathcliff's son; but he, a child of hate, is not a fit match for her, and after his death she turns to the rightful heir (the Victorian cliché comes to life here) her cousin Hareton, whom Heathcliff has disinherited and degraded. In their marriage, life, simple and normal, reasserts itself after the moral storm of Heathcliff's career. He at last, in his lust for revenge, has become a skinflint and a bully; the loss of Catherine has laid his life waste ('Oh, God! would *you* like to live with your soul in the grave?' he had cried to her), until, watching for her ghost, seeming at last to see her, he dies. By now the gentle, patient Edgar is dead too; but it is not he but Heathcliff who 'walks' with Catherine. Yet, if no easy moral judgements are made, the book is not 'amoral'. In it two moral worlds grapple – the Heights and the Grange. In the end, Wuthering Heights is left to its ghosts: Hareton, who is a child of the Heights and Cathy, who is of the valley and yet has something of her mother still, choose to live at Thrushcross Grange. Neither world is victorious over the other.

To investigate the origins of this amazing novel is a critical task worth undertaking. These origins may be found quite specifically in the Gondal poems. Emily Brontë's earliest dated poem was written towards the end of her eighteenth year; by February 1844, when she was nearly twenty-six, she had accumulated enough poetry to begin transcribing it into two manuscript books, which presumably contain all she wished to preserve. Fortunately other manuscripts have survived. . . . Of the two transcript books one bears simply her initials and the date; the other is headed *Gondal Poems*. Of the 151 fully finished poems in Mr Hatfield's edition,[3] these two books account for seventy-six. There is a third manuscript book, now in the British Museum, and there are also three collections of loose sheets, in the hands of various collectors; but neither the third book nor the sheets contains any poem dated later than February 1844. The two transcript books, then, superseded them. The books escaped the holocaust which consumed all the Gondal prose, and were obviously prepared with great care – whether for publication or not it is impossible to say. The story they can be shown to tell is the story of *Wuthering Heights*. . . . Emily Brontë seems to have been a methodical worker. The verse dates back some years. A note written by Anne Brontë in July 1845 says that she and her sister began writing the (presumably prose) Gondal Chronicles 'three and a half years ago';[4] but some of the poems are dated much earlier. The birthday notes written by Emily and Anne in 1845, exchanged, and intended to be opened on Emily's birthday in 1848, suggest that the prose chronicles related to a later generation of Gondalians than that of the chief characters of the verse, the heroes and heroines of *Gondal's Queen* and also, I believe, recognizably the chief characters of *Wuthering Heights*: probably the people belonging to this older generation were evolved in the early stages of the Gondal game, and matured in their creator's mind. If, in 1845, the current Gondal prose might be regarded as an account of contemporary Gondal, the people of the poems were historical figures out of a stormier past. The main action of *Wuthering Heights* takes place in the past – about the year 1775 and onwards. It is in fact a historical novel.

A clue to the Gondal story, then, might be found in the order in which Emily Brontë arranged the poems in her Gondal Poems manuscript. Poems written before 1844 are copied in their sequence in the Gondal story. For poems written after April 1844, however, the order is roughly chronological, as if she copied them in as they were written without regard for their place in the Gondal story. . . .

The first seventeen poems in the manuscript fall into five sections each referring to an episode in the life of the heroine, Augusta Geraldine Almeda or Rosina. Miss Ratchford thinks these are two names for the same heroine, Miss Laura Hinkley thinks they are in fact two people.[5] This sounds like a fundamental and violent difference; but it is unimportant when we are considering the relationship between Gondal and *Wuthering Heights*, since if they were indeed two their personalities coalesced in the figure of Catherine Earnshaw.

Emily Brontë usually refers to the heroine as 'A.G.A.', which is a useful abbreviation for a somewhat cumbersome name. A.G.A.–Rosina, then, has four lovers. The first is Alexander, Lord of Elbë, to whom the first two poems refer. He is killed in battle. An early figure in the saga, he contributes nothing to the *Wuthering Heights* theme, and has no particular interest. . . . The next six poems relate to Lord Alfred of Aspin Castle, another lover of A.G.A. He looks like a prototype of Edgar Linton; and the poems show that the original story of his relationship with the heroine was altered, becoming more like that of Catherine and Edgar in *Wuthering Heights.* This point will be developed later. The third group, of four poems, refers to a political assassination; it is not clear whether the 'sovereign' who has been murdered is a man or a woman, but Miss Ratchford's earlier reconstruction identified him with one Julius Brenzaida, another of A.G.A.'s lovers, who, though apparently of obscure birth, rose to be emperor of Gondal. The poem 'Rosina', which seems to belong to this group, certainly refers to the murder of Julius. The fourth group obviously preceded the third, since it concerns a relationship between Julius and a girl called Geraldine; and the fifth concerns yet another lover, Fernando de Samara, who was driven to suicide by A.G.A. and in whose reproaches we can catch a note of Heathcliff. Thus each group is defined but the groups are not in sequence in the story. It is as if already in 1844 Emily Brontë was dissecting the Gondal story, seeing it as isolated episodes. Possibly she was already considering the regrouping of the episodes into another story, which in the end led her beyond Gondal to the novel.

After these sets of poems come three which have a rather obscure relation to the main story. Then the twenty-first and twenty-third refer to the death of the heroine A.G.A. This brings us to the point at which Emily Brontë caught up with herself in transcribing; from now on most of the poems bear dates which suggest that they were copied into the transcript book as soon as, or soon after, they were written. Two concern Julius, of which one is Rosina's lament 'Cold in the earth, and the deep snow piled above thee . . . ' which has struck many readers as prefiguring the eighteen years of Heathcliff's mourning for Catherine. However, another poem which also occurs late in the manuscript is even closer in verbal expression to Heathcliff; and here, as in 'No coward soul . . .', the reference is not to ordinary human love but to some other order of experience. It is a long Gondal narrative of which some self-contained stanzas were published in the 1846 volume as 'The Prisoner, a fragment':

> Then dawns the Invisible, the Unseen its truth reveals;
> My outward sense is gone; my inward essence feels—
> Its wings are almost free, its home, its harbour found;
> Measuring the gulf it stoops and dares the final bound!
>
> Oh, dreadful is the check – intense the agony
> When the ear begins to hear, and the eye begins to see;
> When the pulse begins to throb, the brain to think again,
> The soul to feel the flesh, and the flesh to feel the chain.[6]

In *Wuthering Heights* Heathcliff's dead love, or rather the sense of her presence, is at the core of the invisible world he cannot reach:

> I have neither a fear, nor a presentiment, nor a hope of death. Why should I? With my hard constitution and temperate mode of living, and unperilous occupation, I ought to, and probably *shall* remain above ground, till there is scarcely a black hair on my head – And yet I cannot continue in this condition! I have to remind myself to breathe – almost to remind my heart to beat! And it is like bending back a stiff spring: it is by compulsion that I do the slightest act not prompted by one thought, and by compulsion that I notice anything alive or dead, which is not associated with one universal idea. I have a single wish, and my whole being and faculties are yearning to attain it. They have yearned towards it so long, and so unwavering, that I'm convinced it *will* be reached – and soon – because it has devoured my existence: I am swallowed up in the anticipation of its fulfilment . . . O, God! It is a long fight, I wish it were over! [ch. 33].

Here is another indication that the love between Catherine and Heathcliff is Emily Brontë's way of giving expression to some all-devouring spiritual experience.

Among several other themes in Gondal Poems, many of which are undeveloped and may or may not have any relation to the novel, we find one emerging as a well-marked interest towards the end of the manuscript. The figures in the foreground are two children, a dark boy and a fair and happy girl, who seem to belong to a different generation. The former is to be found in several very early Gondal poems, but by 1845 he is becoming rather like Hareton Earnshaw, and the girl is beginning to look like Cathy Linton.

In two poems grouped together by Charlotte Brontë in her edition of 1850, and which she called 'The Two Children' it is possible that the second generation theme of *Wuthering Heights* is beginning to appear. This statement assumes that Emily Brontë intended the two poems to be read as one, for which there is some evidence. The first has a Gondal heading, 'A. E. and R. C.' and the date 28 May 1845. The second poem has no heading and no date. It is rare for Emily Brontë not to date a poem, and from the two sets of initials we might expect to find two characters in the poems; but there is only one in the first. It seems safe to assume, then, that A. E. is the boy and R. C. the girl. This double poem is certainly one of the loveliest of Emily Brontë's lyrics – a too-little-known Song of Innocence:

Heavy hangs the raindrop
From the burdened spray;
Heavy broods the damp mist
On uplands far away;

Heavy looms the dull sky,
Heavy rolls the sea—
And heavy beats the young heart
Beneath that lonely tree.

Never has a blue streak
Cleft the clouds since morn—
Never has his grim Fate
Smiled since he was born.

Frowning on the infant,
Shadowing childhood's joy,
Guardian angel knows not
That melancholy boy.

Day is pasing swiftly
Its sad and sombre prime;
Youth is fast invading
Sterner manhood's time.

All the flowers are praying
For sun before they close,
And he prays too, unknowing,
That sunless human rose!

Blossoms, that the west wind
Has never wooed to blow,
Scentless are your petals,
Your dew as cold as snow.

Soul, where kindred kindness
No early promise woke,
Barren is your beauty
As weeds upon the rock.

Wither, brothers, wither,
You were vainly given—
Earth reserves no lessing
For the unblessed of Heaven!

Child of Delight! with sunbright hair,
And seablue, seadeep eyes;
Spirit of Bliss, what brings thee here,
Beneath these sullen skies?

Thou should'st live in eternal spring,
Where endless day is never dim;
Why, seraph, has thy erring wing
Borne thee down to weep with him?

'Ah, not from heaven am I descended,
And I do not come to mingle tears;
But sweet is day, though with shadows blended;
And, though clouded, sweet are youthful years.

'I, the image of light and gladness
Saw and pitied that mournful boy,
And I swore to take his gloomy sadness,
And give to him my beamy joy.

'Heavy and dark the night is closing;
Heavy and dark may its biding be:
Better for all from grief reposing,
And better for all who watch like me.

'Guardian angel he lacks no longer;
Evil fortune he needs not fear:
Fate is strong, but Love is stronger;
And more unsleeping than angel's care.'

Another poem, written much earlier – in May 1842 – is placed nearly next to 'The Two Children' in the manuscript and, like it, is concerned with a dark boy and fair girl:

In the same place, when Nature wore
The same celestial glow,
I'm sure I've seen those forms before
But many springs ago;

And only *he* had locks of light,
And *she* had raven hair;
While now, his curls are dark as night,
And hers as morning fair . . .

The place of this poem is obscure; but the older generation sound like Edgar and Catherine, and the children might well foreshadow

Hareton and Cathy. It is interesting to see Emily Brontë working out that relation between inner self and personal appearance which is so important in *Wuthering Heights*.

Thus we may summarise the parts of the Gondal story which concern A.G.A. After the death of Alexander Elbë the heroine is associated with three men, one of whom, Julius Brenzaida, emperor of Gondal, is murdered, leaving her to lament him through 'fifteen wild Decembers'. At some period in her career she has deserted him for the gentle, fair-haired Lord Alfred (whose fate will be discussed later). She is also loved by the guitar-player Fernando de Samara, who commits suicide. After her death a dark boy is rescued from some kind of misery by a fair girl.

In the unfolding story of Lord Alfred of Aspin Castle as it is told in Gondal Poems I believe we can see a significant modification of both the Gondal people and the story – a change which entails a much deeper scrutiny of the motives of the characters than is usual in Gondal and which also brings the Gondal plot much closer to that of the novel. Other Gondal poems not in the transcript book help to make the stages of this revision clear. ... We find ... the following poems, in the order in which they are placed in Gondal Poems; the numbers are those given the poems by Mr Hatfield in his edition:

I. No. 137. A.G.A. To A.S. 6 May 1840
28 July 1843

Here the heroine expresses her happiness in the love of Alfred, for whom she feels something like veneration [*quotes* 'At such a time in such a spot. ...]. This recalls Catherine in the first days of her marriage in the summer world of Thrushcross Grange – 'almost over-fond' of Edgar. Again, the mainspring of Edgar's character is a gentle, firm Christianity, at the opposite pole from the hell-fire cant of old Joseph: ineffectual against Heathcliff and Catherine, but none the less real. He might well have developed from the Alfred of this poem. It would seem that the mood of this poem, highly uncharacteristic of A.G.A., is shattered by the appearance of another lover, who is to Lord Alfred as the sun is to the moon.

II. No. 110. To A.G.A.

This poem is undated. In it someone taxes A.G.A. with unfaithfulness and she replies that 'morning ... and ardent noon' have destroyed her 'moon of life' [quotes 'Thou standest in the greenwood now . . .'].

III. No. 169. A.G.A. To A.S., is a farewell, penitent but irrevocable, to the gentle lover she is deserting. Its date is 2 March 1844 [quotes 'This summer wind with thee and me . . .'].

IV. No. 61. A.G.A. To A.S. 20 March 1838

In this much earlier poem, A.G.A. laments not her desertion but the death of her lover. . . . The poem suggests the same gentle personality in the same summery setting as the first of the Lord Alfred poems. . . .

V. No. 100. A.G.A. To the Bluebell. 9 May 1839

Miss Ratchford takes this to be a lament for a child; but there seems no reason why, coming where it does in the manuscript, it should not refer to Lord Alfred [quotes 'Sacred watcher, wave thy bells! . . .'].

VI. No. 154. Written in Aspin Castle. There are two dates at the head of this long semi-narrative poem: 20 August 1842 and 6 February 1843.

It would seem that the ghost of Lord Alfred 'walks' unquietly: that he died far away and in despair; and that the heroine of the saga in some way destroyed him. This poem may thus be taken to refer to the desertion of A.G.A.'s 'moon of life'. In passing, we may notice that a portrait of Lord Alfred is described, and it sounds not unlike the portrait of Edgar which Nelly shows Lockwood in *Wuthering Heights*.

While it is not certain that all these poems refer to Lord Alfred it is clear that they all refer to some gentle, fair character, the prototype of Edgar Linton. It seems that as late as May 1839 the Gondal story included the death of this character simply; the more intricate situation in which A.G.A. forsakes him for another man is worked out by 1842; Emily Brontë was in Brussels this year, away from Anne with whom she planned new stories. Perhaps it was a time for meditating on past Gondal games and even modifying the story. The undated poem 'Thou standest in the greenwood now . . .' contains a hint of the kind of contrast which is drawn in *Wuthering Heights* between Heathcliff and Linton. In her confession to Nelly, Catherine says:

I've no more business to marry Edgar Linton than I have to be in heaven ... It would degrade me to marry Heathcliff now; so he shall never know how I love him: and that, not because he's handsome, Nelly, but because he's more myself than I am. Whatever our souls are made of, his and mine are the same; and Linton's is as different as a moonbeam from lightning, or frost from fire. [ch. 9]

The mention of heaven here, and its association with Linton, seems a link with the cruder personality of the Gondal man as we see it in the poem 'At such a time, in such a spot. ...'; but the main point is the use of natural imagery to point the contrast. The stanzas about the 'cloudless moon' and the bright day, which suggest two kinds of love, appear only in the later draft of the poem, the one which was copied into Gondal Poems. It seems as if some new experience is being worked into the story of A.G.A. and Alfred. ...

As for the sunlike lover, Miss Ratchford argues convincingly that he is Julius Brenzaida, the low-born emperor of Gondal. Julius wins power by violence and treachery; so Heathcliff deliberately corrupts Hindley, gets possession of the Heights, possibly murders him, or at least does not encourage him to live, traps Isabella and later Cathy, ruthlessly exploits his own son, and so becomes master of the fate of all the people round him. Julius, like him, is vivid, unscrupulous and violent.

Gondal Poems also contains two songs 'by Julius Brenzaida' addressed to 'Geraldine': the first is a kind of serenade, in which he recalls to her the moors where they have once been happy:

Wild the road, and rough and dreary;
Barren all the moorland round;
Rude the couch that rests us weary;
Mossy stone and heathy ground.

But, when winter storms were meeting
In the moonless, midnight dome,
Did we heed the tempest's beating,
Howling round our spirits' home?

No; that tree with branches riven,
Whitening in the whirl of snow,
As it tossed against the heaven,
Sheltered happy hearts below ...[7]

There is no need to labour the parallel; in October 1838 the two figures who were to become Heathcliff and Catherine in their childhood at the Heights were already sketched out in Emily

Brontë's mind. And the second 'Song', of the same date, shows how the story was shaping:

> I knew not 'twas so dire a crime
> To say the word, Adieu;
> But this shall be the only time
> My slighted heart shall sue.
>
> The wild moorside, the winter morn,
> The gnarled and ancient tree —
> If in your breast they waken scorn,
> Shall wake the same in me. . . .'

Miss Ratchford's reconstruction, in which the heroine first loves Julius, then abandons him for various lovers the last of whom is Lord Alfred, and finally leaves Alfred and returns to him, seems justified, among other reasons, because it is a sketch of the relations between Catherine, Heathcliff and Edgar in the first part of *Wuthering Heights*.

The actual process by which this blurred story, revealed as it is in a series of lyric moments, was transformed into the novel is one at which we can only guess. It is instructive enough to set the two side by side. In Gondal, the uncomplicated heroine can go from one man to another with few words of apology – often trite enough: but for Catherine Earnshaw the betrayal of Heathcliff sets her inevitably on the road that ends in virtual self-destruction, and yet she cannot spiritually desert Edgar without remorse. That she does so desert him there is no doubt.

> 'Ah! you are come, are you, Edgar Linton?' she said with angry animation . . . 'You are one of those things that are ever found when least wanted, and when you are wanted, never! I suppose we shall have plenty of lamentations now – I see we shall – but they can't keep me from my narrow home out yonder: my resting-place, where I'm bound before spring is over! There it is: not among the Lintons, mind, under the chapel-roof, but in the open air, with a headstone; and you may please yourself, whether you go to them or come to me!'
>
> 'Catherine, what have you done?' commenced the master. 'Am I nothing to you any more? Do you love that wretch Heath —'
>
> 'Hush!' cried Mrs Linton. 'Hush, this moment! You mention that name and I end the matter instantly, by a spring from the window! What you touch at present you may have; but my soul will be on that hill-top before you lay hands on me again. I don't want you, Edgar: I'm past wanting you. Return to your books. I'm glad you possess a consolation, for all you had in me is gone.' [ch.12]

She is delirious here, of course, and in her convalescence she tries her best to be kind to him; but it is clear that he is cut out of her life. There are no such hesitations, as far as one can see, in A.G.A.'s behaviour. For her, the autonomy of passion is enough. Gondal, by its very absence of social constraints, is too constricting a setting for the passions of its heroes; Emily Brontë needs the actuality of the novelist's world. So she reduces Gondal into Yorkshire, and transforms an infantile dream into an adult novel. The farm kitchen with its great fire, its white sanded floor, the dressers with their 'gaudily-painted canisters', the battered works of evangelical piety which the children are condemned to read on Sundays, the roast goose and apple sauce at Christmas, Joseph counting out his market-gains using his Bible as a convenient flat surface, Nelly's repertory of ballads and folk-songs, the carving-knife Hindley holds at her mouth in his drunken madness – all these things have a kind of individual solidity. The isolated splendours of Thrushcross Grange, as the two ragamuffins from the Heights see it, brings before our eyes the more familiar world of the eighteenth-century country house:

> . . . we saw – ah! it was beautiful – a splendid place carpeted with crimson, and crimson-covered chairs and tables, and a pure white ceiling bordered by gold, a shower of glass-drops hanging in silver chains from the centre, and shimmering with little soft tapers. [ch. 6]

Wuthering Heights has often been called 'timeless'; but its tragic poetry is set deep in eighteenth-century Yorkshire. It has been called a wild, chaotic book; but the passions of Catherine and Heathcliff dash themselves against the unperceptive common sense and the long-suffering kindness of Nelly Dean, and the whole story as Nelly tells it is thrust against the bogus posturings and trite *idées reçues* of Lockwood, who spends his summers 'at the sea-coast' and assumes a saturnine pose and a capacity for hopeless passion which is soon set off by the reality of Heathcliff's brutality and of his love. . . . Their ordinary and commonplace views of the central tragedy serve to make it more credible. It is amazing to realize that Emily Brontë, who could write so unselfconsciously in 1845 about the Gondal people who she and Anne 'were' on their journey,[8] should so have understood, and forestalled, criticism of her material. Knowing, by some experience of her own, the truth of the inward story she had to tell, she took pains to make it at every point credible in novel-terms. For example, Gondal abounds in ghosts: the unforgettable wraith of

Catherine Linton besets Lockwood in a dream, and we may if we so wish write it off. At the end a little boy driving sheep on the moors sees 'Heathcliff and a woman, younder, under t' Nab'; but Nelly puts this down to the foolish talk of the child's elders, and so may we. If Emily Brontë fed her imagination on German horror stories[9] she nevertheless knew that she must not tax her readers' credulity in the wrong places. Again, as C. P. Sanger's classic essay 'The Structure of *Wuthering Heights*' demonstrates, the framework of the novel, the legal, genealogical and chronological machinery of the plot, is unshakeably established.[10]

That her story had its rise in some personal experience seems most likely. When speaking of such a writer, whose outer life looks both meagre and satisfactory (kneading the Parsonage bread with her German grammar stuck up over the trough,[11] picking fruit, feeding the animals), and whose inner life is revealed only in hints and glimpses, we are not likely to put a crude interpretation on the word 'experience'. What is recorded in the central stanzas of 'The Prisoner' is clearly as real as anything that could happen to the outward form of 't' Parson's Emily'. The god whom she addresses in her poems is a creedless, immortal energy. Presumably the parson's daughter paid her formal respects to Christianity, but the mystical experiences of this sense of infinity and immortality are not, in her poetry, couched in Christian terms or given Christian explanations. She sought to find expression for them not through orthodox religion, but through the fantasy of Gondal. We have seen how closely Catherine's expression of her identity with Heathcliff echoes 'No coward soul...' and that Heathcliff's longing for Catherine is like the Prisoner's agony as she is dragged back to the life of the senses. Somewhere in this realm of her consciousness there was formed some kind of experience of the strife between night and day between the cool and gentle and the hot and vital.

There are at least three attempts to express this strife in words. Two try to express it in terms of human personalities clashing; she is feeling her way towards it in the modifications of the Lord Alfred story in Gondal and she sets it out at length in *Wuthering Heights*. The third attempt is in a poem written in 1845 and called, in the 1846 volume, 'Stars'. Its relation to Gondal suggests that it is more than a 'nature-lyric', that it is in fact a developed symbol for destructive vitality. The visonary may seek out the night, but inevitably morning comes. So Catherine may seek out the soul of Edgar, which she compares to moonlight and frost, but she cannot escape the lightning and fire of Heathcliff. Let us not commit the crudity of looking in Emily Brontë's biography for some kind of emotional upheaval: the poem is self-consistent and self-explanatory, and incidentally it utters a warning to any critic who would draw an absolute dividing line between the Gondal and the non-Gondal verse. The poet herself copied it into the non-Gondal volume, but perhaps she could not have written it were it not for the preliminary sketches of the theme ('I gazed upon the cloudless moon . . .' and so on), which belong to Gondal. Only through the Gondal people, perhaps, could Emily Brontë realize her vision, but 'Stars' is emancipated from Gondal:

Ah! why, because the dazzling sun
Restored my earth to joy
Have you departed, every one,
And left a desert sky?'

All through the night, your glorious eyes
Were gazing down in mine,
And with a full heart's thankful sighs
I blessed that watch divine!

I was at peace, and drank your beams
As they were life to me
And revelled in my changeful dreams
Like petrel on the sea.

Thought followed thought – star followed star
Through boundless regions on,
While one sweet influence, near and far,
Thrilled through and made us one.

Why did the morning rise to break
So great, so pure a spell,
And scorch with fire and tranquil cheek
Where your cool radiance fell?

Blood-red he rose, and arrow-straight
His fierce beams struck my brow:
The soul of Nature sprang elate,
But mine sank sad and low!

My lids closed down – yet through their veil
I saw him blazing still;
And bathe in gold the misty dale,
And flash upon the hill.

I turned me to the pillow then
To call back Night, and see
Your worlds of solemn light, again
Throb with my heart and me!

It would not do – the pillow glowed
And glowed both roof and floor,
And birds sang loudly in the wood,
And fresh winds shook the door.

The curtains waved, the wakened flies
Were murmuring round my room,
Imprisoned there, till I should rise
And give them leave to roam.

O Stars and Dreams and Gentle Night;
O Night and Stars return!
And hide me from the hostile light
That does not warm, but burn —

That drains the blood of suffering men;
Drinks tears, instead of dew:
Let me sleep through his blinding reign,
And only wake with you![12]

Miss Ratchford takes this as a straight Gondal monologue; but its author did not call it a Gondal poem. It is indeed, like the central stanzas of 'The Prisoner', a poem which suggests that Gondal had served its purpose. The poet no longer needs to wear the mask of A.G.A., and nowhere does that passionate but uncomplicated young woman speak with the voice of this poem. It is the quintessence of the Gondal situation, but, paradoxically, once she had grasped the means of expressing it Emily Brontë ceased to need the Gondal people. For the most part they disappeared, but the moments in which they lived most intensely were regrouped, and out of the regrouping rose *Wuthering Heights*, in which the central Gondal people themselves were reborn as Catherine, Heathcliff and Edgar, Cathy, Hareton and Isabella.

SOURCE: *The Genesis of Wuthering Heights* (1958).

NOTES

1. *The Great Tradition* (1948), p. 27.
2. See above, p. 68n.
3. *The Complete Poems of Emily Jane Brontë*, ed. C. W. Hatfield (New York and London, 1941).

4. Anne's diary-paper, 31 July 1845, *Life and Letters*, Shakespeare Head Brontë, II, 52–3.
5. In *The Brontës: Charlotte and Emily* (New York, 1945).
6. For details of this poem, see above p. 108n.
7. This and the following 'song' are dated 17 October 1838: see *Poems*, ed. Hatfield, pp. 82–3.
8. Emily's diary-paper, 30 July 1845, 'Anne and I went our first long journey by ourselves together, leaving home on the 30th June, Monday, sleeping at York, returning to Keighley Tuesday evening . . . during our excursion we were, Ronald Macalgin, Henry Angora, Juliet Angusteena, Rosabella Esmaldan, Ella and Julian Egremont, Catherine Navarre, and Cordelia Fitzaphnold, escaping from the palaces of instruction to join the Royalists who are hard driven at present by the victorious Republicans. The Gondals still flourish bright as ever. . . . We intend sticking firm by the rascals as long as they delight us, which I am glad to say they do at present' (*Life and Letters*, II, 49–51).
9. See above, pp. 158–9.
10. See above, p. 109.
11. Mrs Gaskell's *Life of Charlotte Brontë*, ch. 8.
12. Dated 14 April 1845: *Poems*, ed. Hatfield, p. 225.

Philip Drew Charlotte Brontë's Insight into *Wuthering Heights* (1964)

Of the critics who comment explicitly on the book's subject and its moral import, one of the earliest is Charlotte Brontë. . . . The points she makes in her Preface to the edition of 1850[1] are so different from those which trouble modern critics that they are worth careful attention on their own account, to say nothing of their unique value as the comments of an intelligent and informed contemporary, who was peculiarly well placed to understand the nature of the authoress's achievement.

At the beginning of her Preface, Charlotte Brontë apologizes ironically to those too delicately brought up to enjoy the story of unpolished moorland people and to those who are offended by seeing words (presumably 'damn', 'devil' and 'hell') written out in full. She continues by apologizing in the same vein for the rusticity of *Wuthering Heights*, although she is in fact defending it as authentic and inevitable. . . .

This point established, she explains how Emily became obsessed with the more 'tragic and terrible traits' of Yorkshire life, and how her character was such that she could not understand why anyone should object to the depiction of scenes so vivid and so fearful. Charlotte's next step is to discuss the characters of the book in the light of her knowledge of her sister's imagination and of the atmosphere of the Yorkshire moors: it is here that she is most at variance with modern criticism.

She begins, 'For a specimen of true benevolence and homely fidelity, look at the character of Nelly Dean.' A feature of recent criticism of the book has been the suggestion that Nelly is far from an adequate character – that Emily Brontë wishes us to set her uncultivated, undemanding, homespun, conventional morality in unfavorable contrast to the passion of Heathcliff and the elder Catherine. In support of this, one may observe that she plays a crucial part in the action and that this part is often weak and temporizing. So that Nelly-as-actor often annoys us and disposes us to distrust and even to resist the explicit judgements of Mrs Dean-as-narrator. There are three reasons for supposing that this is not a deliberate effect contrived by Emily Brontë to cast doubt on Mrs Dean's value as a source of moral standards. First, she is honest about her own failures, admitting her errors of judgement and her complacency; in fact she so often reflects ironically on her own inadequacies that James Hafley is able to suggest, in a most entertaining article,[2] that she is the villain of the book. Second, many of the foolish things she does are required by the necessities of the plot, and are more accurately seen as clumsiness or obviousness of contrivance than as deliberate devices to discredit her.[3] Third, Lockwood is already set up as the source of conventional urban judgements and Joseph as the source of narrow moral judgements. If we must choose either Mrs Dean's morality or Heathcliff's, there is no doubt which we are to prefer. Nelly Dean is *of* the moors: Heathcliff is an incomer. She is shown to be fairly perceptive, kindly, loyal, and, in particular, tolerant. Thus she finds many good things to say about Heathcliff, but on balance she feels bound to condemn him. Since we see the story through her eyes and she is not presented ironically, her verdict carries great weight with the reader. But for her the book would hardly have any point of normal reference. Isbella uses a significant phrase in her letter to Nelly in chapter 13,

'How did you contrive to preserve the common sympathies of human nature when you resided here?'

Charlotte's Preface continues, 'For an example of constancy and tenderness, remark [the character] of Edgar Linton.' This view of Edgar is more favorable than that of most modern critics, who generally regard him as 'a poor creature', but there is good warrant for it in the novel. For example, in chapter 18 Nelly describes Linton's demeanor after Catherine's death: 'he was too good to be thoroughly unhappy long. *He* didn't pray for Catherine's soul to haunt him. Time brought resignation and a melancholy sweeter than common joy. He recalled her memory with ardent, tender love, and hopeful aspiring to the better world, where he doubted not she was gone.' A little later she contrasts him favorably with Hindley: 'Linton . . . displayed the true courage of a loyal and faithful soul. He trusted God, and God comforted him. One hoped, and the other despaired. They chose their own lots, and were righteously doomed to endure them.' I find it impossible to believe that Emily Brontë intended either of those passages to be read as ironical.

Charlotte Brontë's comments on Joseph and young Catherine are unremarkable, but of the older Catherine she has this to say: 'Nor is even the first heroine of the name destitute of a certain strange beauty in her fierceness, or of honesty in the midst of perverted passion and passionate perversity.' This surprising judgement must be considered in conjunction with Charlotte Brontë's verdict on Heathcliff, which may be summed up by the beginning of its first sentence: 'Heathcliff, indeed, stands unredeemed; never once swerving in his arrow-straight course to perdition.'

This is the crucial point in her criticism of the novel. Her assessment of Heathcliff depends on a recognition of his superhuman villainy, whereas modern critics, if they move away from a consideration of the book's mechanism to a consideration of the moral relations of the characters, usually choose to minimize or justify Heathcliff's consistent delight in malice in order to elevate him to the status of hero. . . .

In the early part of the book, we are led to suspect him of nothing worse than a hot temper, a proud nature and a capacity for implacable hatred. Indeed until he is sixteen the balance of sympathy is with him, since he has been treated so ill. . . . However, when he returns after three years' absence to find Catherine married to Edgar, it is clear that his character has changed. Catherine herself says [ch. 10]. 'He's a fierce, pitiless, wolfish man,' and Nelly confirms that he is leading Hindley to perdition. The remarkable thing about this is that Heathcliff has been back at Wuthering Heights for at most four months (September 1783–January 1784) and has not yet quarrelled with Catherine: yet she describes his nature so.

He courts Isabella not so much for her property as for revenge on Edgar. That he does not love her he makes plain in chapter 10, when he says of her, 'You'd hear of odd things if I lived alone with that mawkish waxen face. The most ordinary would be painting on its white the colours of the rainbow, and turning the blue eyes black, every day or two.' Later Catherine says to him, 'I won't repeat my offer of a wife. It is as bad as offering Satan a lost soul. Your bliss lies, like his, in inflicting misery' [ch. 11]. She goes on to say that Heathcliff is destroying her happiness with Edgar: his conduct in the succeeding chapters bears this out. He runs off with Isabella through malice, despising her as he does so, and before he leaves, hangs her pet spaniel. He says himself, 'The first thing she saw me do on coming out of the Grange was to hang up her little dog, and when she pleaded for it, the first words I uttered were a wish that I had the hanging of every being belonging to her, except one.' Isabella writes of him, 'He is ingenious and unresting in seeking to gain my abhorrence. I sometimes wonder at him with an intensity that deadens my fear, yet I assure you a tiger or a venomous serpent could not rouse terror in me equal to that which he wakens' [ch. 13]. . . . Of this treatment Heathcliff says, 'I've sometimes relented, from pure lack of invention, in my experiments on what she could endure and still creep shamefully cringing back' [ch.14]. Later in the same chapter he says, 'I have no pity! I have no pity! The more the worms writhe, the more I yearn to crush out their entrails! It is a moral teething; and I grind with greater energy in proportion to the increase of pain.'

Even in his grief for Cathy's death he still behaves cruelly to Isabella; when she has fled from Wuthering Heights after Heathcliff has thrown a dinner-knife at her, she remarks temperately, 'Catherine had awfully perverted taste to esteem him so dearly, knowing him so well'. Heathcliff must also fall under strong suspicion of murdering Hindley Earnshaw, whom he has already ruined and driven to the brink of madness. . . .

There is then a gap of twelve years while the younger generation grows up. During this time, Heathcliff carries out his plan to degrade and pervert Hareton. Later he insists on possession of his son, Linton, and treats him with notable callousness. Finally he lays his plans to trap the younger Catherine into marriage with his son, first prompting Linton into a correspondence with her, and then telling her that Linton is dying for love of her. He uses his son, who is close to death, simply as a bait for Catherine, not because she will have money (all she will bring Linton is what Edgar has set aside for her, although this is referred to as a 'fortune'), but to make her wretched. When Linton is very ill, Heathcliff compels him by terror to lure Catherine into Wuthering Heights. . . . When they are in the house and the door is locked, Heathcliff says of Linton and Catherine, 'It's odd what a savage feeling I have to anything that seems afraid of me. Had I been born where laws are less strict and tastes less dainty, I should treat myself to a slow vivisection of these two as an evening's amusement' [ch. 27]. He seizes Catherine and administers 'a shower of terrific slaps on both sides of the head': he then imprisons her for four or five days, although her father is on his deathbed. 'Miss Linton, I shall enjoy myself remarkably in thinking your father will be miserable; I shall not sleep for satisfaction.' He thus forces her to marry his son (exactly how this was done is not made clear) and then sets him against her: he knocks Catherine down and takes her locket. After Catherine's escape he punishes Linton [quotes from ch. 29; 'I brought him down . . . together . . .']. When Linton is dying, Heathcliff refuses to send for the doctor ('His life is not worth a farthing, and I won't spend a farthing on him'), and his son dies. When Heathcliff is himself on the point of death, he says, 'As to repenting of my injustices, I've done no injustice, and I repent of nothing' [ch. 34].

His whole career from the time of his return (September 1783) to his death (May 1802) is one of calculated malice: during this time he does not perform one single good or kindly action,[4] and continually expresses his hatred of all the other characters. So extreme is his malevolence indeed that one might expect him to impress critics as a grotesque villain, like Quilp in *The Old Curiosity Shop*. But this is far from the case. Melvin R. Watson's article on '*Wuthering Heights* and the Critics'[5] provides a convenient conspectus. He speaks approvingly of the opinion of Mrs Robinson: 'She insists rightly that Heathcliff is the central figure and that he harms no one seriously who had not either harmed him or asked for trouble.' One can see that this is simply an inaccurate account of the novel, but as Watson's article shows, it may fairly be taken as representative of much recent criticism of *Wuthering Heights*. How are we to account for the fact that, although Charlotte Brontë describes Heathcliff's conduct accurately, her judgement of his character has commanded virtually no support from later writers, and the very transactions on which this judgement is based are ignored? Why, in short, have critics responded so readily to Heathcliff as the hero of the novel and paid so little attention to his more conspicuous qualifications to be considered the villain?[6]

Most obviously, the characters set in opposition to him are gentle to the point of weakness. Isabella, the younger Catherine and his own son are powerless to resist him, Hindley seems a frail old man, Edgar is not a man of action, and Nelly herself, who is Heathcliff's most persistent opponent, often behaves foolishly at vital points in the action. The reader is thus tempted to admire Heathcliff, as the Romantic critics admire Satan, for his energy and decisiveness, even his ruthlessness. ...

It is frequently argued that Heathcliff is redeemed by his passionate love for Catherine Earnshaw. This is Charlotte Brontë's comment:

> His love for Catherine ... is a sentiment fierce and inhuman: a passion such as might boil and glow in the bad essence of some evil genius; a fire that might form the tormented centre – the ever-suffering soul of a magnate of the infernal world: and by its quenchless and ceaseless ravage effect the execution of the decree which dooms him to carry Hell with him wherever he wanders.

... I shall hope to show that this is a literally accurate description of Heathcliff's passion for Catherine.

... When Catherine is fifteen and Heathcliff sixteen, he hears her say that it would degrade her to marry him. She has in fact already accepted Edgar Linton. Heathcliff leaves Wuthering Heights then for over three years: the implication is that he is in love with Catherine. Before she knows that he has left, Catherine makes an impassioned declaration of her feelings for him [quotes from ch. 9, 'If all else perished ... I *am* Heathcliff.'] This speech is a fine one; it is quoted *ad nauseam*, and part of its power is transferred to Heathcliff. He is supposed to reciprocate Catherine's selfless love for him and to be redeemed by it. In fact, he reveals to Nelly and

Isabella the selfishness of his love for Catherine and of the means he uses to convince himself that he is actually behaving more nobly than Edgar. This is especially plain in chapter 14, and culminates in Heathcliff's derisive comment on Edgar, 'It is not in him to be loved like me.' . . . Catherine dies when she is eighteen and Heathcliff nineteen. As adults they are together for barely a sixth of the novel: they meet seldom and when they do they usually quarrel, until finally Heathcliff is goaded into marrying Isabella.

There is no doubt that this bond between Catherine and Heathcliff is extraordinarily powerful, but it is not a *justifying* bond. . . . On Heathcliff's side at least, it is selfish, which should warn us not to confuse it with love; it expresses itself only through violence – notice, for example, the extraordinary series of descriptions of violent physical contact during and immediately after Heathcliff's last meeting with Catherine; their passion for each other is so compounded with jealousy, anger and hatred that it brings them only unhappiness, anguish and eventually death. . . . In short, while we must recognise that the forging and breaking of the bond between Catherine and Heathcliff provides the novel with all its motive energy, it is fallacious to argue that this proves that Emily Brontë condones Heathcliff's behavior and does not expect the reader to condemn it. Charlotte's phrase 'perverted passion and passionate perversity' is exact.

We must consider next the argument, as advanced by Cecil, for example, that it was not Emily Brontë's intention that the reader should condemn Heathcliff, since he dictates the whole course of the novel, brings his schemes to a successful conclusion and dies happily. A bitter remark of the younger Catherine's is relevant here. In chapter 29 she says:

> Mr Heathcliff, *you* have *nobody* to love you; and however miserable you make us, we shall still have the revenge of thinking that your cruelty arises from your greater misery! You *are* miserable, are you not? Lonely, like the devil, and envious like him? *Nobody* loves you – *nobody* will cry for you when you die! I wouldn't be you!

Later in the same chapter, Heathcliff himself admits, talking of the older Catherine,

> She showed herself, as she often was in life, a devil to me! And, since then, sometimes more and sometimes less, I've been the sport of that intolerable torture – infernal! – keeping my nerves at such a stretch that, if they had not

resembled catgut, they would long ago have relaxed to the feebleness of Linton's. . . . It racked me. I've often groaned aloud, till that old rascal Joseph no doubt believed that my conscience was playing the fiend inside of me. . . . It was a strange way of killing – not by inches, but by fractions of hairbreadths – to beguile me with the spectre of a hope through eighteen years!

'Strange happiness,' as Nelly says. At the end of the book, Heathcliff's domination over the other characters fails, and he finds himself unable to plan further degradation for Catherine and Hareton [quotes from ch. 33, 'It is a poor conclusion . . . for nothing']. . . . It is clear that his thwarted love of and vain grief for Catherine became perverted into the sadistic desire for revenge which sustained him for so many years. As soon as cruelty lost its savor, he lost all that was keeping him alive. At the end of his life, Nelly reproaches him for his wickedness [ch. 34], and her remarks are clearly just. They accord precisely with the spirit of Charlotte Brontë's Preface.

The only point which Charlotte urges in Heathcliff's favor is what she calls 'his rudely confessed regard for Hareton Earnshaw – the young man whom he has ruined'. There is a strong resemblance between Hareton and Heathcliff, for both were poor dependents – half servant, half adopted-son. Heathcliff perceived the likeness at the time of Hindley's death. 'Now, my bonny lad, you are *mine*! And we'll see if one tree won't grow as crooked as another with the same wind to twist it' [ch. 17]. He takes full advantage of the position [quotes from ch. 21, 'I've a pleasure . . . and weak'].

The crucial difference is that Hareton does not allow his ill-treatment to make him bitter; he even acquires a kind of fondness for Heathcliff. But this tells in his favor, not Heathcliff's, for it shows that Heathcliff was not *necessarily* brutalized by his environment, but rather that Hindley's ill-treatment of him encouraged a vindictiveness which he later deliberately fostered.

These are the strongest arguments I have found in justification of Heathcliff's conduct, and, as I have shown, none of them is of sufficient force to avert the reader's natural censure of his consistent malice and cruelty. The problem therefore is to reconcile our condemnation of his behavior with his dominant place in the novel and in the reader's sympathies. Clearly, our attitude to the main character of a work of fiction need not be one of moral approval (e.g. Macbeth, Giles Overreach, Tamburlaine, Giovanni, Beatrice-

Joanna, Becky Sharp, Pincher Martin), but he must in some way act with the reader's understanding and sympathy. In the remainder of this article, I should like to suggest one way in which Emily Brontë powerfully develops the reader's feelings in Heathcliff's favor.

In the earlier chapters our sympathies go naturally to Heathcliff (i.e. Lockwood's narrative and the first part of Nelly Dean's story – up to chapter 9) since he is seen only as the victim of ill-treatment. As Charlotte wrote to W. S. Williams,

> [Heathcliff] exemplified the effects which a life of continued injustice and hard usage may produce on a naturally perverse, vindictive, and inexorable disposition. Carefully trained and kindly treated, the black gipsy-cub might possibly have been reared into a human being, but tyranny and ignorance made of him a mere demon.[7]

Heathcliff vanishes for three years, and these years are wrapped in mystery. Lockwood makes some historically plausible conjectures about them. 'Did he finish his education on the Continent, and come back a gentleman? Or did he get a sizar's place at college, or escape to America, and earn honours by drawing blood from his foster-country, or make a fortune more promptly on the English highways?' [ch. 10]. Mrs Dean has to admit that she does not know: all she can say is that between the ages of sixteen and nineteen Heathcliff converted himself from an ignorant penniless servant to a man with money and black whiskers, a man of whom Catherine says, 'It would honour the first gentleman in the country to be his friend.' The mystery remains throughout the book.

After Heathcliff's return, he dominates the other characters, but, although he is now strong and his enemies weak, his life is one of continual torment. His sufferings engage the reader's natural sympathies, the more so as he suffers in a particular way, and one that accounts for, even if it cannot excuse, his wickedness. For Emily Brontë implies very strongly that if Heathcliff during his absence has not in fact sold his soul to the devil, he has effectively done so. Every description of him reinforces this implication, starting from Nelly's first meeting with him on his return. He appears suddenly in a patch of shadow, startling her [quotes from ch. 10, 'I have waited . . . in hell till you do.'].

Thereafter, hardly a chapter passes without some indication that Heathcliff is suffering the torments of a lost soul; from the moment of his return he is referred to as 'ghoulish', 'a devil', 'a goblin', 'Judas' and 'Satan'. Edgar says that his presence is 'a moral poison that would contaminate the most virtuous'. After his marriage Isabella writes to Nelly, 'The second question I have great interest in – it is this – Is Mr Heathcliff a man? If so, is he mad? And if not, is he a devil?' Hindley calls Heathcliff 'hellish' and 'a fiend'. 'Fiend' or 'fiendish' is applied to him some seven times thereafter. Hindley is a powerful instrument for stressing the damnation of Heathcliff. He says,

> 'Am I to lose *all* without chance of retrieval? Is Hareton to be a beggar? Oh, damnation! I *will* have it back, and I'll have his gold too, and then his blood, and hell shall have his soul! It will be ten times blacker with that guest than ever it was before!'

Heathcliff himself makes a revealing comment when he learns of Catherine's illness. He says that if he were ever to lose her, if, for example, she forgot him completely, 'Two words would comprehend my future – *death* and *hell*; existence after losing her would be hell.' Shortly afterwards Isabella introduces the other word commonly used to refer to Heathcliff – 'diabolical'. Heathcliff is described as 'diabolical' or 'devilish' no fewer than six times: some comment on his infernal powers is thus made virtually every time he appears. Heathcliff's own outbursts to Catherine have a similar effect [quotes from ch. 15, 'Are you possessed . . . soul in the grave?']. This idea of souls being separated from bodies and its extension into the idea of ghosts walking the earth because there is no peace for them in the grave are pervasive in the book, and do much to reinforce the suggestion that evil powers are abroad. Heathcliff is particularly given to a belief in ghosts [ch. 29].

For the rest of the book, Heathcliff is referred to variously as 'an incarnate goblin', 'a monster', 'not a human being', and 'a hellish villain'; Iabella refers to his 'kin beneath', and talks of Hell as 'his right abode'. She says to Hindley, 'His mouth watered to tear you with his teeth, because he's only half man – not so much – and the rest fiend!' [ch. 17].

Other characters refer to him as a 'devil' (twice) and 'a goblin'. Nelly wonders whether he is wholly human. '"Is he a ghoul or a vampire?" I mused. I had read of such hideous incarnate demons.' He says of himself to Catherine, 'To you I've made myself worse than the devil.' All through his adult life he undergoes what he describes as 'that intolerable torture – infernal!' He says to Nelly when he is near death, 'Last night I was on the threshhold of hell,' and when he dies Joseph exclaims, 'Th' divil's harried off his soul.'

This network of references and comment serves to mark out Heathcliff as a possessed soul. If the story were expressly narrated on a supernatural level, his career could be described by saying simply that he sells his soul to the devil in exchange for power, power over others, and specifically power to make himself fit to marry Catherine. When however he attempts to claim his share of the bargain he finds that the devil is, as always, a cheat. He has the power he asked for but loses Catherine herself. He is left simply with power, the exercise of which he finds necessary but intolerably painful. Thereafter, he is consumed inwardly by hellfire and the knowledge of his own damnation.

This would be a metaphorical way of describing what in fact happens. Heathcliff's personality begins to disintegrate when he allows himself to become obsessed by a physical passion for Catherine and deliberately fosters this passion to the point of mania. He sacrifices every other part of his personality to the satisfaction of his passion, until by its very violence it destroys its own object. Once Catherine has gone, Heathcliff is left with no possible emotions except those into which he can pervert his previous obsession with Catherine. He finds that he can demonstrate that he has feelings only by expressing them as cruelty. This brings him no happiness: on the contrary his power for wickedness *is* his punishment, rather than his prize, just as his passion for Catherine was not a blessing but a curse. In short, he is destroying himself throughout the book: each act of wanton brutality is a further maiming of himself. 'Treachery and violence are spears pointed at both ends. They wound those who resort to them worse than their enemies' [ch. 17]. Time moves swiftly on the moors, and senility sets in very early (Hindley is only 27 at his death), but nobody else ages as fast as Heathcliff. Towards his death, he seems to be consuming his life ever more rapidly, as if the processes of nature had been accelerated by the fires within. He acts like a fiend incarnate, but his actions torture him as much as they torture his victims: they are a part, and the worst part, of the torments of the damned which Heathcliff suffers during his life. When he finds himself capable of a good act, even one so neutral as not persecuting Hareton and Catherine, it is as though his sentence had been at last worked out, and he dies almost joyfully.

The sympathy that we give to him is thus not the sort that we give to the noble tragic hero, nor is it the same as our reluctant admiration of a powerfully defiant villain like Vittoria. It is more nearly akin to the compassion we feel for those who are fated to work out their doom in torment and despair, characters such as Satan himself, Marlowe's Faustus and Mephistopheles, the Wandering Jew, Vanderdecken, or even Captain Ahab.[8] It does not lead us to approve of Heathcliff's actions or even to condone them. Emily Brontë's achievement is to arouse our sympathy for a lost soul while making it quite clear that his actions are damnable.

All this is comprehended in Charlotte's preface. She sees that Heathcliff is embarked on an 'arrow-straight course to perdition', and that his love for Catherine is a fire 'that might form the tormented centre – the ever-suffering soul of a magnate of the infernal world' doomed 'to carry Hell with him wherever he wanders'. She concludes her remarks on his character by saying that but for one or two slight redeeming features 'we should say he was child neither of Lascar nor gipsy, but a man's shape animated by demon life – a Ghoul – an Afreet'. She thus identifies the novel's main source of evil energy and its central metaphor, which is the parallel between diabolical possession and embittered passion. Her concluding paragraph expresses with some subtlety the extent of Emily Brontë's achievement in liberating this terrifying energy and yet controlling it [quotes the passage, '*Wuthering Heights* . . . giant's foot': see pp. 63–4 above].

SOURCE: *Nineteenth-Century Fiction* (1964).

NOTES

1. See above, p. 60.
2. 'The Villain in *Wuthering Heights*', in *Nineteenth-Century Fiction*, XIII (1958), pp. 199–215. For a rebuttal of the essay, see further John Fraser on 'Nelly Dean and *Wuthering Heights*', referred to p. 34n above, p. 236 below.
3. Cp. Mrs Humphry Ward on Nelly Dean, pp. 99–100 above.
4. The author comments, 'But notice that E. F. Shannon (op. cit.) makes the following point in Heathcliff's favour: "Although a reluctant host he provides Lockwood with a glass of wine, tea and dinner on separate occasions; and during the narrator's illness, he sends him a brace of grouse and chats amiably at his 'bedside a good hour'" . . .'
5. *Trollopian*, III (1948) see p. 1 and n.
6. But they have not always done so. See Introduction, pp. 19–21 above.
7. 14 August 1848: see above, p. 53.

8. The author notes: 'Mrs Allott [see above, p. 174 and n] suggests that Heathcliff sometimes reminds us of Byron's Manfred or Cain. Muriel Spark and Derek Stanford [*Emily Brontë*, 1953] note this also, but as a major weakness in the drawing of Heathcliff who, they say, "is Byron in prose dress".' See also Jacques Blondel on Heathcliff and Byron, p. 160 above.

Terry Eagleton (1) Passion, Social Rebellion, Capitalist Villainy: Contradiction Incarnate in Heathcliff (1976)

... Heathcliff is a self-tormentor, a man who is in hell because he can avenge himself on the system which has robbed him of his soul only by battling with it on its own hated terms. If as a child he was outside and inside that system simultaneously, wandering on the moors and working on the farm, he lives out a similar self-division as an adult, trapped in the grinding contradiction between a false social self and the true identity which lies with Catherine. The social self is false, not because Heathcliff is only apparently brutal – that he certainly is – but because it is contradictorily related to the authentic selfhood which is his passion for Catherine. He installs himself at the centre of conventional society, but with wholly negative and inimical intent; his social role is a calculated self-contradiction, created first to further, and then fiercely displace, his asocial passion for Catherine.

Heathcliff's social relation to both Heights and Grange is one of the most complex issues in the novel. Lockwood remarks that he looks too genteel for the Heights; and indeed, in so far as he represents the victory of capitalist property-dealing over the traditional yeoman economy of the Earnshaws, he is inevitably aligned with the world of the Grange. Heathcliff is a dynamic force which seeks to destroy the old yeoman settlement by dispossessing Hareton; yet he does this partly to revenge himself on the very Linton world whose weapons (property deals, arranged marriages) he deploys so efficiently. He does this, moreover, with a crude intensity which is a quality of the Heights world; his roughness and resilience link him culturally to *Wuthering Heights*, and he exploits those qualities to destroy both it and the Grange. He is, then, a force which springs out of the Heights yet subverts it, breaking beyond its constrictions into a new, voracious acquisitiveness. His capitalist brutality is an extension as well as a negation of the Heights world he knew as a child; and to that extent there is continuity between his childhood and adult protests against Grange values, if not against Grange weapons. Heathcliff is subjectively a Heights figure opposing the Grange, and objectively a Grange figure undermining the Heights; he focuses acutely the contradictions between the two worlds. His rise to power symbolises at once the triumph of the oppressed over capitalism and the triumph of capitalism over the oppressed.

He is, indeed, contradiction incarnate – both progressive and outdated, at once caricature of and traditionalist protest against the agrarian capitalist forces of Thrushcross Grange. He harnesses those forces to worst the Grange, to beat it at its own game; but in doing so he parodies that property-system, operates against the Lintons with an unLinton-like explicitness and extremism. He behaves in this way because his 'soul' belongs not to that world but to Catherine; and in that sense his true commitment is an 'out-dated' one, to a past, increasingly mythical realm of absolute personal value which capitalist social relations cancel. He embodies a passionate human protest against the marriage-market values of both Grange and Heights at the same time as he callously images those values in caricatured form. Heathcliff exacts vengeance from that society precisely by extravagantly enacting its twisted priorities, becoming a darkly satirical commentary on conventional mores. If he is in one sense a progressive historical force, he belongs in another sense to the superseded world of the Heights, so that his death and the closing-up of the house seem logically related. In the end Heathcliff is defeated and the Heights restored to its rightful owner; yet at the same time the trends he epitomises triumph in the form of the Grange, to which Hareton and young Catherine move away. Hareton wins and loses the Heights simultaneously; dispossessed by Heathcliff, he repossesses the place only to be in that act assimilated by Thrushcross Grange. And if Hareton both wins and loses, then Heathcliff himself is both ousted and victorious.

Quite who has in fact won in the end is a matter of critical contention. Mrs Leavis and Tom Winnifrith both see the old world as having yielded to the new, in contrast to T. K. Meier, who reads the conclusion as 'the victory of tradition over innovation'.[1] The critical contention reflects a real ambiguity in the novel. In one sense, the old values have triumphed over the disruptive usurper: Hareton has wrested back his birthright, and the qualities he symbolises, while preserving their authentic vigour, will be fertilised by the civilising grace which the Grange, in the form of young Catherine, can bring. Heathcliff's career appears from his perspective as a shattering but short-lived interlude, after which true balance may be slowly recovered. In a more obvious sense, however, the Grange has won: the Heights is shut up and Hareton will become the new squire. Heathcliff, then, has been the blunt instrument by which the remnants of the Earnshaw world have been transformed into a fully-fledged capitalist class – the historical medium whereby that world is at once annihilated and elevated to the Grange. Thrushcross values have entered into productive dialogue with rough material reality and, by virtue of this spiritual transfusion, ensured their continuing survival; the Grange comes to the Heights and gathers back to itself what the Heights can yield it. This is why it will not do to read the novel's conclusion as some neatly reciprocal symbolic alliance between the two universes, a symmetrical symbiosis of bourgeois realism and upper-class cultivation. Whatever unity the book finally establishes, it is certainly not symmetrical: in a victory for the progressive forces of agrarian capitalism, Hareton, last survivor of the traditional order, is smoothly incorporated into the Grange.

There is another significant reason why the 'defeat' of Heathcliff cannot be read as the resilient recovery of a traditional world from the injuries it has suffered at his hands. As an extreme parody of capitalist activity, Heathcliff is also an untypical deviation from its norms; as a remorseless, crudely transparent revelation of the real historical character of the Grange, he stands askew to that reality in the very act of becoming its paradigm. It *is* true that Heathcliff, far from signifying some merely ephemeral intervention, is a type of the historically ascendant world of capital; but because he typifies it so 'unnaturally' the novel can move beyond him, into the gracefully gradualistic settlement symbolised by the union of Hareton and young Catherine. Heathcliff is finally fought off, while the social values he incarnates can be prised loose from the self-parodic mould in which he cast them and slowly accommodated. His undisguised violence, like the absolutism of his love, come to seem features of a past more brutal but also more heroic than the present; if the decorous, muted milieu of the Grange will not easily accommodate such passionate intensities, neither will it so readily reveal the more unpleasant face of its social and economic power. The 'defeat' of Heathcliff, then, is at once the transcending of such naked power and the collapse of that passionate protest against it which was the inner secret of Heathcliff's outrageous dealings.

We can now ask what these contradictions in the figure of Heathcliff actually amount to. It seems to me possible to decipher in the struggle between Heathcliff and the Grange an imaginatively transposed version of that contemporary conflict between bourgeoisie and landed gentry which I have argued is central to Charlotte's work. The relationship holds in no precise detail, since Heathcliff is not literally an industrial entrepreneur; but the double-edgedness of his relation with the Lintons, with its blend of antagonism and emulation, reproduces the complex structure of class-forces we found in Charlotte's fiction. Having mysteriously amassed capital outside agrarian society, Heathcliff forces his way into that society to expropriate the expropriators; and in this sense his machinations reflect the behaviour of a contemporary bourgeois class increasingly successful in its penetration of landed property. He belongs fully to neither Heights nor Grange, opposing them both; he embodies a force which at once destroys the traditional Earnshaw settlement and effectively confronts the power of the squirearchy. In his contradictory amalgam of 'Heights' and 'Grange', then, Heathcliff's career fleshes out a contemporary ideological dilemma which Charlotte also explores: the contradiction that the fortunes of the industrial bourgeoisie belong *economically* to an increasing extent with the landed gentry but that there can still exist between them, socially, culturally and personally, a profound hostility. If they are increasingly bound up objectively in a single power-bloc, there is still sharp subjective conflict between them. I take it that *Wuthering Heights*, like Charlotte's fiction, needs mythically to resolve this historical contradiction. If the exploitative adult Heathcliff belongs economically with the capitalist power of the Grange, he is culturally closer to the traditional world of the Heights; his contemptuous response to the Grange as a child, and later to Edgar, is of a piece with Joseph's scorn for the finicky Linton Heathcliff and the haughty young Catherine. If Heathcliff exploits Hareton culturally and economically, he nevertheless feels a certain rough-and-ready *rapport* with him. The contradiction Heathcliff embodies, then, is brought home in the fact that he combines Heights violence with Grange methods to gain power over both properties; and this means that while he is economically progressive he is culturally outdated. He represents a turbulent form of capitalist aggression which must historically be civilised – blended with spiritual values, as it will be in the case of his surrogate Hareton. . . .

SOURCE: from '*Wuthering Heights*', *Myths of Power. A Marxist Study of the Brontës* (London, 1976).

NOTE

1. Q. D. Leavis, *Lectures in America* (1969), pp. 128–9; Tom Winnifrith, *The Brontës and their Background* (1973), p. 192; T. K. Meier, *Brontë Society Transactions*, no. 78 (1968).

(2) Afterword (1988)

. . . The theoretical model with which this book [*The Myths of Power*] works is not in itself, I think, class-reductionist. On the contrary, true to its Althusserian background,[1] it emphasises the 'overdetermination' of the Brontës' fiction, the multiple, interacting constituents of its making. In practice, however, many of these non-class determinants, and gender above all, are given notably short shrift. . . . I would want to argue now that the question of gender, far from figuring in the Brontës as one among many social determinants, is nothing less than the *dominant medium* in which, in much of their writing at least, other social conflicts are actually lived out; and it has its own high degree of autonomy of those other conflicts too. To fail to recognise this is not only to produce a seriously limited analysis, but to err in *tone* . . . because . . . attending less to the woman than to the *petty bourgeoise*, displacing the focus from gender to class, and thus directing towards the former negative judgements and responses which might have a certain justification in the case of the latter.

This is not to argue, on the other hand, that the class status of the Brontës' protagonists should be simply suppressed – that they can be exculpated because of their gender, in some falsely chivalric gesture. On the contrary, there are indeed negative, even offensive aspects of these characters which spring more or less directly from their class positions; the Charlotte Brontë who has been properly redeemed and valorised by feminist criticism is also the woman who deeply feared workers' revolution in Britain and indulged in the crudest travesty of working-class characters. What feminist criticism of the Brontës has appeared since the first publication of this book has not, on the whole, addressed itself to these issues. Indeed it has been in general as unhistorical and class-blind as traditional Marxist criticism has been obstinately oblivious of gender. Feminist criticism may have good reasons for this omission, as Marxist criticism does not: its understandable fear of appropriation by male radicals has led it perhaps to give somewhat less than full attention to those aspects of women's oppression about which Marxism has something relevant to say. But it cannot be ignored either that the brunt of contemporary feminist criticism has emerged from the society in the world today most deeply hostile to socialism, and these political conditions may well have left their mark. Since the later 1970s, such Marxist criticism, however blunderingly, externally or even patronisingly, has sought to engage with questions of women's oppression, and in this way to make what reparation it can for past omissions. The same, to date at least, cannot in general be said of feminist criticism's relation to Marxism.

Feminist criticism in our time has struck up a kind of logical alliance with psychoanalytical theory; and the latter is another palpable silence in this book. The chapter on *Wuthering Heights*, though not, I think, a 'Romantic' reading of the text, is nevertheless too ready to take on board such essentially Romantic concepts as 'the imagination', 'authenticity' and 'liberation', without submitting these notions to Freud's sceptical, rigorously materialist reading. Despite its own materialist bias, there is an aura of idealism about that whole account, which a judicious dose of Freudianism might well have tempered. The disruptive force of the unconscious is evident enough in the libidinal exchanges of that text; but its traces can also be found in the curious nature of the *writing*, another matter to which I here give insufficient consideration. The implicit epistemology of this book is in many ways more idealist than materialist: high marks are awarded to works which achieve some 'balance' of subjective and objective, and censorious comments are provoked by texts which are in some sense disjunctive, subjectively 'excessive' or non-totalised. *Wuthering Heights* is accordingly congratulated on its high degree of formal unity; but this simply overlooks the fact that, with its 'Chinese boxes' effect of narratives-within-narratives, its constant regression of perspectives and instabilities of viewpoint, it is a strangely 'decentred' fiction which subverts the dominance of the conventional authorial 'voice' as markedly as aspects of its subject-matter threaten to undermine the received forms of bourgeois society. In concentrating on the bizarre features of the world of the Heights, I miss the most bizarre phenomenon of all: the elusive, enigmatic text of *Wuthering Heights* itself. . . .

Finally, I would now want to qualify what seems to me rather too rigid a contrast between the 'politics' of Emily's text, and those of Charlotte's. In the end, Charlotte emerges here as a compromiser and canny strategist, in contrast with the unflinching absolutism I discern in *Wuthering Heights*. Such a judgement not only passes over the powerfully 'incorporative' aspects of the latter work, but underplays the radicalism of the former. In *social* terms, Charlotte's novels indeed negotiate adroitly for an acceptable settlement; but this decorous resolution is constantly jeopardised by a *sexual* demand – an angry, wounded, implacable desire for full personal acceptance and recognition – which breaks beyond the boundaries of any social or narrative closure. The book's strategy tends to generate too severe an opposition between the two sisters in this respect; and I leave it to the reader to deconstruct that polarity as he or she might wish.

SOURCE: from Introduction to the Second Edition of *Myths of Power* . . . (London, 1988).

NOTE

1. Louis Althusser's influential essay 'Ideology and Ideological State Apparatuses' appeared in 1969; his *Lenin and Philosophy and Other Essays*, transl. Ben Brewster, was published in 1971. A critique of his structuralist Marxism is included in E. P. Thompson, *The Poverty of Theory and Other Essays* (1978).

Margaret Homans Transcending the Problem of Sexual Identity (1980)

. . . In Charlotte's account of [the Brontë sisters'] choice of the sexually ambiguous pesudonyms, Currer, Ellis, and Acton, she says that they did not want to declare themselves women, because of a tendency among critics to condescend to 'authoresses', 'without at that time suspecting that our mode of writing and thinking was not what is called "feminine"'. Contemporary reviewers of *Wuthering Heights* spoke of Ellis Bell's 'power' and 'mastery'. If Charlotte means that later on they did come to understand that their writing was not 'what is called "feminine",' it is not clear whether she welcomed this distinction, thinking of 'the poetry women generally write', or whether this distinction was an affront to her sense of identity and integrity as a woman. They did not want to abdicate their proper identity and assume 'Christian names positively masculine', yet they could hardly wish, in the world in which they lived, to be grouped with authoresses.[1]. . .

The choice to be named 'Ellis', assuming that Emily participated in the decision, must represent the poet's wish not to have, as a writer, a determinate sexual identity. This wish may result partly from the desire not to be judged on the basis of gender, but sexual identification is problematic also because the two origins of poetry that she perceives as being available to her are sexually defined, and she can consider neither to be identifiable with the self. Feminine nature and forms of the masculine Word present her with a choice she does not wish to make. The arrangement of this choice is of course her own, but it may express her frustration at the sexual restriction of so many aspects of literary tradition and practice. Brontë's separation from the two sources of her power may be, then, the result not of any fragmentation of her own sense of identity, but of her uneasiness about their sexual orientation. She may not be able to, but also perhaps does not wish to, claim identification with either one.[2]. . .

Unable to identify with the masculine Word or breath of God, Brontë portrays herself as its passive object in 'The Night-Wind' and in 'Shall Earth no more inspire thee'. Where in 'Aye, there it is' a female figure is united with an intellectual breeze, her assumption promotes thoughts of death, not of power. . . .

Brontë's myth of imaginative possession and her sense of obligatory deference to higher powers create great difficulties in her poems. Self-alienation in the poetry causes her to feel as much threatened as delighted by her gift. One cure for self-alienation is simply to give in to it and 'sleep/Without identity', and in *Wuthering Heights* death's project is the reuniting, not of parts of the self, or of poet and poetic spirit, but of two individuals. Heathcliff is eager for death so that he and Cathy may 'be lost in one repose'. Loss of the self, the dispersal of identity, leads to the merging and reunion of identities. . . . The form of the novel is fitted for dispersiveness as the Romantic lyric is not, and it may be that Brontë . . . found in the novel the proper place for turning it to use. This transformation of a former difficulty may account, in part, for the novel's superiority to the poetry.

Many critics, writing on diverse aspects of the novel, have noted its drive both toward diffusion and toward reunion. Robert Kiely finds in it an underlying principle of dynamism that causes motion to be valued exclusively over stasis.[3] The novel defies its own potential categories, because it is constantly fusing polarities, whether of character, of landscape, or of morality (hell is heaven and heaven is hell). Leo Bersani's chapter on *Wuthering Heights* is about the dissolution and transference of identity, particularly in the exchange of identity between Cathy and Heathcliff.[4] Although Cathy insists 'I *am* Heathcliff', and Heathcliff calls Cathy 'my soul' and 'my life', Bersani points out how different they are in character, a difference that transcends particular qualities because Heathcliff is the archetypal outsider in the story. Their fusion of identity is not a natural reunion, but a self-alienation and an identification with otherness that is both terrifying and appealing. Because death is the final form of dissolution, especially in Heathcliff's plan for the physical merging of his corpse with Cathy's, 'death is the most appropriate metaphor for that radical transference of the self to another . . .' [pp. 211–212]. The two houses, Wuthering Heights and Thrushcross Grange, are not the polarities they are usually taken to be, but have interchangeable characteristics. Even sexual distinctions cease to pertain: the second Linton is more conventionally feminine than any character in the novel, except his mother Isabella. The boundaries of identity are dissolved by the repetition of the generations and the recombination of family traits resultant from intermarriage. And the diffuse narrative structure dissolves this dissolution even further. There is no single controlling point of view that might preserve a remnant of stability.

There are novels by men that exhibit the same traits of diffuseness to be found in *Wuthering Heights*, though perhaps not to so great a degree. The novel is generically a more scattered form than the lyric, and it would be impossible definitively to trace this difference to sexual difference. Kiely points out that Nelly's success as a narrator has to do with her lack of egotism: 'The fact is that neither Lockwood nor Heathcliff could possibly tell the story without focusing almost exclusively on himself. Nelly can do otherwise' [p. 237]. This lack of egotism may, however, originate in her being a domestic rather than in her femininity; neither of the Cathys would do much better as narrator than Lockwood and Heathcliff. But in so far as the diffuseness of *Wuthering Heights* provides a successful answer to difficulties in the poems that arise from the poet's femininity . . . it tentatively may be connected to the novelist's femininity. The poet is never confident of her power over language and over imagination because both are, to her, alien and masculine, therefore dangerous to the self's integrity. Whereas the poetic speaker must always fear her own death, characters in the novel may die without impinging on the continued life of the whole, and in fact their deaths may contribute to continuity. There is no single self in the novel to compare with the poems' troubled selves. The only comparable figure is the surface of the entire text. If the novel's text is like a psyche, this psyche is so diffuse as to include, and therefore not be threatened by, its own potential destroyers.

In the poems the poet is obliged, unwillingly, to value possession positively by characterizing it as transcendence. She can overcome the threat of invasion or of possession only by pretending that it is not threatening but welcome, deferring to it either way. But the novel's inclusiveness allows her to avoid having to overvalue external powers. There is an almost exact correspondence between Cathy's words about Heathcliff and the transcendent belief represented in 'No coward soul is mine':

> If all else perished, and *he* remained, I should still continue to be; and, if all else remained, and he were annihilated, the Universe would turn to a mighty stranger. I should not seem a part of it.

Though Earth and moon were gone
And suns and universes ceased to be
And thou wert left alone
Every Existence would exist in thee.

The similarity between these two passages is startling, but there are important differences as well. The prose passage consists of a pair of complementary statements whereas the verse is a single gesture, a stylistic difference that underscores a more basic difference. Cathy's speech is punctuated by an alternation of emphatic 'I' and 'he', but there is no 'I' in the verse, only a 'thou'. Cathy's and Heathcliff's relation is reciprocal, but after an initial equality with the 'God within my breast' the 'I' in the poem defers to what she knows is a higher principle.[5]

Life, that in me has rest
As I Undying Life, have power in Thee. . . .

The symmetry of 'in me . . . in Thee' suggests mutual dependence, but that life rests in her and she draws power from it is not an equal relation but a hierarchical devotion that operates only in one direction. All the sources of poetry seem to be external, and the poetic self invariably loses any competition with a divine figure external to the poem. The novel has better success, not by winning, but by avoiding the competition altogether.

When Charlotte Brontë mentions Heathcliff in the preface to her edition of *Wuthering Heights* [p. 63 above] it is as an example of the horrors that a mind possessed by its creative gift may produce, and her theory of possession develops from her desire to excuse Heathcliff's presence in the novel. Heathcliff is himself daemonic, and although he hardly represents his author's creative powers, he is the main character and much of the action is presented from his point of view. He is in many ways similar to the figures of imaginative power in the poetry, in that he is powerful, at times visionary, and alien. This similarity may be Brontë's way of announcing that in the novel she has discarded her myth of visionary possession, because there Heathcliff is only a character, dissociated from the creative process. He may retain the shape of the daemon of creativity, but his significance lies elsewhere. Heathcliff is himself possessed and driven to death by Cathy's ghost. In his human shape, the visitant is as much victim as victor, and his power is relative, not absolute. . . .

In the earlier passages, from Cathy's delirium [ch. 12] the purpose of returning to childhood and to nature is to return to Heathcliff, the 'earth' alternative in her earlier cosmic comparison between the two suitors. Nature is associated with Heathcliff, and is entirely free of the maternal associations that trouble the poetry. This may be because the novel affords the author a way to step outside poetic traditions. Free to create her own symbolic landscape, she can more easily discard the feminized nature she inherits from the Romantic tradition. Furthermore it is Cathy, not the poetic self, who sees nature in this new way. Although the poems' speaker is not to be identified with Emily Brontë, a fictive character is much further from the self. Heathcliff's vision of nature is feminized, in a way, but that is because he sees Cathy there (and everywhere), not a mythic maternal presence.

> What does not recall her? I cannot look down to this floor, but her features are shaped on the flags! In every cloud, in every tree – filling the air at night, and caught by glimpses in every object by day, I am surrounded with her image! [ch. 33]

Like Cathy during the first part of her illness, Heathcliff is eager to be out of doors, just before his death, to commune with her spirit.

Both of them believe in a very physical union or reunion with one another after death, a merging of identity through the dissolution of physical entity. Cathy associates this reunion in death with regression to childhood. . . .

That death should fulfill both the desire for reunion and the desire for regression is exactly what Freud shows in *Beyond the Pleasure Principle*, and Leo Bersani finds in *Wuthering Heights* the characteristics of the Freudian death instinct. Bersani's primary interest is in the relation between the death instinct and the notion of self-alienation as proposed in the second section of *Beyond the Pleasure Principle*, but his argument leads back from 'being different from ourselves' to the strange nature of the relationship between Heathcliff and Cathy, which appears to represent other aspects of the death instinct as well. The death instinct is a desire for 'the restoration of an earlier state of things' [p. 37], and at the end of his discussion Freud shows how the sexual instincts also share this regressive character, by referring to Plato's primordial unity of the sexes in the *Symposium*. Regression thus provides a ground for connecting and perhaps identifying the sexual instincts and the death instinct. . . .

The difficulty with Freud's theory, for a woman author and her female characters, is that the feminine desire to be reunited with the mother is considerably less fervent than it is for males. The significance of Cathy's death instinct is that, at the same time that it is a sexual instinct, it is not the same as a desire for a return to first things. The reunion that Cathy and Heathcliff seek is not primordial, but a reunion with each other as consciously known and loved individuals, however the reader may qualify that love. Both Cathy and Heathcliff are reborn on the occasion of their becoming friends as children, and their identification with each other forms a new origin that replaces parental origins. Their regressive wishes go back only to that second origin, and no further. It is this invented origin that permits the novel to value Cathy's desire for death so highly. Were nature associated with the maternal figure and were Cathy's death wish as Freud describes it, it would have all the ambivalence of the attitude toward death in 'I see around me tombstones grey' and elsewhere in the poetry. . . . The novel permits Brontë to depart from the poetic traditions that enforce maternal origins, and allows her to remake nature in the form of a chosen beloved.

During her delirium Cathy sees Nelly as a witch who inhabits and commands nature.

> 'I see in you, Nelly,' she continued, dreamily, 'an aged woman – you have grey hair, and bent shoulders. This bed is the fairy cave under Penistone Crag, and you are gathering elf-bolts to hurt our heifers; pretending, while I am near, that they are only locks of wool.' [ch. 12]

Later, when she half understands that Nelly has been keeping the knowledge of her illness from Linton, she exclaims, 'Nelly is my hidden enemy. You witch! So you do seek elf-bolts to hurt us!' [ch. 12]. In a novel in which biological mothers die off rapidly and in obscurity, Nelly is the only durable maternal figure. She points out that the second Cathy and Hareton are 'in a measure, my children' [ch. 33] but she also helped raise the older generation of which she was a part. Nelly as a 'withered hag' in the landscape represents Cathy's fearful image of motherhood, both her neglected maternal origins and the maternal presence buried in nature. The withered hag is also Cathy herself, however, and that recognition renders the image maddening. Directly after the speech about the aged woman Cathy looks in a mirror across the room and recognizes neither herself in it, nor that it is a mirror. Literally self-alienated, her own image 'haunts' and terrifies her. Nelly's persuasion that the face is really Cathy's own is even more terrifying than an unknown demon: '"Myself!" she gasped, "and the clock is striking twelve! It's true, then; that's dreadful!"' [ch. 12]. What it is that is dreadful, we are not explicitly told. During her delirium, Cathy habitually imagines that she is back at Wuthering Heights as a child, and it is her adult self that frightens her and from which she is alienated. The ghostly face in the mirror might be the image of her own impending motherhood.

This reading may be extravagant, but one of the late poems ['Stars'] requires a similar reading. . . . The speaker is lamenting the night's departure and the intrusion of the dazzling sun, who is associated with violent masculinity:

> Blood-red he rose, and arrow-straight
> His fierce beams struck my brow:
> The soul of Nature sprang elate,
> But mine sank sad and low!

The sun's presence is painful because of his fierce beams and scorching fire, but even more because of the response he evokes in nature, the proper mate for this phallic sun. . . . Nature as a feminine figure so readily and so efficaciously empowered by a masculine one is more threatening than the sun himself.

This image of nature should not of itself threaten the speaker's self-image, but nature gives the speaker an unfavorable image of herself as jailor, through wakening those flies that are 'Imprisoned there, till I should rise/And give them leave to roam'. Usually nature is the jailor. In 'I see around me tombstones grey' maternal nature is a hypocritical jailor who uses love to prevent the speaker from passing natural limits. The prison is the commonest image for the mortal condition, as when in 'Silent is the House' the soul is imprisoned in the body or in natural life. Nature can also be a liberator, but to be identified with nature in her character of jailor is to see oneself not as a poet but as the antagonist of poetry. Nature as jailor definitively resists propriation by human act or language, by turning propriation back on humanity. It is that final otherness that the human poet cannot and should not try to grasp, like the natural violence that Dorothy Wordsworth depicts in her *Journal of a Tour on the Continent*. . . . In *Wuthering Heights*, Brontë does not entirely forget nature's ominous maternal configuration, but she presents it as a function of madness. As the witch of Penistone crags, Nelly is only a vestigial and distorted image of Mother Nature. Like repressed material that surfaces in a dream, the image vanishes after a brief appearance, clearly a figment of Cathy's fevered brain and not adopted by the rest of the novel.

Excluding from the novel the poetic tradition of maternal nature permits the novel to abandon the poems' investment in transcendence after death that defaces the authenticity of many of the poems. The poems' unconvincing belief in transcendence is made necessary because the image of maternal nature makes natural death horrific. In the novel, free from maternal characterization, the earth need hold no particular terrors. It ceases to threaten the author's powers because nothing about it is predetermined, and she is free to characterize it as she chooses. It holds no thematic terrors for Cathy and Heathcliff because they are free to identify it with each other and with a restoration of their childhood. Instead of an investment of belief in transcendence after death, images of continuance in the novel are all invested in heterosexual love, regardless of how the reader judges the specifics of Cathy and Heathcliff's relationship. Freed from the poems' distorted and distorting fixation on the extremes of hyperbolic transcendence and tellurian darkness, the novel locates in Cathy and Heathcliff a compromise that is both conducive to writing and humanly convincing.

SOURCE: from *Women Writers and Poetic Identity. Dorothy Wordsworth, Emily Brontë, and Emily Dickinson* (Princeton, NJ, 1980).

NOTES

1. Author's note: 'Carol Ohmann discusses the way critics trivialized *Wuthering Heights* once its author's identity had been revealed, in "Emily Brontë in the Hands of Male Critics", *College English*, 32 (1971), pp. 906–13.' But see, e.g., pp. 19–20; 65; 69–70; 70–1; 74–5.

2. The author compares C. Day Lewis on Emily Brontë's dissatisfaction with the world as a projection of her frustration at not being a man, 'The Poetry of Emily Brontë', *Brontë Society Transactions*, 13 (1957), pp. 94–7.

3. Robert Kiely, *The Romantic Novel in England* (1972), pp. 233–51 (the author notes especially pp. 237, 245).

4. Leo Bersani, *A Future for Astyanax: Character and Desire in Literature* (Boston: Little, Brown, 1976), pp. 197–223.

5. The author's note refers to J. Hillis Miller, *The Disappearance of God': Five Nineteenth-Century Writers* (Cambridge: The Belknap Press of Harvard University Press, 1963), p. 174.

Hillis Miller *Wuthering Heights* and the 'Uncanny' (1982)

There have been explanations of *Wuthering Heights* in terms of its relation to the motif of the fair-haired girl and the dark-haired boy in the Gondal poems; or by way of the motifs of doors and windows in the novel (Dorothy Van Ghent); or in terms of the symmetry of the family relations in the novel or of Brontë's accurate knowledge of the laws of private property in Yorkshire (C. P. Sanger); or in more or less orthodox and schematic Freudian terms, as a thinly disguised sexual drama displaced and condensed (Thomas Moser); or as the dramatization of a conflict between two cosmological forces, storm and calm (Lord David Cecil); or as a moral story of the futility of grand passion (Mark Schorer); or as a fictional dramatization of Brontë's religious vision (J. H. Miller); or as a dramatization of the relation between sexuality and death, as 'l'approbation de la vie jusqu'à la mort', the approbation of life all the way to death (Georges Bataille); or as the occult dramatization of Brontë's lesbian passion for her dead sister, Maria, with Brontë as Heathcliff (Camille Paglia); or as an overdetermined semiotic structure which is irreducibly ambiguous by reason of its excess of signs (Frank Kermode); or as Brontë's effacement of nature in order to make way for specifically female imaginative patterns (Margaret Homans); or as the expression of a multitude of incompatible 'partial selves' dispersed among the various characters, thereby breaking down the concept of the unitary self (Leo Bersani), or in more or less sophisticated Marxist terms (David Wilson, Arnold Kettle, Terry Eagleton).[1] . . .

All these interpretations are, I believe, wrong. This is not because each does not illuminate something in *Wuthering Heights*. Each brings something to light, even though it covers something else up in the act of doing so. . . .

The essays . . . seem to me insufficient, not because what they say is demonstrably mistaken, but rather because there is an error in the assumption that there *is* a single secret truth about *Wuthering Heights*. This secret truth would be something formulable as a univocal principle of explanation which would account for everything in the novel. The secret truth about *Wuthering Heights*, rather, is that there is no secret truth which criticism might formulate in this way. No hidden identifiable ordering principle which will account for everything stands at the head of the chain or at the back of the back. Any formulation of such a principle is visibly reductive. It leaves something important still unaccounted for. This is a remnant of opacity which keeps the interpreter dissatisfied, the novel still open, the process of interpretation still able to continue. . . .

Wuthering Heights produces its effect on its reader through the way it is made up of repetitions of the same in the other which permanently resist rational reduction to some satisfying principle of explanation. The reader has the experience, in struggling to understand the novel, that a certain number of the elements which present themselves for explanation can be reduced to order. This act of interpretation always leaves something over, something just at the edge of the circle of theoretical vision which that vision does not encompass. This something left out is clearly a significant detail. There are always in fact a group of such significant details which have been left out of any reduction to order. The text is over-rich.

This resistance to theoretical domination, both in the sense of clear-seeing and in the sense of conceptual formulation, is not accidental, nor is it without significance. It is not a result of Brontë's inexperience or of the fact that she overloaded her novel with elements which can be taken as having meaning beyond their realistic references. The novel is not incoherent, confused, or flawed. It is a triumph of the novelist's art. It uses the full resources of that art against the normal assumptions about character and about human life which are built into the conventions of realistic fiction. The difficulties of interpreting *Wuthering Heights* and the superabundance of possible (and actual) interpretations do not mean that the reader is free to make the novel mean anything he wants to make it mean. The fact that no demonstrable single meaning or principle of meaningfulness can be identified does not mean that all meanings are equally good. Each good reader of *Wuthering Heights* is subject to the text, coerced by it. The best readings, it may be, are those, like Charlotte Brontë's, which repeat in their own alogic the text's failure to satisfy the mind's desire for logical order with a demonstrable base. *Wuthering Heights* incorporates the reader in the process of understanding which the text mimes in Lockwood's narration. It forces him to repeat in his own way an effort of understanding that the text expresses, and to repeat also the baffling of that effort.

Wuthering Heights presents an emblem for this experience of the reader in a passage describing Lockwood's reaction to Nelly's proposal to skip rapidly over three years in her narration: 'No, no', says Lockwood. 'I'll allow nothing of the sort! Are you acquainted with the mood of mind in which, if you were seated alone, and the cat licking its kitten on the rug before you, you would watch the operation so intently that puss's neglect of one ear would put you seriously out of temper?' [ch. 7]. This, I take it, is an oblique warning to the reader. Unless he reads in the 'mood of mind' here described he is likely to miss something of importance. Every detail counts in this novel. Only an interpretation which accounts for each item and puts it in relation to the whole will be at once specific enough and total enough. The reader must be like a cat who licks her kitten all over, not missing a single spot of fur, or rather he must be like the watcher of such an operation, following every detail of the multiple narration, assuming that every minute bit counts, constantly on the watch for anything left out. There is always, however, a neglected ear, or one ear too many.

Nelly describes Lockwood's anxiety about the neglected ear as 'a terribly lazy mood', to which Lockwood replies: 'On the contrary, a tiresomely active one. It is mine, at present, and, therefore, continue minutely. I perceive that people in these regions acquire over people in towns the value that a spider in a dungeon does over a spider in a cottage, to their various occupants' [ch. 7]. The kitten's neglected ear, like the spider in the dungeon, is not a 'frivolous external thing'. It is a small thing on the surface which bears relation to hidden things in the depths. This opposition between surface and depth is suggested when Lockwood says people at Wuthering Heights 'live more in earnest, more in themselves' [ch. 7]. To live in oneself is to be self-contained. This is opposed to living in terms of surface change and frivolous external things. Where people live in themselves, external things are not superficial or frivolous. They are rather the only signs outsiders have of the secret depths. Each passage must be concentrated upon with the most intense effort of the interpreting mind. . . . Each detail must be taken as a synecdoche, as a clue to the whole. . . .

Take, for example the following passages:

The ledge, where I placed my candle, had a few mildewed books piled up in one corner; and it was covered with writing scratched on the paint. This writing, however, was nothing but a name repeated in all kinds of characters, large and small – *Catherine Earnshaw*, here and there varied to *Catherine Heathcliff*, and then again to *Catherine Linton*.

In vapid listlessness I leant my head against the window, and continued spelling over Catherine Earnshaw–Heathcliff–Linton, till my eyes closed; but they had not rested five minutes when a glare of white letters started from the dark, as vivid as spectres – the air swarmed with Catherines. [ch. 3]

I had remarked on one side of the road, at intervals of six or seven yards, a line of upright stones, continued through the whole length of the barren: these were erected, and daubed with lime on purpose to serve as guides in the dark, and also when a fall, like the present, confounded the deep swamps on either hand with the firmer path: but, excepting a dirty dot pointing up here and there, all traces of their existence had vanished; and my companion found it necessary to warn me frequently to steer to the right or left, when I imagined I was following, correctly, the windings of the road. [ch. 3]

I sought, and soon discovered, the three head-stones on the slope next the moor – the middle one grey, and half buried in the heath – Edgar Linton's only harmonized by the turf, and moss creeping up its foot – Heathcliff's still bare.

I lingered round them, under that benign sky; watched the moths fluttering among the heath, and hare-bells; listened to the soft wind breathing through the grass; and wondered how anyone could ever imagine unquiet slumbers for the sleepers in that quiet earth. (ch. 20]

These three texts are similar, but this similarity is, in part at least, the fact that each is unique in the structural model it presents the reader. This uniqueness makes each incommensurate with any of the others. Each is, in its surface texture as language, 'realistic'. It is a description of natural or manmade objects which is physically and sociologically plausible. Such things are likely to have existed in Yorkshire around 1800. All three passages are filtered through the mind and through the language of the narrator. In all three, as it happens, this is the mind of the primary narrator of the novel, Lockwood. As always in such cases, the reader must interrogate the passages for possible irony. This irony potentially arises from discrepancies between what Lockwood knows or what he makes out of what he sees, and what the author knew and made, or what the reader can make out of the passages as he interprets the handwriting on the wall. All of the passages possibly mean more than their referential or historical meaning. They may be signs or clues to something beyond themselves. This possibility is opened up in the fissure between what Lockwood apparently knows or intends to say, and what the author may have known or intended to say. None of these passages, nor any of the many other 'similar' passages which punctuate the novel, is given the definitive closure of a final interpretation within the text of the novel. In fact they are not interpreted at all. They are just given. The handwriting on the wall is not read within the novel. The reader must read it for himself.

When he does so, he finds that each such passage seems to ask to be taken as an emblem of the whole novel. Each is implicitly an emblem of the structure of the novel as a whole and of the way that whole signifies something beyond itself which controls its meaning as a whole. Each such passage leads to a different formulation of the structure of the whole. Each is exclusive and incongruous with the others. It seems to have an imperialistic will to power over the others, as if it wished to bend them to its own shape. It expands to make its own special reading of the whole. . . .

The first passage would lead to an interpretation of the novel in terms of the permutation of given names and family names. This reading would go by way of the network of kinship relations in symmetrical pedigree and by way of the theme of reading. The critic might note that there do not seem to be enough names to go around in this novel. Relations of similarity and difference among the characters are indicated by the way several hold the names also held by others or a combination of names held by others. An example is 'Linton Heathcliff', the name of the son of Heathcliff and Isabella. His name is an oxymoron, combining names from the two incompatible families. How can a name be 'proper' to a character and indicate his individuality if it is also held by others? Each character in *Wuthering Heights* seems to be an element in a system, defined by his or her place in the system, rather than a separate, unique person. The whole novel, such a critic might say, not only the destiny of the first Catherine but also of the second Catherine, as well as the relation of the second story to the first, is given in emblem in Lockwood's encounter with the names scratched on the windowsill and in his dream of an air swarming with Catherines. The passage is a momentary emblem for the whole. That whole, as it unfolds, is the narrative of the meaning of the emblem.

The second passage offers a model for a somewhat different form of totalization. The passage is a 'realistic' description of a country road in Yorkshire after a heavy snow. If the reader follows Lockwood's example and considers every detail as possibly a clue to the whole and to what stands behind or beneath the whole, then the passage suggests that the novel is made of discrete units which follow one another in a series with spaces between. The reader's business is to draw lines between the units. He must make a pattern, like the child's game in which a duck or a rabbit is magically drawn by tracing lines between numbered dots. In this case, the line makes a road which leads the reader from here to there, taking him deeper and deeper across country to a destination, away from danger and into safety. The only difficulty is that some of the dots are missing or invisible. The reader must, like Lockwood, extrapolate. He must make the road to safety by putting in correctly the missing elements.

This operation is a dangerous one. If the reader makes a mistake, guesses wrong, hypothesizes a guidepost where there is none, he will be led astray into the bog. This process of hypothetical interpretation, projecting a thesis or ground plan where there is none, where it is faint or missing, hypotrophied, is risky for the interpreter. He must engage in the activity Immanuel Kant, following rhetorical tradition, calls 'hypotyposis', the sketching out of a ground plan where there is no secure indication of which line to follow.[2] Such an operation gives figurative names to what has no literal or proper name. The reader's safety somehow depends on getting it right. There is a good chance of getting it wrong, or perhaps there is no secure foundation for deciding between right and wrong. . . .

The third passage quoted makes explicit the situation of the survivor. This too may be taken as emblematic of the whole text in relation to what lies behind the events it narrates, or as emblematic of the narrator's relation to the story he tells, or as a figure of the reader's relation to the story told. Just as many of Wordsworth's poems, 'The Boy of Winander', for example, or the Matthew poems, or 'The Ruined Cottage', are epitaphs spoken by a survivor who stands by a tombstone musing on the life and death of the one who is gone, so all of *Wuthering Heights* may be thought of as a memorial narration pieced together by Lockwood from what he can learn. The first Catherine is already dead when Lockwood arrives at the Heights. Heathcliff is still alive as the anguished survivor whose 'life is in the grave'. By the end of the novel Heathcliff has followed Catherine into death. At the end, Lockwood stands by three graves. These, like the three versions of Catherine's name in my first emblematic text, can stand in their configuration for the story of the first Catherine: Catherine Earnshaw in the middle torn by her love for Edgar Linton, in one direction, and for Heathcliff, in the other, destroying their lives in this double love and being destroyed by it.

A gravestone is the sign of an absence. Throughout the whole novel Lockwood confronts nothing but such signs. His narration is a retrospective reconstruction by means of them. This would be true of all novels told in the past tense about characters who are dead when the narration begins, but the various churchyard scenes in *Wuthering Heights*, for example the scene in which Heathcliff opens Catherine's grave and coffin, keep before the reader the question of whether the dead still somewhere live on beyond the grave. The naïveté of Lockwood, even at the end of the novel, is imaged in his inability to imagine unquiet slumbers for the sleepers in the quiet earth. The evidence for the fact that this earth is unquiet, the place of some unnamable tumultuous hidden life, is there before his eyes in the moths fluttering among the heath and hare-bells. It is there in the soft wind breathing through the grass, like some obscurely vital creature. These are figures for what can only manifest itself indirectly. If Lockwood survives the death of the protagonists and tells their story, it may be this survival which cuts him off from any understanding of death. The end of the novel reiterates the ironic discrepancy between what Lockwood knows and what he unwittingly gives the reader evidence for knowing. . . .

Different as are the several schematic paradigms for the whole, they share certain features. Each is a figure without a visible referent. Whatever emblem is chosen as center turns out to be not at the center but at the periphery. It is in fact an emblem for the impossibility of reaching the center. Each leads to a multitude of other similar details in the novel. Each such sequence is a repetitive structure, like the echoes from one to another of the lives of the two Catherines, or like the narrators within narrators in Lockwood's telling, or like the rooms inside rooms he encounters at the Heights. Each appearance is the sign of something absent, something earlier, or later, or further in. Each detail is in one way or another a track to be followed. It is a trace which asks to be retraced so that the something missing may be recovered.

The celebrated circumstantiality of *Wuthering Heights* is the circumstantiality of this constant encounter with new signs. The reader of *Wuthering Heights*, like the narrator, is led deeper and deeper into the text by the expectation that sooner or later the last veil will be removed. . . .

A further feature of this web of signs behind signs is that they tend to be presented in paired oppositions. Each element of these pairs is not so much the opposite of its mate as . . . a differentiated form, born of some division within the same, as the different Catherines in the passage discussed above are forms of the same Catherine; or as Heathcliff and Lockwood are similar in their exclusion from the place where Catherine is, as well as opposite in temperament, sexual power, and power of volition; or as Cathy says of Heathcliff not that he is her opposite, other than she is, but that 'He's more myself than I am'; or as, in the passage describing the three graves, Edgar on one side of Catherine or Heathcliff on the other each represents one aspect of her double nature. The novel everywhere organizes itself according to such patterns of sameness and difference, as in the opposition between stormy weather and calm weather; or between the roughness of the Heights and the civilized restraint of Thrushcross Grange, or between inside and outside, domestic interior and wild nature outside, beyond the window or over the wall; or between the stories of the two Catherines, or between those who read and those who scorn books as weak intermediaries, or between people of strong will like Heathcliff, who is 'a fierce, pitiless, wolfish man' [ch. 10] and people of weak will like Lockwood.

These apparently clear oppositions have two further properties. The reader is nowhere given access to the generative unity from which the pairs are derived. The reader never sees directly, for example, the moment in childhood when Cathy and Heathcliff slept in the same bed and were joined in a union which was prior to sexual differentiation. This union was prior to any sense of separate selfhood, prior even to language, figurative or conceptual, which might express that union. As soon as Cathy can say, 'I *am* Heathcliff', or 'My love for Heathcliff resembles the eternal rocks beneath' [ch. 9], they are already divided. This division has always already occurred as soon as there is consciousness and the possibility of retrospective storytelling. Storytelling is always after the fact, and it is always constructed over a loss. What is lost in the case of *Wuthering Heights* is the 'origin' which would explain everything.

Another characteristic of the oppositions follows from this loss of the explanatory source. The separated pairs, differentiations of the same rather than true opposites, have a tendency to divide further, and then subdivide again, endlessly proliferating into various nuances and subsets. Once the 'primal' division has occurred, and for Brontë as soon as there is a story to tell it has already occurred, there seems to be no stopping a further division. Once this primitive cell is self-divided it divides and subdivides perpetually in an effort to achieve reunification which only multiplies it in new further-divided life cells. . . .

The special form of 'undecidability' in *Wuthering Heights* or in other narratives in which repetition takes this form lies in the impossibility, in principle, of determining whether there is some extralinguistic explanatory cause of whether the sense that there is one is generated by the linguistic structure itself. Nor is this a trivial issue. It is the most important question the novel raises, the one thing about which we ought to be able to make a decision, and yet a thing about which the novel forbids the reader to make a decision. In this *Wuthering Heights* justifies being called an 'uncanny' text. To alter Freud's formulas a little, the uncanny in *Wuthering Heights* is the constant bringing into the open of something which seems familiar and which one feels ought to have been kept secret, not least because it is impossible to tell whether there is any secret at all hidden in the depths, or whether the sense of familiarity and of the unveiling of a secret may not be an effect of the repetition in difference of one part of the text by another, on the surface.[3] In the oscillation between the invitation to expect the novel to be an example of the first, grounded form of repetition and the constant frustration of that expectation, *Wuthering Heights* is a special case of the intertwining of two forms of repetition described in chapter 1.[4]

Any repetitive structure of the 'uncanny' sort, whether in real life or in words, tends to generate an irrational sense of guilt in the one who experiences it. I have not done anything (or have I?), and yet what I witness makes demands on me which I cannot fulfill. The mere fact of passive looking or of reading may make one guilty of the crime of seeing what ought not to have been seen. What I see or what I read repeats or seems to repeat something earlier, something deeper in. That something hidden is brought back out into the open in a disguised repetition by what I see. It should be brought out now into full clarity. At the same time perhaps it should be kept secret, since it may possibly be one of those things which, to paraphrase Winnie Verloc in Conrad's *The Secret Agent*, does not stand much looking into. . . . The situation of the reader of *Wuthering Heights* is inscribed within the novel in the situations of all those characters who are readers, tellers of tales, most elaborately in Lockwood. The lesson for the reader is to make him aware that he has by reading the novel incurred a responsibility like that of the other spectator-interpreters. . . .

The double guilt of Lockwood's narration as of any critic's discourse is the following. If he does not penetrate all the way to the innermost core of the story he tells, he keeps the story going, repeating itself interminably in its incompletion. This is like the guilt of the one who keeps a grave open, or like the guilt of a sexual failure. On the other hand, to pierce all the way in is to be guilty of the desecration of a grave, to be guilty, like Heathcliff when he opens Cathy's grave, of necrophilia. . . . The reader's sense of guilt is systematically connected to the swarm of other emotions aroused in any good reader of *Wuthering Heights* as he makes his way through the book: affection for the two Catherines, though in a different way for each, and mixed with some fear of her intransigence in the case of the first Catherine; scorn for Lockwood, but some pity for his limitations; awe of Heathcliff's suffering; and so on.

The line of witnesses who feel one or another form of this complex of emotions goes from the reader-critic to Charlotte Brontë to Emily Brontë to that pseudonymous author 'Ellis Bell' to Lockwood to Nelly to Heathcliff to Cathy, the inside of the inside, or it moves the other way around, from Cathy out to the reader. The reader is the last surviving consciousness enveloping all these other consciousnesses, one inside the other. The reader is condemned, like all the others, to be caught by a double contradictory demand: to bring it all out in the open and at the same time to give it decent burial, to keep the book open and at the same time to close its covers once and for all, so it may be forgotten, or so it may be read once more, this time definitively. The guilt of the reader is the impossibility of doing either of these things, once he has opened the book and begun to read: '1801 – I have just returned from a visit to my landlord' [ch. 1].

The reading of the first present-tense words of the novel performs a multiple act of resurrection, an opening of graves or a raising of ghosts. In reading those first words and then all the ones that follow to the end, the reader brings back from the grave first the fictive 'I' who is supposed to have written them or spoken them, that Lockwood who has and had no existence outside the covers of the book. With that 'I' the reader brings back also the moment in the fall of 1801 when his 'I have just returned' is supposed to have been written or spoken. By way of that first 'I' and first present moment the reader then resurrects from the dead, with Lockwood's help, in one direction Hindley, Nelly, Joseph, Hareton, the two Catherines, Heathcliff, and the rest, so that they walk the moors once again and live once again at the Heights and the Grange. In the other direction are also evoked first Ellis Bell, the pseudonymous author, who functions as a ghostly name on the title page. Ellis Bell is a male name veiling the female author, but it is also the name of a character in the book: someone who has survived Lockwood, an 'editor' into whose hands Lockwood's diary has fallen and who presents it to the public, or, more likely, the consciousness surrounding Lockwood's consciousness, overhearing what he says to himself, what he thinks, feels, sees, and presenting it again to the reader as though it were entirely the words of Lockwood. In doing this Ellis Bell effaces himself, but he is present as a ghostly necessity of the narrative behind Lockwood's words. The name Ellis Bell functions to name a spectator outside Lockwood, who is the primary spectator. Ellis Bell is another representative of the reader, overhearing, overseeing, overthinking, and overfeeling what Lockwood says, sees, thinks, feels, and writing it down so we can in our turns evoke Lockwood again and raise also that thin and almost invisible ghost, effaced presupposition of the words of the novel, Ellis Bell himself. Behind Ellis Bell, finally, is Brontë, who, the reader knows, actually wrote down those words, '1801 – I have just returned . . .' at Haworth on some day probably in 1846. Brontë too, in however indirect fashion, is brought back to life in the act of reading. . . .

The most powerful form of repetition in fiction, it may be, is not the echoes of one part of the book by another, but the way even the simplest, most representational words in a novel ('1801 – I have just returned . . .') present themselves as already a murmuring repetition, something which has been repeating itself incessantly there in the words on the page waiting for me to bring it back to life as the meaning of the words forms itself in my mind. Fiction is possible only because of an intrinsic capacity possessed by ordinary words in grammatical order. Words no different from those we use in everyday life, 'I have just returned', may detach themselves or be detached from any present moment, any living 'I', any immediate perception of reality, and go on functioning as the creators of the fictive world repeated into existence, to use the verb transitively, whenever the act of reading those words is performed. The words themselves, there on the page, both presuppose the deaths of that long line of personages and at the same time keep them from dying wholly, as long as a single copy of *Wuthering Heights* survives to be reread.

SOURCE: from '*Wuthering Heights*. Repetition and the "Uncanny"', *Fiction and Repetition: Seven English Novels* (1982; Blackwell, 1984).

NOTES

1. See Dorothy Van Ghent, *The English Novel: Form and Function* (New York, Rinehart, 1953) pp. 153–70; C. P. Sanger, *The Structure of Wuthering Heights* (London, 1926); Thomas Moser, 'What is the Matter with Emily Jane', *Nineteenth-Century Fiction*, 17 (June 1962), pp. 1–19; David Cecil, *Early Victorian Novelists* (London, 1948), pp. 136–82; Mark Schorer, 'Introduction' to *Wuthering Heights* (New York, 1950), pp. iv–xviii; J. Hillis Miller, *The Disappearance of God* (Cambridge, Mass., 1963), pp. 157–211; Georges Bataille, *La Littérature et le mal* (Paris, 1957), pp. 11–31; Camille Paglia, *Sexual Personae: The Androgyne in Literature and Art*, Diss. Yale 1974, pp. 321–33; Frank Kermode, *The Classic* (New York, 1975), pp. 117–41: Margaret Homans, 'Repression and Sublimation of Nature in *Wuthering Heights*', *PMLA*, 93, no. 1 (Jan. 1978), pp. 9–19; Leo Bersani, *A Future for Astyanax: Character and Desire in Literature* (Boston, 1976), pp. 197–223; David Wilson, 'Emily Brontë, First of the Moderns', *Modern Quarterly Miscellany*, no. 1 (1947), pp. 94–115; Arnold Kettle, '*Wuthering Heights*', in *Introduction to the English Novel*, I (London, 1965), pp. 139–55; Terry Eagleton, *Myths of Power: A Marxist Study of the Brontës* (London, 1975), pp. 97–121.

2. See paragraph 59 of Kant, *Critique of Judgment*, trans. J. H. Bernard (New York, 1951), pp. 196–8. See also Paul de Man's discussion of this paragraph in 'The Epistemology of Metaphor', *Critical Inquiry*, 5, no. 1 (Autumn 1978), pp. 26–9.

3. The uncanny in literature is firmly opposed by Freud to situations in real life which are uncanny. Nevertheless, the uncanny, both in literature and in life, is defined by Freud as 'nothing else than a hidden, familiar thing that has undergone repression and then emerged from it', Sigmund Freud, 'The "Uncanny"' (1919), *Collected Papers*, IV (New York, 1959), p. 399.

4. See Introduction, p. 33 above [Ed.]

SELECT BIBLIOGRAPHY

For a full bibliography of studies of the Brontës see *The New Cambridge Bibliography*, III (1969) and for other and later bibliographical listings see the Introduction, pp. 30–1 above. The following studies of Emily Brontë are of special interest and include several which the editor would have represented in this edition had space allowed. For the same reason, some items included in the 1970 edition listings have been excluded to make room for more recent studies based on new findings. Certain essays not included below but connected with particular areas of debate are cited in notes to the texts above; see especially Introduction 12n, pp. 34–5 above.

The best scholarly editions are Hilda Marsden and Ian Jacks (eds), *Wuthering Heights* (Oxford University Press, 1976), and *Wuthering Heights: An Authoritative Text with Essays in Criticism*, a Norton Critical Edition, ed. William M. Sale (New York, 1965). The standard edition of the poems is *The Complete Poems of Emily Jane Brontë*, ed. C. W. Hatfield (Columbia University Press and Oxford University Press, 1941).

Edward Chitham, *A Life of Emily Brontë* (Basil Blackwell, Oxford, 1987).

——, *The Brontës' Irish Background* (Macmillan, London, 1986).

The most recent biographical studies, notable for providing carefully documented and readable accounts of the available material, with some fresh details uncovered by the author. See p. 24 above.

Inga-Stina Ewbank, *Their Proper Sphere: a study of the Brontë sisters as Early Victorian female novelists* (Arnold, London, 1966).

An early attempt to look at the Brontës' work in the light of received ideas about the social and familial role of women, drawing some lively details from contemporary sources including periodicals and conduct books. Notwithstanding the sense of limitation Emily Brontë is felt to have gained strength from resisting containment within the 'proper sphere'. See p. 31 above.

John Fraser, 'The Name of Action: Nelly Dean and *Wuthering Heights*', *Nineteenth-Century Fiction*, XX (1965).

Contributes to discussion about Nelly Dean's role in the novel, arguing against a 'sentimental disengagement' which simultaneously encourages the uncritical acceptance of 'wickedness' in Catherine and Heathcliff, and the depreciation of Nelly Dean as 'an agent of repression'. See p. 208n. above.

Winifred Gérin, *Emily Brontë: A Biography* (Oxford, 1972).

The fourth in this author's series for Oxford University Press: *Anne Brontë* (1959); *Branwell Brontë* (1961); *Charlotte Brontë* (1967).

Sandra Gilbert and Susan Gulbar, *The Madwoman in the Attic: The Woman Writer and the Nineteenth-Century Literary Imagination* (1979).

The chapter on *Wuthering Heights* discusses its author as a striking example of resistance to patriarchal writing, the central theme in this work of feminist criticism. The novel shows Emily Brontë reversing patriarchal ideas of Heaven and Hell, Milton's in particular, and thus reaching her own synthesis and sense of identity.

Lew Girdler, '*Wuthering Heights* and Shakespeare', *Huntington Library Quarterly*, XIX, no. 4 (Aug. 1946).
A short paper rehearsing the principal Shakespearian allusions, verbal echoes and 'general resemblances in character, plot structure and motifs' in *Wuthering Heights*. The principal references are to *Twelfth Night*, *Macbeth*, *King Lear*, *The Taming of the Shrew* and *Hamlet*.

John Hagan, 'The Control of Sympathy in *Wuthering Heights*', *Nineteenth-Century Fiction*, XX (1966).
Our 'double view of Catherine and Heathcliff with its blend of moral disapproval and compassion' is chiefly determined by Emily Brontë's 'ability to convince us that cruelty is not innate in [them] . . . but is the consequence of extreme suffering'. Cp. p. 156n. above.

John Hewish, *Emily Brontë: a critical and biographical survey* (1969).
A good resumé of most of the material concerning Emily Brontë available since 1847. It includes 'An Emily Brontë Reading List', a substantial survey of works appearing between that date and the 1960s, covering editions of her works, textual and bibliographical studies, biographical sources and studies, works of criticism, and nineteenth-century reviews. See p. 24 above.

N. B. Jacobs, 'Gendered and Layered Narrative in *Wuthering Heights* and *The Tenant of Wildfell Hall*', *Journal of Narrative Technique*, XVI (1986).
Extends discussion of the 'multiple perspectives' in *Wuthering Heights* by examining the different assumptions and conventions informing the 'male' and 'female'narratives, noting especially the relationship between the Domestic and the Gothic as unwittingly revealed by Lockwood in his framing narrative.

James H. Kavanagh, *Emily Brontë* in Rereading Literature series (Basil Blackwell, Oxford 1985).
A psycho-social study informed by feminist, Lacanian and Marxist ideas which manages to formulate some lively comments on aspects of the text in spite of the constraints imposed by its ideological preoccupations and specialist vocabulary. See p. 31 above.

Frank Kermode in *The Classic: Literary Images of Permanence and Chance* (Harvard University Press, Cambridge and London, 1983).
Chapter IV is devoted to *Wuthering Heights* as a 'classic' because exemplifying particular qualities which the author seeks to explore and demonstrate in his series of studies. The novel survives precisely because of its inherent liberating plurality and multiplicity of readings, remaining 'unaffected by time yet offering itself to be read under our particular temporal disposition'. See further under Leavis below and pp. 11, 33 above.

U. C. Knoepflmacher, *Emily Brontë: Wuthering Heights* in Landmarks of World Literature series (Cambridge University Press, Cambridge, New York, New Rochelle, Melbourne, Sydney, 1989).

An informative study, including a detailed chronology of Emily Brontë's life and work, a chronological account of the events in her novel; an innovative survey of the novel's 'after-life', headed 'Unquiet ghosts', 'Victorian domestications' and 'A fable for modernists'; and a guide to further reading (see p. 31 above). The critical emphasis is on the novel's multiplicity and insistence on contradiction. Emily Brontë 'never upholds one polarity over its counterpart; nor does she dissolve contraries into some synthesis'; she 'challenges our partial constructions of truth'.

Q. D. Leavis, 'A Fresh Approach to *Wuthering Heights*', in *Lectures in America* by F. R. Leavis and Q. D. Leavis (London, 1969).
Provokes strong disagreement along with admiration for particular insights. The essay celebrates the novel's 'truly human centrality', its provision of 'a specific and informed sociological' context for its portrayal of passionate Romantic rebellion, and its technical skill and virtuosity in unfolding human and sociological 'truths' in a time of change (an 'old rough farming culture based on a *naturally* patriarchal family life' is yielding to the forces that would produce 'the Victorian class consciousness and the *unnatural* idea of gentility'). This emphasis on health, wholeness and 'fine awareness of human relations' means getting rid of unaccommodating areas in the text, especially the portrayal of Heathcliff, 'an unsatisfactory composite' which belongs with other 'unregenerate' elements surviving from what are assumed to be earlier versions of the text. Recent critics who acknowledge the essay's stature while firmly rejecting this partial reading include notably Frank Kermode in the essay mentioned above. There is a pointed short summary of Mrs Leavis's essay and the issues it raises by Lyn Pykett (see below). See p. 31 above.

Philippa Moody, 'The Challenge of Maturity in *Wuthering Heights*', *Melbourne Critical Review*, v (1962).
'It seems to me a mistake to assume too readily that the love of Catherine and Heathcliff is necessarily outside normal experience. In duration it may be, but in essence it is closely related to the extreme, intense, but not necessarily sexual involvement that is most frequently felt in adolescence.'

Lyn Pykett, *Emily Brontë* in Women Writers series (Macmillan, London, 1989). Succinct and informative, placing in social and historical perspective the problems of gender, genre and the Woman Poet while maintaining a good grip of, and respect for, textual detail. See p. 31 above.

Fanny E. Ratchford, *The Brontës' Web of Childhood* (Columbia University Press, 1941; Oxford University Press, 1941).
——, *Gondal's Queen: A novel in verse* (Austin, 1955).
Seminal studies of the Brontë children's creative fantasies, including Emily's and Anne's world of Gondal. See above, p. 34n.

Charles Simpson, *Emily Brontë* (Country Life, 1929).
In spite of its early date, worth noting for its level-headedness and for discussion of the possible influence on her novel of Emily Brontë's stay at Law Hill.

David Wilson, 'Emily Brontë: First of the Moderns', *Modern Quarterly Miscellany*, No. 1 (1947).

One of the first 'social' readings of the novel. See p. 31 above.

Tom Winnifrith, *The Brontës and their Background: Romance and Reality* (Macmillan, London, 1973).

One of the staple works in Bronte criticism, assembling a wide range of material in its attempt to distinguish firmly between the 'Brontë story' and the stories the Brontës wrote. It deals with cruces such as the nature of their religion, their much talked-of 'coarseness', which is linked with Victorian ideas of snobbery and prudery, their reading, their reviewers, and the transmission of the texts of their work. See pp. 24, 30 above.

NOTES ON CONTRIBUTORS

MIRIAM ALLOTT is Emeritus Professor of English at London University and Honorary Senior Research Fellow in English at Liverpool University. Her publications have included *Novelists on the Novel*, *Elizabeth Gaskell*, the Casebook on *Charlotte Brontë: Jane Eyre and Villette*, and complete annotated editions of the poems of John Keats and Matthew Arnold. She is currently completing *Poets on Poetry* for Faber and Faber.

JACQUES BLONDEL was formerly Professor of English Literature in the University of Clermont-Ferrand. His studies of Emily Brontë include his French translation of *Wuthering Heights* (1851), *Emily Brontë: expérience spirituelle et création poétique* (1955, and *Nouveaux regards sur Emily Brontë* (1959). His *Imaginaire et croyance: études de poésie anglaise* appeared in 1976.

PHILIP DREW, Emeritus Professor of English in the University of Glasgow, is the author of *The Meaning of Freedom* (1982). His earlier studies include work on Browning, notably an edition of collected critical essays, *The Poetry of Robert Browning* (1966), and *The Poetry of Robert Browning: A Critical Introduction* (1970).

TERRY EAGLETON is Warton Professor of English at Oxford. Among his most recent publications are *The Rape of Clarissa: Writing, Sexuality and Class* (1982); *Literary Theory: An Introduction* (1985); and *Ideology: An Introduction* (1990).

MARGARET HOMANS is Professor of English at Yale University. Her recent studies, notably on the work of women writers, include *Bearing the Word: Language and Female Experience in Nineteenth-Century Women's Writing* (1986), which has a chapter on 'The Name of the Mother in *Wuthering Heights*' ('the narrators, in order to produce a coherent narrative, distance themselves from the maternal, but ... the first Cathy identifies herself with it to her peril').

J. HILLIS MILLER is Professor of English in the University of California at Irvine. He has contributed widely to the study of Victorian and modern fiction, especially in relation to critical theory and the question of imagination and belief. His *The Disappearance of God* (1963), on nineteenth-century writers, includes a chapter on Emily Brontë.

MARK SCHORER, formerly Professor of English at the University of California in Berkeley, has published novels and short stories as well as literary criticism. His books include a biography of Sinclair Lewis, editions of novels by Jane Austen and the Brontë sisters, and critical and scholarly studies of D. H. Lawrence.

DEREK TRAVERSI, writer and critic, has written extensively on Shakespeare, Chaucer and Renaissance drama. His *Literary Imagination: Studies in Dante, Chaucer, and Shakespeare* appeared in 1983, and *Chaucer: The Early Poetry – A Study in Poetic Development* in 1987.

DOROTHY VAN GHENT was Professor of English Literature in the University of Buffalo at the time of her death in 1967. Her publications include *The English Novel: Form and Function*, and editions of collections of essays on novelists, including Hardy and Henry James.

INDEX